Italian design is coming home. To Switzerland.

Polyedra Presents:
Italian Design Is Coming Home.
To Switzerland.

A Will and Tommaso publication
Made possible by Polyedra

Published by Actar and Polyedra.

Printed on Hello Hot Silk
Cover: 300 gr/m^2
Text block: 150 gr/m^2

Amsterdam, Barcelona,
London, Milan, Zurich.
ISBN: 978-84-92861-74-3

Contents.

Welcome to Italian Design Is Coming Home. To Switzerland.
A celebration of the past, current and future generations
of Swiss and Italian graphic design talent.

Celebrate the past

Essays & interviews on the history of Swiss & Italian design.

Celebrate the present

11 collaborations between 22 of the best contemporary
Swiss & Italian graphic designers.

Celebrate the future

The next generation of Swiss & Italian creative talent.

Preface.

Will and Tommaso.
Amsterdam/Milan, 2011.

FR

Quand nous avons commencé ce projet dans un jardin au nord d'Amsterdam, nous n'avions aucune idée de la façon dont il serait perçu.

La réaction fut écrasante. Tous ceux avec qui nous avons travaillé, en allant de Polyedra aux 22 designers dont le travail honore ce livre, ont saisis ce projet avec un enthousiasme qui nous a vraiment touchés.

Nous sommes parfaitement conscients que ça n'a rien à voir avec à quel point nous sommes charmants ou à quel point nous sommes doués au téléphone, mais avec la passion que l'Italie et la Suisse ont pour le design et la fierté qu'ils partagent au travers de leur histoire commune.

Nous nous sentons privilégié d'avoir pu écrire ce que nous espérons être un nouveau chapitre dans cette illustre histoire.

ENG

When we first began this project in a garden in North Amsterdam, we had no idea how it would be received.

The response was overwhelming. Everyone who we've worked with, from Polyedra to the 22 designers whose work graces this book, has embraced this project with an enthusiasm that has truly touched us.

We're well aware that it's got nothing to do with how charming we are or how good we are on the phone, but the passion that both Italy and Switzerland have for design and the pride they share in their history.

We're privileged to have written what we hope will be a new chapter in this illustrious history.

DE

Als wir mit diesem Projekt in einem Garten im Norden Amsterdams begannen, hatten wir keine Vorstellung davon, wie es ankommen würde.

Die Reaktion war einfach überwältigend. Alle, mit denen wir zusammengearbeitet haben - von Polyedra bis zu den 22 Designern, dessen Werke dieses Buch schmücken - sind diesem Projekt mit einem Enthusiasmus begegnet, der uns wahrlich gerührt hat.

Wir wissen nur zu gut, dass es nichts damit zu tun hat, wie charmant wir sind oder wie nett wir am Telefon reden, sondern mit der Leidenschaft Italiens und der Schweiz für Design und dem Stolz für ihre gemeinsame Geschichte.

Wir fühlen uns privilegiert, dieses Buch geschrieben zu haben und hoffen, dass es ein neues Kapitel in dieser glorreichen Geschichte darstellt.

ITA

Quando abbiamo cominciato questo progetto in un giardino nel nord di Amsterdam, non avevamo idea di come sarebbe stato accolto.

La risposta è stata travolgente. Tutte le persone con cui abbiamo lavorato, da Polyedra ai 22 designer le cui opere abbelliscono questo libro, hanno accolto il nostro progetto con un entusiasmo che ci ha veramente commosso.

Siamo ben coscienti del fatto che questo non c'entra con quanto siamo carismatici o quanto siamo bravi a parlare al telefono, ma con la passione che sia l'Italia che la Svizzera hanno per il design e con l'orgoglio che condividono nella loro storia.

Abbiamo avuto il privilegio di scrivere quello che speriamo diventerà un nuovo capitolo di questa storia gloriosa.

A word from our sponsors, Polyedra.

Milan, 2011.

FR

Ce livre est une collection de travaux d'un groupe d'artistes qui ont acceptés l'invitation de Polyedra à célébrer le passé, le présent et le future de la proche collaboration entre designers Suisses et Italiens. Le résultat est une galerie d'images extraordinaires inspirée par les maîtres Suisses des années 1950 qui ont créés le célèbre Style Typographique International. Beaucoup d'eux sont allés travailler en Italie dans les années 1940, surtout au légendaire Studio Boggeri à Milan, pour créer ce qui deviendra un mouvement symbolique dans le monde du graphisme. Un mouvement qui est aussi pertinent aujourd'hui qu'il l'était hier.

ENG

This book is a collection of the work of a group of artists who accepted Polyedra's invitation to celebrate the past, present and future of the close collaboration between Swiss and Italian designers. The result is an extraordinary gallery of images inspired by the Swiss masters of the 1950s who founded the famous International Typographic Style. Many of them went to work in Italy in the 1940s, particularly at the legendary Studio Boggeri in Milan, to create what would become a iconic new movement in graphic design. One that is as relevant today as it was yesterday.

DE

Dieses Buch ist eine Grafiksammlung verschiedener Künstler, die Polyedras Einladung akzeptierten, die Vergangenheit, Gegenwart und Zukunft der engen Zusammenarbeit zwischen schweizerischen und italienischen Designern zu feiern. Das Ergebnis ist eine außergewöhnliche Bildersammlung, inspiriert durch die Schweizer Meister der fünfziger Jahre, die den berühmten Internationalen Typografie Stil gründeten. Viele von ihnen gingen in den vierziger Jahren nach Italien, um dort zu arbeiten, insbesondere im legendären Studio Boggeri in Mailand, und kreierten eine ikonische neue Grafikdesign-Bewegung, die heute genauso relevant ist wie gestern.

ITA

Questo libro raccoglie le opere e le voci di un gruppo di artisti che hanno accettato l'invito promosso da Polyedra a celebrare il presente, il passato e il futuro della stretta collaborazione tra designer svizzeri e italiani. Il risultato é una straordinaria galleria diimmagini originali ispirate dal segno intellettuale e creativo delle opere dei grandi maestri svizzeri che negli anni '50 fondarono l'International Typographic Style. Molti di loro giá negli anni '40 andarono in Italia, specie a Milano presso il mitico studio Boggeri, per creare quelle che sarebbero diventate le icone del rinnovamento dell'arte grafica. Oggi piú che mai.

Celebrate the Past.

On the left:
Illustration by Elena Xausa,
after the work of Walter Ballmer (left)

On the opposite page:
Illustrations by Elena Xausa,
after the work of Josef Muller-Brockmann (right),
Carlo Vivarelli (left)

There's been a strong link in design between Switzerland and Italy (particularly Milan) going back to the 1940s. Max Huber, Carlo Vivarelli, Walter Ballmer were just a few of the legendary Swiss designers who crossed the Alps to help create the International Typographic School for which Italian (and Swiss) design became renowned. This section explores the situation in both countries after the Second World War that created one of the most fruitful creative environments of the 20th century.

A Beginner's guide to Swiss and Italian design.

William Georgi

Being an English copywriter working in Amsterdam, albeit with an Italian art director, gives me a unique position on which to comment on Swiss and Italian design. For if I can begin to understand its wonderful complexity and significance, then so, dear reader, can you. Especially after you've read the essays that follow. Essays from people who really know what they're talking about: Bettina Richter and Maurizio Vitta, a pair of academics from Switzerland and Italy respectively, who provide an intelligent perspective on what happened in both countries after the Second World War; while Giancarlo Iliprandi and Felix Humm are a pair of designers who were actually there at the time, did that and designed the metaphorical t-shirt.

But for the next couple of pages, you'll be riding with me. Hooray. Because as a copywriter, I wanted this book to be for everyone, not just designers, or people who know what the difference between a graphic designer and an art director is without having to look it up in a dictionary or ask one of their designer friends like I did.

So I'd like to ask for your patience in explaining why we're here and what we're going to celebrate. Because everyone, I mean absolutely everyone, knows that Italian and Swiss design are great. But not everybody knows how close they are. Or even what Swiss and Italian design actually are.

To be clear, what we're talking about is graphic design. The art of making, well, art, out of visual communication to relay a message as clearly, effectively and attractively as possible. It could be a poster, a logo, packaging, a shop display, a bird, a plane, whatever. If you can print or draw on it, then it's graphic design. And as you'll see, it doesn't matter whether it's to promote a typewriter, a supermarket or a tyre, you can make something beautiful out of it.

And what we're here to celebrate is the huge influence that a group of Swiss and Italian designers and artists working together in Milan after the second world war would have on the world.

Basically two worlds collided - the technical Swiss and the arty Italians (you've got to love a good old national stereotype or two). But in this case it was true; the Swiss had long placed a high value on design and even had schools dedicated to design, something we now take for granted, but at the time was something that Italy, at least, didn't have.

So to break it down somewhat crudely, the Swiss were more technical because they relied on a grid-based system, while the Italians were more artistic because they learnt their trade in art schools.

The grid-based system, you ask? Well, it's a system for designing artwork that's based on a grid. Everything you stick in the design (text, photography, images, etc) has to conform to the lines of the grid. Simple. Except it's not really. Depending on your point of view it's either indispensable or a killer of creativity. Either way, to use it properly, you need to learn how to do it. And that takes time. And education. Which is why the Swiss, and the grid's main proponent, Josef Müller-Brockmann, were so very good at it. And exactly why the art-school trained Italians complemented the more formal Swiss so well. Because as we all know, rules (and grids) are made to be broken.

But what Italy, and Milan in particular, did have was a magnetic effect for creative people after the Second World War. The Swiss designers came to Milan because they were a) in demand and b) that's where the most exciting

work was. Clients who offered you carte blanche to do what you wanted. Fellow designers and intellectuals with whom you could shoot the breeze over lunch.

What comes across most clearly when reading the essays that follow this, is that people like Iliprandi were fortunate to be present at one of those times where everything comes together to create something truly amazing. The right people – from the top to the bottom, from illustrators to musicians, from Zurich to Milan – in the right place together. Ideas were exchanged and barriers weren't merely broken down, they simply didn't exist. Creatives and clients were equals and bartered ideas instead of money. John Steinbeck once said that creative people always go where they're appreciated. And Milan between 1945 and 1960something was one of those special places. The world of design would never be the same again.

Italian Influence in Post-War Swiss Graphic Design.

Bettina Richter

Curator of the Poster Collection at the Museum für Gestaltung in Zurich.

Zürich and Milan, c.1945: worlds apart

Shortly after the end of the Second World War, Switzerland experienced an economic boom that had immediate need of a workforce to sustain it. Countless people – many from the south of Italy – flocked to Switzerland in search of employment and a better life. To chase this dream they had to endure hard work as well as Swiss political racism, while working conditions and the number of workers in demand changed constantly, making it impossible for the Italians to feel welcome in their new country.

But for a group of Swiss graphic designers who made the reverse journey to Milan at the same time, it was a completely different story. The *Dolce Vita* atmosphere that pervaded the city promised a new beginning for immigrants, all of who were made very welcome, despite the differences between Switzerland and Italy at that time.

Switzerland (neutral during World War II) had become increasingly conservative since 1939 and politically and culturally isolated from the rest of Europe. It had ground to an intellectual standstill and was engulfed by a creative slump that ran contrary to the economic boom.

But in the 1950s the Modernism of the pre-war years began to thrive again in graphic design. In Zürich, Josef Müller-Brockmann developed his mix of Concrete Art and typography, while in Basel Armin Hofmann and Emil Ruder offered a more sensual and playful vision of Swiss graphics.

They were the main protagonists of a "Swiss Style" that would become famous around the world. Its foundations were a grid system of horizontal and vertical lines in which the composition of image and text was considered more important than the creative content itself.

However these principles were often applied too rigidly, producing rather limp and conventional graphics. It was a trend that would even pervade the later work of such a pioneer as Müller-Brockmann.

The Milan of 1945, on the other hand, basked in the glow of a new open, progressive, atmosphere, made all the richer by the same economic boom that Switzerland was enjoying.

And just as in Switzerland, the Avant-garde picked up where it had left off before the war. Moreover, there was much discussion about what had happened during the war, especially amongst the intelligentsia, leading to radical shifts in society and politics. This duly affected the business world, where the predominant harbinger of change was Adriano Olivetti.

Olivetti started working in 1926 in the firm founded by his father and began building his concrete utopia of a *città degli uomini*, where profits were of secondary importance to employees' wellbeing. Olivetti was exiled to Switzerland in 1944 because of his ideals, but upon his return after the war he expanded his concept of visual communication, fusing ethics with aesthetics and making these two principles the cornerstones of his company. A significant development was the creation of an advertisement and communications division for Olivetti in 1933.

Swiss Graphic Designers in Milan

Xanti Schawinsky and Max Huber were the first ambassadors of Swiss design to venture to Italy. Schawinsky was a gifted man who had studied music and painting in Germany and was keen on experimenting and reforming the arts and society.

He fled Germany for Switzerland in 1933, before moving to Italy later that year, where he met Antonio Boggeri. Boggeri is another vital piece of the puzzle in the Swiss-Italian story. He was a passionate musician and photographer who was profoundly influenced by the work of leading avant-garde artists like El Lissitzky and Jan Tschichold.

Inspired by their sensitive mixing of typography, illustration, graphic design and photography, Boggeri opened his own studio in 1933. Schawinsky was one of his first employees, while Huber joined in 1940. A multitude of Swiss designers followed in their footsteps, including Carlo Vivareli, Walter Ballmer, Serge Libiszewski, Lora Lamm and Bruno Monguzzi. Many used their employment at Studio Boggeri as a springboard to further their career or to start their own studio, so none of the employees at Boggeri's stayed very long. But all shared a creative curiosity and openness that would become a hallmark of the studio.

Boggeri's only real competitor in Milan was the studio of graphic designer Franco Grignani, where most of the employees were Swiss as well. Together they formed an intimate scene of young designers who would convene for lunch at noon in small trattorias, where they would hold intense discussions with writers and other artists on the social value of design and art and the social responsibility of the designer.

Meanwhile, Max Huber, who had been forced to return to Switzerland during the war, once again sought inspiration in Italy after 1945. Together with graphic designer Albe Steiner he worked from 1950 to 1954 in the advertising division of the renowned department store La Rinascente.

In the 1950s La Rinascente embodied Italy's cultural and economic renaissance. Fashion and furniture became synonymous with design and quality with La Rinascente products blending aesthetics, innovation and affordability. The architect and designer Giò Ponti held his exhibitions at La Rinascente from 1953 and the prestigious design award, the *Compasso d'Oro*, was another La Rinascente initiative. Huber designed the company logo as well as their integral communication concept.

Lora Lamm was one of the few Swiss women working in Milan in the 1950s. She worked at Studio Boggeri from 1953 until 1954, when Max Huber brought her into La Rinascente's advertising department. In 1956 she designed the promotional materials for an exhibition of Japanese products at La Rinascente that would establish her as a major designer. After Huber's departure from La Rinascente, she was manager of the advertising department from 1958 to 1962.

Photographer Serge Libiszewski was another invited by Huber to work at La Rinascente. Libiszewski had studied at the Kunstgewerbeschule in Zürich before working at the Müller-Brockmann Studio. Because of the lack of commercial photographers in Northern Italy, Libiszewski was keen to accept Huber's invitation. However their working relationship began inauspiciously: there were no commissions so Libiszewski was reduced to helping Huber around his studio.

Success finally came when Libiszewski started his own studio in 1962. Orders flooded in from La Rinascente, Studio Boggeri, Olivetti and Pirelli. At this time photography was evolving into a new and independent artistic form within advertisement graphics. Together with Salvatore Gregorietti and Giancarlo Iliprandi (at La Rinascente) and Walter Ballmer (at Olivetti) he worked on many innovative poster campaigns.

All the graphic designers and photographers who came to Milan after 1950 shared the same thirst for new challenges that they couldn't find in the conservative and orthodox artistic circles in Switzerland. They wanted to be creative, regardless of boundaries between the different art forms. However, sadly periods of such intensity and innovation never last long.

At the beginning of the 1970s this social utopia gradually disappeared. Marketing concepts based on effectiveness, with less art and bigger logos, began to dominate communication campaigns. Accounts were given to leading advertisement agencies rather than to individual designers. The relationship between the management of a large company and individual designers and photographers was at an end.

Elena Xausa, after Lora Lämm

Contemporary Swiss Graphic Design

The reputation that Swiss graphic design enjoys today owes much to the influence it absorbed from Italy during the 1950s and 1960s. The solid education of Swiss designers laid the foundations, but it was their inspirational interaction with their Italian counterparts that allowed Max Huber, Lora Lamm, Walter Ballmer et al to flourish.

This, and the distinctly favourable conditions in Milan during this period: the economic boom, ambitious studios and enthusiastic clients all contributed to the stylistic richness in graphic design. A tradition of formal severity thrown together with an experimental curiosity, colour, poetry wit and lust for life made for a heady combination that was highly fruitful for both sides and continues to inspire Swiss graphic design today.

Its aesthetic variety shows that the even in a time of political turbulence like the 1980s, the design tradition of

Aufbruch (departure) can still survive. The strict application of Helvetica is still questioned provocatively by designers.

And graphic design in Switzerland continues to blossom through the cultural exchanges with other art forms such as music, literature, all of which are mutually enriched. These trends, which began post war, continue today and still lead to many wonderful and exciting experiments, at least as far as design is concerned.

Even more encouragingly, a young generation of graphic designers has emerged since the 1990s that doesn't restrict itself to computer-generated graphic solutions; just like their predecessors they use their hands and get back to the basics.

When touching and feeling materials, different and more creative solutions emerge, leading to a more personal, subjective and less orthodox result.

Everything imperfect, coincidental and spontaneous can influence the everyday practice of design positively.

Freehand-illustrations, handwriting, the development of new letter types, and unusual blends of letters all have their echoes in contemporary posters. Playing with other mass media, such as photography and the fine arts, reflect the various ways of dealing with the images and texts of today.

As regards content, contemporary cultural posters show a different understanding of the poster as mass media. The old laws of the poster as a medium of communication (such as readability and an immediate understanding of the message) no longer apply.

People are once again challenged to assess the traditional way of interpreting texts, messages and images.

Elena Xausa, after
Max Huber

Italian Graphic Design post 1945.

Maurizio Vitta

Professor of Design History and Culture at the Design Faculty of Politecnico di Milano University.

The history of Italian graphic design in the second half of the 20th century begins not in 1950, but in the first half of the century. In 1933 to be precise, when Studio Boggeri opened, the first issue of *Campo Grafico* (Graphic Field) was published and the fifth *Triennale di Milano* was held, where the German graphic design section designed by Paul Renner aroused keen interest. So right from its very beginning, Italian graphic design did not develop linearly, but grew from a series of cultural exchanges established via networks formed in two urban hubs.

Through its close links with industrial design, mutual fields of experimentation with modern architecture and constant comparisons with contemporary art, Italian graphic design gained a thorough and knowledgeable professional approach, as well as a keen sense of internationalism from a lively exchange of experiences with European designers, particularly Swiss ones.

This was the crucible in which contemporary Italian graphic design formed: a seething cauldron in which the long-awaited modern age would finally come into being. It wasn't the result of a search for new ways of expression, but an attempt to build the foundations of what might best be called a visual culture. This visual culture was set in the intellectual landscape of the time, yet linked back to classicism and formal balance; all the way from Luca Pacioli's Golden Ratio and Aldus Manutius' printing revolution, to the ground-breaking innovations of the first phase of the Futurist movement and the refined experiments of its second phase, led mainly by Fortunato Depero.

After the desolation of the post-war period, the imperative for economic and social development in Italy necessitated the creation of new communication and information protocols able to cope with the demands of an industrialized and democratic mass society. It was no coincidence that the graphic design network centred on the publishing capitals of Italy, Milan and Turin; two cities that had the cultural and industrial capacity to power the rapid spread of consumerism across the country.

Despite their apparent polarity, the two entrepreneurial and cultural worlds shared an ideology that united them: a desire for clear, logical communication. A simple message expressed as directly as possible. Albe Steiner's work is the most representative example of this approach. He started in 1945 with the poster designed for the *Mostra della ricostruzione* (The Rebuilding Exhibition) and continued with the design of *Politecnico*, a magazine created by Elio Vittorini to be a vehicle for the new visual culture.

This desire for rationality had begun with the experiments, reflections and international contacts made in the previous decades. The brief life of *Campo Grafico* lived on in the memory of its protagonists, while Milan's Triennale museum immediately established itself as a place for experimentation and new initiatives. The large group of Swiss graphic designers at Studio Boggeri before the war (Schawinski, Ballmer, Huber, Calabresi, Vivarelli, Monguzzi) not only bequeathed a rich heritage that would become the reference point for their Italian successors, but would also assure the possibility of continuity by staying in Milan. Besides the Swiss Boggeri contingent, Bauhaus was a key influence, as was the Dutch school (Bob

Elena Xausa, after Lora Lämm

Noorda moved to Milan in the early fifties) and the teachings of Max Bill.

A comparison of the story of Italian graphic design with the 'stars' of that period - industrial design and architecture (together with cinema) - reveals how closely connected it is to the more general development of design culture.

The man who most embodied this holistic approach to design was Olivetti.

His industrial values were directly mirrored in the work he commissioned for his company: the architecture of Gabetti and Isola, the design of Sottsass, the consultancy work of intellectuals like Giudici or Volponi, and last, but not least, the legendary graphical identity for Olivetti led by Giovanni Pintori.

Other large companies followed Olivetti in implementing refined brand strategies, although not on the same scale: Pirelli, for example, focused on an in-house graphic design studio (helped by designers such as Pino Tovaglia), and communicated through a magazine called simply *Pirelli*, which expressed

the company's dynamic nature through a rigorous graphic style - magnified by the building of the Pirelli Tower skyscraper designed by Gio Ponti - and its attention to the arts.

The rapidly growing television industry gave much of its graphic production to Erberto Carboni, who interpreted the new mass medium by translating its technological complexity into a simple and appealing visual language for Rai, foreshadowing the later iconic work he would create for Barilla.

Thus by the 1960s, the modern age entered in the first half of the century finally came to maturity and Italian graphic design was firmly rooted in the professional establishment, its position guaranteed by the proliferation of schools, publications and public popularity.

This paved the way for a new generation of designers to rise to the forefront of the visual communication industry: A.G. Fronzoni, with his absolute mastery of *Gestaltung* and a refined use of black and white; Franco Grignani, who conducted sophisticated optical experiments

searching for a new visual language; Pino Tovaglia, a fine interpreter of the new business landscape; Giancarlo Iliprandi, a visual language scholar; Michele Provinciali, Ilio Negri, Giulio Confalonieri and many others, including Armando Testa, in Turin, whose name began to be noticed in those early days.

Each of those names conjures up a different style, but they all share common cultural influences. Beneath the subjective differences there was a homogeneous conceptual layer that made graphic design the dominion of Cartesian logic, supported by a clear set of rules: every image was constructed in a logical order through a carefully calculated geometric model. This model ensured that every image produced was minimalistic; a result achieved through a skilful metonymic process.

Hence the common desire to reduce the visual discourse to its bare bones by tirelessly removing any excess material. This technique made the message emerge as if from nothing, from a silence that spoke as loudly as the message itself.

From this perspective it is possible to identify individual inclinations: Fronzoni's obsession with the simplest forms of communication; Iliprandi's quest for the tools to build a new visual rhetoric; Grignani, who played with perception and geometry to create a whirlwind of language assemblages.

The developments in contemporary modern art, from the rigours of Op Art, to the technological aesthetics of programmed art, also found an echo in the burgeoning world of graphic design. As did the dialectic in architecture, still struggling between its feelings for Wright and the teachings of Giuseppe Terragni. Or industrial design, in which every edition of the Compasso d'Oro awards marked a significant advance in the field.

It is not difficult to discern a red thread in this process; a new tradition of design that had its roots in the Northern European design culture of the first half of the 20th century. The progress of this new tradition was temporarily suspended by the closure of the Ulm School of Design, an event marked by the heated debate between Max Bill and Tomas Maldonado, which planted doubts into many over the design process.

But by this time were there already new changes on the horizon, announced by the emergence of new forms and media for communication. It was no accident that television advertising, for example, was best understood by minds like Armando Testa, a lively creative genius, who could transform a sign into a character, a character into a communication icon, transformed into a poster with vivid imagery, ranging from metamorphosis (the elephant tyre for Pirelli) to conceptual abstraction (the Punt e Mes logo). Pop art's energy was in the air, but beyond it a new production landscape was emerging, set to change the rituals of consumption and consequently the patterns of communication.

Meanwhile, editorial graphics were undergoing a slow but fundamental evolution - as the media itself required - perfectly exemplified in the work that Unimark (Massimo Vignelli and Bob Noorda) did for Mondadori and Feltrinelli.

Between the end of the 20th century and the beginning of the 21st, Italian graphic design faced an even more changeable and unstable world (marked by major structural changes and increasing awareness of other aesthetic models from the East and West), but it did so by adopting a policy of continuous refreshment without renouncing its ties with tradition.

In fact, in the work of Massimo Dolcini, Armando and Maurizio Milani, Italo Lupi and Pierluigi Cerri, you can see an indisputable continuity; a classical background, discreet, implicit, tenacious, to which design schemes still refer, even when addressing new issues. This same classical approach is flexible enough to allow designers to retain a strong link with regional cultures (Franco Balan) and address issues relating to the new political and social climate (Michele Spera, Ettore Vitale), as well as transcend the decline of the poster as a form of media due to the seismic changes in the urban landscape (despite a temporary rebirth thanks not to a graphic designer, but a photographer, Oliviero Toscani).

In one way or another, this classical foundation allows Italian graphic design to keep its distinguishing characteristics in a world where cultural differences tend to dissolve in the cloud of globalization and the relentless advance of digital technology hints at the rise of a new world, yet to be explored.

This reveals another aspect of Italy's cultural tradition: its intellectual cosmopolitanism. It has sustained the country's national creativity for centuries and still helps solve problems today; problems that are ever more European rather than national.

Elena Xausa, after
Giancarlo Iliprandi

An interview with Giancarlo Iliprandi.

Italian designer working in Milan since the 1950s.

The late '50s and '60s were a particularly fertile time in Italy. Everything came together at the same time: design flourished, companies were innovative and, of course, many people were attracted by the situation, including the Swiss.

When they arrived we had no idea that their influence would change the history of Italian graphic design. Italians interested in design usually had an artistic background then, like Bigani, Carboni and Italo Lupi, who were all architects. On the other side of the Alps however, everything was more rigorous, formal and technical.

Graphic design in Switzerland was already seen as a profession, while here we were still considered "advertising artists." A lot of people had already tried (and were still trying) to break away from the concept of "graphic art", like Munari, who, like many others, thought this definition cheapened the profession. The start of a real change in this situation only came when the Swiss arrived, or after their method became more widespread. For people like me, who wanted to be a designer a method, a set of rules, was essential. We felt the design process was vital, and that it should be based on a method that could match form and function throughout the whole design, and finally we'd found someone, or lots of people, who thought like us, who had even thought about it before us!

As for me, I started to think seriously about graphic design when I was working at Castiglioni's architectural firm. That's where I discovered this thing called visual communication and graphic design and where I met Max Huber for the first time. Before then I had studied medicine, done four years of painting and four years of set design at the Academy of Fine Arts of Brera, but I still hadn't found something that really interested me. I was deeply unsatisfied. Sure, set design was better than painting, as it gave me the opportunity to work with music, but ultimately a set designer always works under a director, so unless you're someone like Zeffirelli, who switched successfully from one role to another, it was limiting. At least for me.

My relationship with Max was inspirational. Not that Max and I would always talk about graphics, we'd go out a lot together to jazz clubs and concerts as well. In those years, when I was always at the Studio, I had the opportunity to get to know Steiner and Boggeri and I remember that one day I said to myself "yes, this is something interesting." That was when I really began to apply myself to graphic design. Watching Max working design displays made me want to learn, so I began to experiment with this "Swiss graphic design", buying books, and magazines like *Neue Grafik*, all set

in Helvetica. I bought them at Salto bookshop, a very significant place, not just for me. The two Salto brothers (of Swiss origin) ran the shop and were very knowledgeable. You could talk with them about what was happening in other countries, and when one of them was in the shop, the other would visit the studios with a bag full of the latest books on graphic design. In all honesty, I believe that much of the influence of Swiss design is due to them, and Castiglioni's studio of course.

There was really a lot of us working there, all working on many different display design projects: Max on some things, Heinz Waibl, who at the time was Max's assistant, on others, Tovaglia, Munari and Bianconi too. It was a place where we exchanged ideas, so we'd also go to see what others were doing. The atmosphere wasn't competitive, but friendly and collaborative in way that would have been impossible in the pure and rigid philosophy of the various Müller-Brockmanns.

Another key role in this Italy-Switzerland relationship was played by the graphic design course for assistants held at Humanitaria, the school founded in 1961 by Michael Provinciali and directed in its eight years of existence by Bauer first, and Melino later. And talking about crucial experiences,

we have to mention Rinascente, a department store that with its great exhibitions on Japan, India and Central America, taught the Milanese that different cultures existed. That affected everything from 1955 onwards.

Rinascente has always provided stimuli to make exchanges possible between people, designers, musicians, graphic designers, writers and its management. There were two families who alternated in the Managing Director and Presidency chairs, the Borletti's and the Bruschi's, and both played an important role in all of this. They always had an eye on what other department stores in London and Paris were doing, and had a curiosity and an openness that proved fruitful in many ways and represented an ideal combination for Swiss influences, from Zurich and Basel, to leave a mark.

Max Huber had a gifted hand and a benevolent eye; he appreciated everyone's work, and it was fascinating to see him working on large displays. He'd put a colour layer on top of another using huge sheets of cellophane. Then he'd brush them with water (in which he would have diluted some glue) and stretch them with a spatula. We were all delighted to see how quickly he could fix this and that. Steiner, however, would often criticize others. For him, communication had to have a social value and if it didn't,

An interview with Giancarlo Iliprandi.

it was nothing but wasted time. He was certainly more Swiss than Huber, despite being Italian. It was only later that I found out that everyone called me "small Steiner", as they said that I was picky as him.

Apart from and Max and Steiner, I admired Gfeller, but particularly Serge Libiszewski, a true innovator in photography. He was a still life and fashion photographer and had this incredible way of shooting people as if they were still life subjects too. He cared a lot about composition and lighting, and anything that appeared casual in his work was far from accidental. That was his great ability.

We all got to know each other when Mrs. Latis, Rinascente's art director, chose me to work on a design display instead of Steiner. Maybe she did it because I used to work on sets. Actually, working on a department store was like working on a set for me, with paints and big brushes. I remember once I set up the whole shop for Christmas, including the entrance. Lamm took care of the design of the small beauty shops. She was chosen to replace Max, mainly as her feminine way of doing things suited Latis' vision better. Then after Latis came along a new, young art director, Adriana Botti, and she began working with many other young people like Massimo Vignelli and Salvatore Gregorietti, who was Vignelli's assistant before the foundation of Unimark.

The shift in graphic design became evident in the next generation of designers: the mutual Swiss/Italian influences had left their trace. Certainly in Vignelli, who was probably the strongest supporter of the Haas foundry's Helvetica; conversely Max began to use Futura and Bodoni as soon as he got to Italy. Then there was the group formed by Cappelli, Bonini and Calabrese or the CNTP group - Confalonieri, Negri, Provinciali and Tovaglia - who had a way of expressing themselves through italics that was more humanistic and less Swiss.

At the time I was a critic of Sans Serif typefaces as I was convinced that many used them thinking they would be enough to make work look fashionable and contemporary. I've always been opposed to trends and convinced that designers should adapt their style to the customer and product, but Massimo used Helvetica well. He asked Nava to go to Switzerland and buy the lead blocks for that typeface. The operation worked the second time, but Nava wasn't the only one with Helvetica in Milan. Tipocromo, which later became Cromotipo, also had it in their catalogue.

A typeface that gave us a lot of trouble was Times New Roman. I liked it a lot, mainly when it was still unavailable in Italy. It was copyright protected at the time, so to use it we had to cut out the letters from The Times newspaper, assemble the text then photograph it all.

In those days there weren't any managers in Italy either. We had a direct relationship with the *Padrun* (boss): we'd take care of the idea, write the copy and in the case of larger companies, even talk to the client ourselves. Franco Fortini from Pirelli, Siniscaldi and Volponi from Olivetti or Vittorio Sereni were all intellectuals, and you could discuss stuff with them, explain why things were written in a certain order or why a single photograph wasn't enough. Well, let's say that for a while we did a little 'teaching' in certain companies.

When the *Padruns* were gone however, the multinational agencies came along and ate up all the market. There was a time when we had a good relationship with them - Milan's Art Directors Club was founded in 1967 by people from different disciplines: Pino Tovaglia, Blachian from Young & Rubicam, Flavio Lucchini (Vogue's art director) and me – but things didn't work for long. Everything slowly faded away, including the experimentation that created our small movement. We were just looking to find a new way of doing things with the people we met and worked with and make some connections, maybe some friends, along the way.

An Interview with Felix Humm.

Swiss designer working in Switzerland and Italy since the 1960s.

Graphic design had a starring role in the Milan of 1945-1970. Many Swiss designers emigrated to the city from Basel and Zurich during these years. Others came from Germany (inspired by the Bauhaus school), but no matter their origin, many passed through Studio Boggeri, where I had the honour to work as a very young man.

However, after I graduated, I didn't go straight to Milan, but to Turin. While I was still in Switzerland, I worked for an advertising agency called Reiwald, in Basel. I was part of the team that worked on the Fiat Switzerland account. After a little while the agency won the Fiat Italy account as well, so they transferred me to Turin. I was 21 years old. I was meant to stay in Italy for three days, but I ended up staying for forty years, first in Turin then in Milan. At that time there was a bit of a cultural renaissance in Italy, led mainly by companies like Olivetti, La Rinascente and Pirelli, all of who shared an enlightened corporate philosophy.

An Interview with Felix Humm.

The effects of this enlightenment also spread to us at Fiat in Turin, thanks mainly to the person leading the Fiat communications department at the time, Odone Camerena. He was related to the Olivetti family and studied at Oxford University, England. It created a new atmosphere that you could taste everywhere. In Turin and Milan it manifested itself in entrepreneurial initiatives (of course) and new opportunities on a social level. Today it would be impossible to propose work as extravagant, and with the same expressive freedom, that I did at the time. The photographic collages that I realised for a book called *70 Years Of Fiat* for example, were made into large prints to be placed on the walls of the office of Gianni Agnelli (the president of Fiat) alongside other paintings by Rauschenberg and Lichtenstein.

During my time in Turin I was personally particularly inspired by an exchange of ideas I had with a young product designer called Pio Manzù, son of the famous sculptor Giacomo Manzù. I really liked him. He arrived at Fiat after graduating from the Ulm School of Design (in Switzerland), and our relationship was made easier by our shared knowledge of German. I was also fascinated by typographers; by their machines, the smell of their workshops and the way our professions interacted.

But to go more in-depth into the graphic design scene, I believe that the relationship between the avant garde (both artistic and intellectual) and the work of a few graphic designers who were trying to produce a symbiosis between art and visual communication, was fundamental to the development of a new style.

As for my own style, I think it was mainly influenced by my studies in Basel. Once in Italy, I was inspired by the beauty of the tombstones in the Roman Forum in Rome and the elegance of Roman architecture, which taught me about the Golden Ratio. But every part of Italy you went to was so beautiful that you risked being affected by Stockholm syndrome!

Surely my studies had a foundation in a country (Switzerland) where graphic design was firmly established as a profession and wasn't considered 'art', as was often the case in Italy. But I don't believe that there's such a thing as a "Swiss" graphic design style. Swiss graphic design is derived from a mix of the Russian constructivism of El Lissitzky, Moholy-Nagy's Bauhaus, Piet Zwart's *de Stijl*, the *Neue Graphik* of Jan Tschichold and Max Bill's first Ulm School of Design.

The Swiss schools and institutions that taught graphic design passed on the principles of these movements, and from that education emerged designers like Max Huber, Hans Neuberg, Armin Hoffmann, Emil Ruder and Josef Müller-Brockmann and many others. I only met Huber when he was an old man, the same with Castiglioni. When I arrived in Milan the trend was to associate mainly with other foreigners, although I did meet many stimulating Italians, especially A.G. Fronzoni, whose work in typography was truly innovative and broke many boundaries. In those years experimentation and intuition were valued very highly and it's impossible to imagine the same situation being possible today. When marketing arrived on the scene, everything changed drastically. Marketing had a vision contrary to any form of creativity and innovation, ruled by the fear of selling a few less products. Intuition slowly became a taboo. But without intuition, there's no chance of change in the future.

Elena Xausa, after
Max Huber

Schweizerisches und Italienisches Design für Anfänger.

William Georgi

Als englischer Werbetexter, der in Amsterdam arbeitet - obgleich mit einem italienischen künstlerischen Leiter – befinde ich mich in einer einzigartigen Position, um schweizerisches und italienisches Design näher zu betrachten. Denn wenn ich die wundervolle Komplexität und Bedeutung dieser Designformen verstehen kann, dann können Sie, meine lieben Leser, es auch. Besonders nachdem Sie die Aufsätze, die dieser Einleitung folgen, gelesen haben. Diese Aufsätze wurden von Personen verfasst, die wirklich wissen wovon sie reden: die Akademiker Bettina Richter (Schweizerin) und Maurizio Vitta (Italiener) betrachten die Geschehnisse in beiden Ländern nach dem zweiten Weltkrieg aus intelligenter Perspektive; während die Designer Giancarlo Iliprandi und Felix Humm zu der Zeit mitten im Geschehen steckten und aus ganz persönlicher Perspektive schreiben.

Aber auf den nächsten Seiten werde ich Sie begleiten. Hurra. Denn als Werbetexter möchte ich, dass dieses Buch jedem zugänglich ist, nicht nur Designern oder Personen, die den Unterschied zwischen einem Grafikdesigner und einem künstlerischen Leiter kennen, ohne in einem Wörterbuch nachschlagen oder, wie ich es getan habe, Designerfreunde fragen zu müssen.

Also möchte ich Sie um Ihre Geduld bitten, während ich erkläre, warum wir hier sind und was wir feiern. Denn jeder - und ich meine absolut jeder - weiß, dass italienisches und schweizerisches Design fantastisch sind. Aber nicht jeder weiß, wie nah sie einander sind. Oder vielleicht sogar, was genau schweizerisches und italienisches Design eigentlich ist.

Genau gesagt reden wir hier von grafischem Design – die Kunst, aus visueller Kommunikation, nun ja, Kunst zu schaffen, um eine Nachricht so klar, effektiv und attraktiv wie möglich zu übermitteln. Dabei kann es sich um ein Poster, ein Logo, eine Verpackung, ein Schaufenster, einen Vogel, ein Flugzeug, Wenn man auf etwas drucken oder zeichnen kann, dann ist es Grafikdesign. Und wie Sie sehen werden ist es völlig egal, ob Sie für eine Schreibmaschine, einen Supermarkt oder einen Autoreifen werben; man kann mit Grafikdesign etwas Wunderschönes kreieren.

Und was wir hier feiern ist der riesige Einfluss, den eine Gruppe schweizerischer und italienischer Designer, die nach dem zweiten Weltkrieg in Mailand zusammenarbeiteten, auf die Welt haben würde.

Im Grunde genommen kollidierten zwei Welten miteinander – die technischen

Schweizer und die künstlerischen Italiener (wer liebt nicht ein gutes altes Länderklischee). Aber in diesem Fall war es tatsächlich so; die Schweizer legten schon seit jeher hohen Wert auf Design und hatten sogar Schulen, die sich Design widmeten – etwas, was wir jetzt für selbstverständlich ansehen, was es aber zu der Zeit, zumindest in Italien, nicht gab.

Um es etwas technischer auszudrücken, die Schweizer waren eher Grafikdesigner, denn sie nutzen ein Rastersystem, während die Italiener eher Künstler waren, denn sie lernten Ihre Fertigkeiten in Kunstschulen.

Und was genau ist ein Rastersystem? Es ist ein System, bei dem das Material eines Designs einem Raster entsprechend angeordnet wird. Alles, was zu einem Design dazugehört – Text, Fotografie, Bilder, etc. – muss mit den Linien des Rasters übereinstimmen.

Ganz einfach. Oder auch nicht. Je nach dem Standpunkt des Betrachters ist das Rastersystem entweder unentbehrlich oder ein Kreativitäts-Killer. Wie dem auch sei, um es anwenden zu können, muss man es erlernen. Und das braucht Zeit. Und Bildung. Darum waren die Schweizer, und ihr hauptsächlicher Befürworter Josef Müller-Brockmann, so gut darin. Und genau deswegen waren die an Kunstschulen ausgebildeten (oder einfach künstlerischen) Italiener so gut darin, mit ihnen (oder gegen sie) zu arbeiten. Denn wie wir alle nur zu gut wissen, Regeln sind zum brechen da.

Aber es war Italien, und insbesondere Mailand, das nach dem zweiten Weltkrieg eine enorme Anziehungskraft für kreative Leute hatte. Designer aus der Schweiz kamen nach Mailand weil sie a) gebraucht wurden und b) weil es dort die aufregendsten Aufträge gab. Kunden, die ihnen die Carte Blanche und volle künstlerische Freiheit gaben. Designer und Intellektuelle, mit denen man sich zum Mittagessen treffen und herrlich diskutieren konnte.

Die folgenden Aufsätze zeigen, dass Designer wie Iliprandi das Glück hatten, zu einer Zeit dort gewesen zu sein, als alle Elemente zusammenkamen und etwas wahrhaft Erstaunliches geschaffen wurde. Die richtigen Leute – von oben bis unten, von Illustratoren bis zu Musikern, von Zürich bis Mailand – am richtigen Ort. Ideen wurden ausgetauscht und Barrieren wurden nicht abgebaut, sie existierten einfach nicht. Kreative und Kunden waren gleichgestellt und es wurde mit Ideen und nicht mit Geld gehandelt. John Steinbeck hat einmal gesagt, dass kreative Leute dort hingehen, wo man sie schätzt. Und Mailand war zwischen 1945 und den Sechzigern einer dieser besonderen Orte. Die Designwelt würde nie wieder dieselbe sein.

Italienische Inspiration im Schweizerischen Grafikdesign der Nachkriegszeit.

Bettina Richter

Kuratorin Plakatsammlung, Museum für Gestaltung, Zürich.

Zürich und Mailand um 1945: gegensätzliche mentale Welten

Kaum war der Zweite Weltkrieg beendet, setzte in der Schweiz ein wirtschaftlicher Aufschwung ein, dessen Bedarf an Arbeitskräften das Land alleine nicht decken konnte. Unzählige Menschen, meist aus dem tiefsten Süden Italiens stammend, emigrierten in die Schweiz. Die Hoffnung auf Arbeit und ein besseres Leben liess sie viele Strapazen ertragen, nicht zuletzt den Rassismus der Schweizer Politik. Arbeitsbedingungen und Zahl der Arbeitnehmenden wurden an die Konjunkturlage angepasst und verunmöglichten es den Italienern, sich in der neuen Heimat willkommen zu fühlen.

Anders erging es da einigen Schweizer Grafikern, die in der gleichen Epoche den umgekehrten Weg nahmen und sich in Mailand niederliessen. Die Stadt trug das Versprechen von *Dolce Vita* und Neuanfang im Namen. Wenngleich man noch nicht wie heute in knapp vier Stunden von Zürich in die italienische Stadt gelangen konnte, war die örtliche Distanz gering. Dies umso mehr, wenn man bedenkt, welche mentalen und geistigen Welten sich damals zwischen beiden Ländern auftaten.

In der vom Krieg verschonten Schweiz hatten sich in den Jahren nach 1939 konservative Werte verfestigt, die die politische und kulturelle Abschottung vom übrigen Europa verstärkten. Geistige Unbeweglichkeit und kreative Ermattung standen dem ökonomischen Boom gegenüber.

Zwar gelang es in der Grafik der 1950er Jahre, an den Modernismus der Vorkriegsjahre anzuknüpfen. In Zürich formulierte Emil Müller-Brockmann, Hauptprotagonist des sogenannten *Swiss Style*, das Leitbild konkreter Kunst und Typografie. Armin Hofmann und Emil Ruder fanden in Basel zu einer sinnlicheren, verspielten Variante schweizerischer Grafik. Puristische, auf dem Raster basierende Strenge im Bildaufbau, bewusster Einsatz von Typografie, Grafik und Fotografie und der unbedingte Vorrang des Informationsgehalts einer visuellen Mitteilung wurden zu den Prämissen eines Stils, der sich rasch internationales Ansehen verschaffen konnte. In der Schweiz selbst jedoch wurden diese „Gesetze" bald in

orthodoxer Manier weitergegeben und führten zumal bei weniger begabten Gestaltern zu einer blutleeren, routinierten Grafik. Selbst Müller-Brockmanns spätes Werk ist diesem Schicksal nicht gänzlich entgangen.

In Norditalien hingegen, vor allem in Mailand, wurde der wirtschaftliche Aufschwung getragen und begleitet von einem progressiven, offenen Klima. Da der italienische Faschismus in der Kulturpolitik weniger radikal gewirkt hatte als in Deutschland, konnte auch hier an die Avantgarde der Vorkriegszeit angeknüpft werden. Zudem war die Nachkriegszeit von einer intensiven geistigen Auseinandersetzung mit den jüngsten, historischen Ereignissen geprägt, geführt von engagierten Künstlern, Literaten und Intellektuellen. Auch in der Wirtschaft manifestierte sich der radikale gesellschaftspolitische Wandel. Am eindrücklichsten verdeutlicht dies das Wirken von Adriano Olivetti (1901-1960), der die westlich von Mailand gelegene Stadt Ivrea zu einem Symbol für Industrie- und Kulturgeschichte werden liess. Bereits 1926 stieg Olivetti in das väterliche Unternehmen ein und arbeitete an seiner konkreten Utopie einer „città degli uomini". Reines Profitdenken stellte er zugunsten humaner Firmenkonzepte zurück. Aufgrund seines antifaschistischen Engagements wurde Olivetti 1944 kurz ins Schweizer Exil gezwungen, setzte aber seine Ideen nach Kriegsende fort. Olivetti entwickelte nicht zuletzt einen weitgefassten Begriff visueller Kommunikation, der Ethik und Ästhetik verband und ihr einen hohen Stellenwert in der Unternehmenspolitik sicherte. Bereits in den 1930er Jahren schuf er eine betriebseigene Werbe- und Kommunikationsabteilung. Olivettis soziales und kulturelles Engagement wirke vorbildlich auf wie La Rinascente, Pirelli und Montecatini, die nach dem Krieg ebenfalls eigene Werbebüros einrichteten. Damit stieg der Bedarf an professionellen Gestaltern und Fotografen, denn in Italien existierten bis in die 1950er Jahre kaum Designschulen. In den wenigen Ateliers und Werbebüros wirkten Quereinsteiger, die von der Malerei oder der Architektur zur angewandten Gestaltung gefunden hatten. Diese Situation erwies sich als äusserst vorteilhaft für die gut ausgebildeten jungen Grafiker und Fotografen der benachbarten Schweiz. Voll Sehnsucht nach persönlichen und gesellschaftspolitischen Auf- und Umbrüchen bestiegen sie den Zug nach Mailand, um hier ihre berufliche Laufbahn zu beginnen oder fortzusetzen.

Schweizer Gestalter in Mailand

Xanti Schawinsky und Max Huber waren die frühesten Botschafter der Schweiz in Italien. Der charismatische, vielseitig begabte Basler Schawinsky studierte nach frühen Musik- und Malausbildungen am Bauhaus in Weimar und Dessau. Mit seiner Universalbegabung und seiner Experimentierfreudigkeit war er ganz dem Geist des frühen, auf eine umfassende Reform von Kunst und Gesellschaft ausgerichteten Bauhaus verpflichtet. 1933 flüchtete er zunächst zurück in die Schweiz, liess sich aber noch im gleichen Jahr in Italien

nieder, wo er in Künstlerkreisen verkehrte und auch Antonio Boggeri begegnete. Boggeri verkörpert ein weiteres Puzzleteil im schweizerisch-italienischen Zusammenspiel jener Jahre. Durch seine Arbeit im Druckereibetrieb Alfieri & Lacroix begegnete der Musiker und Fotograf dem Werk führender Avantgardisten wie El Lissitzky und Jan Tschichold. Im sensiblen Zusammenspiel von Typografie, Illustration, Grafik und Fotografie erkannte Boggeri neue Wege der visuellen Kommunikation und eröffnete 1933 ein eigenes Studio. Schawinsky zählte zu seinen ersten Mitarbeitern. Als begabter Talent-Scout immer auf der Suche nach neuen Grafikern, knüpfte Boggeri bereits 1935 Kontakte nach Zürich. Durch eine Empfehlung kam Max Huber 1940 nach Mailand und begann mit der Arbeit im Studio Boggeri. Kreative Neugier, gestalterische Offenheit und eine pluralistisch verstandene Avantgarde verband alle Mitarbeiter des Studios. Im weiteren Verlauf seiner Geschichte rückten andere Schweizer nach wie Carlo Vivareli, Walter Ballmer, Serge Libiszewski. Lora Lamm, oder Bruno Monguzzi. Die Rotation war hoch, viele benutzten die Arbeit bei Boggeri als Sprungbrett, um sich anschliessend selbständig zu machen oder in den neu entstandenen Werbeabteilungen verschiedener Unternehmen führende Positionen einzunehmen. Nur das Studio Grignani unter Leitung des ausgebildeten Architekten und Grafiker Franco Grignani konkurrenzierte das Studio Boggeri im Mailänder Zentrum und lockte ebenfalls Schweizer Mitarbeiter an. Die überschaubare Szene junger Grafiker traf sich mittags zu ausgiebigen Essen in kleinen Trattorien. Künstler und Schriftsteller gesellten sich dazu und es fanden regelmässig intensive Diskussionen über den gesellschaftlichen Stellenwert von Design und Kunst und die Verantwortung der Gestalter statt.

Max Huber, der in den Kriegsjahren in die Schweiz zurückkehren musste, suchte nach Kriegsende sofort wieder die italienische Inspiration. Neben dem Grafiker Albe Steiner arbeitete er von 1950 bis 1954 in der Werbeabteilung des Kaufhauses La Rinascente, für das er das Firmenlogo sowie ein integrales Kommunikationskonzept entwickelte. La Rinascente symbolisierte in den 1950er Jahren exemplarisch die kulturelle und wirtschaftliche Wiedergeburt Italiens. Die Angebotspalette an Mode und Möbel stand für Design und Qualität. Giò Ponti, namhafter Architekt und Designer, richtete ab 1953 bei La Rinascente seine Ausstellungen zu ausgezeichneter Produktästhetik aus und vergab dort ab 1954 den Designpreis Compasso d'Oro. Die Synthese von Funktionalität, Ästhetik, Innovation und Erschwinglichkeit auch für weniger Verdienenden war charakteristisch für alle Produkte von La Rinascente.

Lora Lamm war einige der ganz wenigen Schweizer Frauen im umtriebigen Klima der 1950er Jahre in Mailand. Max Huber holte sie 1954 zu La Rinascente, nachdem sie zunächst im Studio Boggeri einen wenig verheissungsvollen Start genommen hatte und nur mit zweitrangigen Arbeiten beschäftigt worden war. Bereits 1956 machte sie mit einer höchst eigenwilligen Werbekampagne für eine Ausstellung japanischer Produkte bei La Rinascente auf sich aufmerksam. Von 1958 bis 1962 war sie Leiterin des Grafikateliers und prägte mit ihren originellen, illustrativen, von Bildwitz strotzenden Arbeiten eine eigene Ära.

Auch der Fotograf Serge Libiszewski, der nach seiner Ausbildung an der Zürcher Kunstgewerbeschule in Müller-Brockmanns Atelier direkt beim Zürcher Hauptbahnhof arbeitete, wurde von Huber für La Rinascente abgeworben. Max Huber machte auf seinen Fahrten von und nach Mailand regelmässige Besuche im Atelier und schwärmte von der dortigen Atmosphäre. Das Fehlen professioneller Werbefotografen in Norditalien bewog Libiszewski zum Aufbruch. Sein Beginn war allerdings ebenfalls enttäuschend, da er zunächst kaum Fotoaufträge erhielt, sondern vielmehr als Handlanger funktionierte. Als er sich 1962 mit einem eigenen Studio selbständig machte, begann sein Erfolg. Er erhielt nun namhafte Aufträge, u.a. von La Rinascente, vom Studio Boggeri, von Olivetti und Pirelli. Die Fotografie emanzipierte sich in just in diesen Jahren vom Versatzstück zum eigenständigen Bildmittel innerhalb der Werbegrafik. Mit seiner künstlerischen Experimentierfreude war Libiszewski in Zusammenarbeit mit Salvatore Gregorietti und Giancarlo Iliprandi für La Rinascente oder Walter Ballmer für Olivetti an vielen innovativen Plakaten und Grafikaufträgen beteiligt.

Allen Schweizer Grafikern und Fotografen, die nach 1950 in Mailand ankamen, waren der Durst nach neuen Anregungen, die Lust zum Ausbruch aus schweizerischer Enge und die Sehnsucht nach kreativem Schaffen ohne Vorgaben und Abgrenzungen zwischen den Künsten gemeinsam. Wie viele Epochen eines historischen Umbruchs, begleitet von gesellschaftlichem und kulturellem Wandel, währte aber auch diese nicht allzu lange. Zu Beginn der 1970er Jahre verloren sich die sozialen Utopien zunehmend. Marketingkonzepte, die vor allem auf ein effektives Logo setzten, begannen die Unternehmenskommunikation zu bestimmen. Anstelle von mutigem Autorendesign wurden Aufträge an führende Werbeagenturen vergeben, der direkte Dialog zwischen Unternehmensleitung und ausgesuchten Grafikern und Fotografen fand sein Ende.

Zeitgenössisches Grafikdesign aus der Schweiz

Die von Italien empfangenen Impulse trugen wesentlich dazu bei, dass Schweizer Grafik in der Geschichte der visuellen Kommunikation der 1950er und 1960er Jahre einen hohen Stellenwert einnimmt. Die fundierte Ausbildung der Schweizer Gestalter bildete wohl eine wertvolle Grundlage. Aber erst durch den inspirierenden Austausch mit italienischen Gestaltern und ihrem frischen Zugriff, der eine ganz andere gestalterische Tradition verriet, konnte sich die Grafik eines Max Huber, einer Lora Lamm oder eines Walter Ballmer entfalten. Und nur die glücklichen Bedingungen im Mailand dieser Jahre, wirtschaftliche Blüte, herausragende Studios und engagierte Auftraggeber, führten zu diesem stilistischen Reichtum im Grafikdesign. Formale Strenge mischten sich mit experimenteller Neugier, Farbigkeit, Poesie, verspieltem Witz und unbekümmerter Lebenslust. In jener Zeit konnte ein Austausch von Mentalitäten stattfinden, der sich für beide Seiten als höchst fruchtbar erwies.

Dieser gelungene Mix bestimmt jedoch bis heute zeitgenössisches Grafikdesign aus der Schweiz. In seiner ästhetischen Vielschichtigkeit liefert es den Beweis, dass spätestens seit den politisch und kulturell bewegten 1980er Jahren der expressive Aufbruch nicht mehr rückgängig gemacht werden kann. Das strenge Regelkorsett von Raster und Helvetica wird hinterfragt, oftmals der provokative Regelbruch geprobt, immer im Sinne einer wachen Auseinandersetzung mit der eigenen Tradition und einem sensiblen Ausloten von Freiräumen, kaum in umstürzlerischer Manier.

Eine Ausweitung der gestalterischen Möglichkeiten im Grafikdesign ergab sich schon immer auch durch die intensive, undogmatische Auseinandersetzung mit anderen kulturellen Äusserungen – Musik, Literatur, bildende Kunst – und durch die Aufnahme von Einflüssen aus anderen Kulturräumen. Diese Tendenzen dauern bis heute an und führen zu Grenzüberschreitungen und lustvollen, gestalterischen Experimenten. Seit den 1990er Jahren vermittelt sich zudem deutlich, dass eine junge Generation von Gestaltern nicht mehr nur der Verführungskraft computergenerierter grafischer Lösungen erliegt. Neuste Technologien werden zwar souverän und spielerisch genutzt, bewusst aber wird auch wieder „Handarbeit" gesucht. Die sinnliche Auseinandersetzung mit dem Material erlaubt andere kreative Versuche und fordert ein höheres persönliches Engagement, die Ergebnisse sind subjektiver und unkonformistischer. Das Unperfekte, der Zufall, das Spontane werden zu Faktoren, die die gestalterische Praxis wesentlich beeinflussen. Freihand-Illustrationen, Handschriften, selbstgesetzte Lettern, ungewöhnliche Schriftmischungen, Collagetechniken etc. feiern ein fröhliches Comeback im zeitgenössischen Plakat. Das Spiel mit Zitaten aus anderen Massenmedien, der Fotografie, der hohen Kunst reflektieren die vielfältigen Aneignungsweisen und Lesarten von Bildern und Texten heute. In formaler als auch inhaltlicher Sicht belegen zeitgenössische Kulturplakate auch ein anderes Verständnis des Massenmediums Plakat. Fernwirkung, Lesbarkeit, unmittelbare Verständlichkeit der Botschaft als lange gültige Gesetze des Kommunikationsmediums Plakat werden durch sie in Frage gestellt.

Mit ihrer Offenheit und Vieldeutigkeit wollen sie ihr Publikum herausfordern, rufen zur Auseinandersetzung auf, stören und irritieren eingefahrene Sehgewohnheiten.

Italienisches Grafikdesign nach 1945.

Maurizio Vitta

Professor für Design Geschichte und Kultur an der Fakultät Gestaltung der Politecnico di Milano University.

Die Geschichte des italienischen Grafikdesigns in der zweiten Hälfte des 20. Jahrhunderts beginnt nicht im jahre 1950, sondern in der ersten Hälfte des Jahrhunderts. Genauer gesagt im jahre 1933, dem Jahr als Studio Boggerie aufmachte, die erste Ausgabe von *Campo Grafico* (Grafikfeld) erschien und die fünfte *Triennale di Milano* stattfand, wo der von Paul Renner entworfene deutsche Grafikdesign-Bereich für reges Interesse sorgte. Italienisches Grafikdesign entwickelte sich also von Anfang an nicht auf lineare Weise, sondern entsprang vielmehr einer Reihe kultureller Austausche durch Netzwerke, die in zwei urbanen Angelpunkten entstanden.

Durch seine enge Beziehung zu industriellem Design, seine Überschneidung mit moderner Architektur im Bereich der Experimentierung und seinem ständigen Vergleich mit moderner Kunst entwickelte italienisches Grafikdesign eine sorgfältige und fundierte professionelle Herangehensweise sowie ein feines Gespür für Internationalität durch den lebhaften Erfahrungsaustausch mit anderen europäischen Designern, insbesondere den Schweizern.

Dies war der Schmelztiegel, in dem das moderne italienische Grafikdesign entstand: ein siedender Kessel, in dem das lang erwartete moderne Zeitalter endlich ins Leben gerufen werden würde. Italienisches Grafikdesign ist nicht das Resultat der Suche nach einer neuen Ausdrucksform, sondern ein Versuch, das Fundament dafür zu schaffen, was man am besten als visuelle Kultur beschreiben kann. Diese visuelle Kultur war zu der Zeit in der intellektuellen Landschaft gegenwärtig, reichte aber auf den Klassizismus und das Prinzip des formalen Gleichgewichts zurück; von Luca Paciolis goldenem Schnitt und Aldus Manutius' Druckrevolution bis zu den bahnbrechenden Innovationen der ersten Phase der Futuristenbewegung und den präzisierten Experimenten der zweiten Phase, hauptsächlich von Fortunato Depero angeführt.

Nach der Trostlosigkeit der Nachkriegszeit war es die Notwendigkeit für wirtschaftliche und soziale Entwicklung, welche die Schaffung neuer Kommunikations- und Informationsprotokolle forderte, die den Anforderungen einer industrialisierten und demokratischen Massengesellschaft gerecht werden konnte. Es war kein Zufall, dass sich das Grafikdesign-Netzwerk auf Mailand und Turin, den Druckzentralen Italiens konzentrierte – zwei Städte, deren kulturelle und industrielle Kapazität die schnelle Verbreitung des Konsumverhaltens im ganzen Land ermöglichte.

Trotz ihrer anscheinenden Gegensätzlichkeit teilten die beiden unternehmerischen und kulturellen Welten eine Ideologie, die sie miteinander verband: ein Verlangen nach klarer, logischer Kommunikation. Eine Nachricht so direkt wie möglich auszudrücken. Albe Steiners Werke veranschaulichen diese Herangehensweise am besten. Er begann 1945 mit dem Entwurf eines Posters für die *Mostra della ricostruzione* (Messe für den Wiederaufbau) und entwarf danach für *Politecnico*, ein von Elio Vittorini ins Leben gerufene Magazin, was als Träger für die neue visuelle Kultur galt.

Dieses Verlangen nach Rationalität hatte mit den Experimenten, Überlegungen und internationalen Kontaktaufnahmen

Italienisches Grafikdesign nach 1945.

in den vorhergehenden Jahrzehnten begonnen. Trotz seiner kurzen Lebensspanne lebte *Campo Grafico* in der Erinnerung seiner Protagonisten weiter, während sich Mailands Triennale Museum sofort als ein Ort für Experimente und neue Initiativen etablierte. Die große Gruppe schweizerischer Grafikdesigner, die vor dem Krieg bei Studio Boggeri gearbeitet hatten (Schawinski, Ballmer, Huber, Calabresi, Vivarelli, Monguzzi), hinterließen nicht nur ein reiches Erbe, das als Anhaltspunkt für ihre italienischen Nachfolger gelten würde, sondern ermöglichten auch Kontinuität indem sie in Mailand blieben. Neben der schweizerischen Boggeri-Gruppe war Bauhaus ein wichtiger Einfluss, als auch die holländische Schule (Bob Noorda zog am Anfang der fünfziger Jahre nach Mailand) und die Lehren von Max Bill.

Wenn man die Geschichte des italienischen Grafikdesigns mit den „Prominenten" dieser Zeit – industrielles Design und Architektur (gemeinsam mit Film) – vergleicht, stellt man fest, wie eng es mit der allgemeinen Entwicklung der Designkultur in Verbindung steht.

Die Person, die diese holistische Herangehensweise an Design am stärksten verkörperte, war Olivetti. Seine industriellen Werte wurden direkt in den Werken, die er für sein Unternehmen in Auftrag gab, widergespiegelt: die Architektur von Gabetti und Isola, das Design von Sottsass, die Beratungsfunktion von Intellektuellen wie Giudici oder Volponi und nicht zuletzt die legendäre grafische Identität für Olivetti, angeführt von Giovanni Pintori.

Andere große Firmen folgten Olivettis Vorbild und implementierten durchdachte Markenstrategien, wenn auch nicht in der gleichen Größenordnung: Pirelli konzentrierte sich zum Beispiel auf ein firmeneigenes Grafikdesign-Studio (mit der Unterstützung von Designern wie Pino Tovaglia) und kommunizierte anhand einer Zeitschrift, schlicht Pirelli genannt, in welcher der dynamische Charakter der Firma durch einen drastischen Grafikstil – verstärkt durch den Bau des von Gio Ponti entworfenen Pirelli-Turm Wolkenkratzers - und ihr Interesse an Kunst ausgedrückt wurde.

Die schnell wachsende Fernsehindustrie überließ den Großteil ihrer grafischen Produktion Erberto Carboni, der das neue Massenmedium interpretierte, indem er dessen technologische Komplexität für Rai in eine einfache und ansprechende Sprache übersetzte; ein Vorreiter der Kultwerke, die er später für Barilla entwarf.

Somit war das moderne Zeitalter, was in der ersten Hälfte des Jahrhunderts seinen Anfang gefunden hatte, in den sechziger Jahren zur vollen Reife gelangt und italienisches Grafikdesign war ein fester Bestandteil der Industrie geworden - sein Status garantiert durch die Verbreitung von Schulen und gedruckter Presse und seiner allgemeinen Beliebtheit.

Dies bahnte den Weg für eine neue Generation an Designern, die es zur Spitze der visuellen Kommunikationsindustrie schaffte: A.G. Fronzoni mit seiner absoluten

Meisterung von *Gestaltung* und einer raffinierten Anwendung von schwarz und weiß; Franco Grignani, der auf der Suche nach einer neuen visuellen Sprache aufwendige Experimente durchführte; Pino Tovaglia, ein ausgezeichneter Deuter der neuen Geschäftslandschaft; Giancarlo Iliprandi, ein Lehrer der visuellen Sprache; Michele Provinciali, Ilio Negri, Giulio Confalonieri und viele andere, unter anderem Armando Testa in Turin, dessen Name schon in diesen frühen Jahren Aufmerksamkeit erregte.

Jeder dieser Namen wird mit einem anderen Stil assoziiert, jedoch teilen sie alle die gleichen kulturellen Einflüsse. Über die subjektiven Unterschiede hinweg existiert eine homogene konzeptionelle Schicht, die aufzeigt, dass Grafikdesign der kartesischen Logik und einer Reihe festgelegter Regeln unterlag: jedes Bild wurde mittels eines sorgfältig berechneten geometrischen Modells in einer logischen Reihenfolge erstellt. Dieses Modell gewährleistete, dass jedes produzierte Bild minimalistisch war – das Ergebnis eines geschickten metonymischen Vorgangs.

Daraus resultierte das gemeinsame Verlangen danach, den visuellen Diskurs auf ein Minimum zu reduzieren, indem alle überflüssigen Elemente entfernt wurden. Dieses Verfahren ließ es so aussehen, als ob die Nachricht aus dem Nichts erschien, aus einer Stille, die so laut sprach wie die Nachricht selbst.

Von dieser Perspektive aus ist es möglich, individuelle Neigungen zu identifizieren: Fronzonis Besessenheit mit den einfachsten

Kommunikationsformen; Iliprandis Suche nach Werkzeugen zum Bau einer neuen visuellen Rhetorik; Grignani, der mit Wahrnehmung und Geometrie spielte, um einen Wirbelwind an Sprachsammlungen zu schaffen.

Die Entwicklungen in zeitgenössischer moderner Kunst, von der Strenge der Op Art bis zu der technologischen Ästhetik der programmierten Kunst, fanden ebenfalls Anklang in der aufkeimenden Welt des Grafikdesigns. Das galt auch für die Dialektik in der Architektur, die einerseits noch mit ihren Gefühlen für Wright und andererseits mit der Lehre Giuseppe Terragnis kämpfte. Und auch für das industrielle Design, wo jede Ausgabe der *Compasso d'Oro* Auszeichnungen einen wesentlichen Schritt auf diesem Gebiet verzeichnete.

Es ist nicht schwer, einen roten Faden in diesem Vorgang zu erkennen; eine neue Designtradition, die ihre Wurzeln in der Designkultur Nordeuropas in der ersten Hälfte des 20. Jahrhunderts hatte. Der Fortschritt dieser Entwicklung wurde vorübergehend durch die Schließung der Ulmer Designschule unterbrochen, begleitet von heftigen Diskussionen zwischen Max Bill und Tomas Maldonado, die bei vielen Zweifeln über den Designvorgang säte.

Aber zu diesem Zeitpunkt zeichneten sich bereits Veränderungen ab, die sich mit der Entstehung neuer Kommunikationsformen und –Medien ankündigten. Es war kein Zufall, dass zum Beispiel Fernsehwerbung am besten von Gemütern wie

Armando Testa verstanden wurde. Testa, ein lebhaftes und kreatives Genie, konnte ein Zeichen in einen Charakter, einen Charakter in ein Kommunikationssymbol und dieses wiederum in ein Poster mit lebhafter Symbolik verwandeln, von Metamorphose (der Elefantenreifen für Pirelli) bis hin zu konzeptioneller Abstraktion (das Punt e Mes Logo). Die Energie der Kunstrichtung Pop Art lag schon in der Luft, aber darüber hinaus entwickelte sich eine neue Produktionslandschaft, die Verbraucherrituale und damit Kommunikationsmuster verändern würde.

Währenddessen erlebten redaktionelle Grafiken eine langsame aber grundlegende Evolution – was für dieses Medium auch notwendig war – perfekt veranschaulicht durch die Arbeit von Unimark (Massimo Vignelli und Bob Noorda) für Mondadori und Feltrinelli.

Zwischen dem Ende des 20. Jahrhunderts und dem Beginn des 21. Jahrhunderts wurde das italienische Grafikdesign mit einer zunehmend wechselhaften und unbeständigen Welt konfrontiert (geprägt von wesentlichem Strukturwandel und wachsender Wahrnehmung anderer ästhetischer Modelle aus dem Osten und Westen), stellte sich dieser aber mit einer Strategie der ständigen Erfrischung, ohne dabei seine Verbundenheit zur Tradition aufzugeben.

Tatsächlich lassen die Werke von Massimo Dolcini, Armando und Maurizio Milani, Italo Lupi und Pierluigi Cerri eine unbestreitbare Kontinuität

erkennen; ein klassischer Hintergrund - diskret, implizit, beharrlich - auf den sich Designschemas noch immer beziehen, selbst wenn sie sich mit neuen Problemen befassen. Dieselbe klassische Herangehensweise ist flexibel genug, so dass Designer eine starke Verbindung mit regionaler Kultur aufrecht erhalten können (Franco Balan) und sich mit Problemen im Zusammenhang mit dem neuen politischen und sozialen Klima auseinandersetzen können (Michele Spera, Ettore Vitale), als auch den Verfall des Posters als Medienform aufgrund seismischer Änderungen in der urbanen Landschaft (trotz einer vorübergehenden Wiederbelebung, nicht durch einen Grafikdesigner, sondern durch den Fotografen Oliviero Toscani) überstehen zu können.

So oder so ist es diese klassische Grundlage, die es dem italienischen Grafikdesign ermöglicht, seine unterscheidenden Charaktereigenschaften in einer Welt beizubehalten, in der kulturelle Unterschiede dazu neigen, sich in der Wolke der Globalisierung aufzulösen und in welcher der erbarmungslose Fortschritt digitaler Technologien den Beginn einer neuen Welt andeuten lässt, die es erst zu entdecken gilt.

Und das enthüllt einen weiteren Aspekt der kulturellen Tradition Italiens: sein Weltbürgertum. Dieses hat die nationale Kreativität des Landes jahrhundertlang aufrecht erhalten und hilft auch heute noch dabei, Probleme zu lösen – Probleme, die zunehmend europäischer anstatt italienischer Natur sind.

Ein interview mit Giancarlo Iliprandi.

Italienische Designer arbeiten in Mailand seit den 1950er Jahren.

Giancarlo Iliprandi, Basta violenza sui bambini, 2009

Die späten fünfziger und sechziger Jahre waren eine besonders fruchtbare Zeit in Italien. Alle Elemente kamen zur gleichen Zeit zusammen: Design gedieh, Firmen waren innovativ und natürlich fühlten sich viele Personen von dieser Situation angezogen, einschließlich der Schweizer.

Als sie ankamen hatten wir verständlicherweise keine Ahnung, dass ihr Einfluss die Geschichte des italienischen Grafikdesigns verändern würde. An Design interessierte Italiener hatten gewöhnlich einen künstlerischen Hintergrund, wie Bigani, Carboni und Italo Lupi, die alle Architekten waren. Auf der anderen Seite der Alpen war alles strenger, formaler und technischer.

Grafikdesign wurde in der Schweiz bereits als ein Beruf angesehen, während wir noch als „Werbekünstler" betrachtet wurden. Viele Personen hatten bereits versucht (und versuchten immer noch), sich von dem Konzept der „Grafikkunst" zu lösen, unter anderem Munari, der wie viele andere der Meinung war, dass diese Definition den Beruf verbilligte. Eine wirkliche Änderung in diesem Bereich vollzog sich erst als die Schweizer ankamen, oder nachdem ihre Methode weiter verbreitet war. Für Personen wie mich selbst, die Designer sein wollten, war eine Methodik, ein Regelwerk, unentbehrlich. Wir waren überzeugt, dass der Designprozess entscheidend war und dass er auf einer Methodik basieren sollte, die mit der Form und Funktion des gesamten Designs übereinstimmt und wir hatten endlich jemanden, oder viele Personen, gefunden, die genau das Gleiche dachten – die sogar schon vor uns auf den Gedanken gekommen waren!

Ich selbst begann ernsthaft über Grafikdesign nachzudenken als ich für Castiglionis Architektenbüro arbeitete. Dort entdeckte ich zum ersten Mal die Konzepte der visuellen Kommunikation und des Grafikdesigns und dort traf ich auch Max Huber zum ersten Mal. Davor hatte ich Medizin studiert und vier Jahre Malerei und vier Jahre Bühnenbild an der Kunstakademie in Brera hinter mir, aber trotzdem nichts gefunden, was mich wirklich interessierte. Ich war zutiefst unzufrieden. Natürlich war Bühnenbildner besser als Maler, weil es mir die Möglichkeit gab, mit Musik zu arbeiten, aber schlussendlich arbeitet ein Bühnenbildner immer unter einem Regisseur – es sei denn, man war jemand wie Zeffirelli, der

erfolgreich zwischen beiden Rollen hin- und herwechselte – und das war einschränkend. Zumindest für mich.

Meine Beziehung zu Max war inspirierend. Nicht, dass Max und ich immer über Grafiken reden würden, wir gingen auch oft zu Jazzclubs und Konzerten. Zu dieser Zeit, als ich immer im Studio war, hatte ich die Gelegenheit, Steiner und Boggeri kennenzulernen und ich erinnere mich, wie ich mir eines Tages sagte „ja, das ist etwas interessantes". Und von da an widmete ich mich der Sache wirklich. Max bei seiner Arbeit an Design-Displays zuzusehen spornte mich zum Lernen an und so begann ich, mit diesem „schweizerischen Grafikdesign" zu experimentieren und kaufte Bücher und Zeitschriften wie *Neue Grafik*, die alle in Helvetica gesetzt waren. Ich kaufte sie in der Buchhandlung Salto, einem sehr bedeutsamen Ort, nicht nur für mich. Die zwei Brüder Salto (schweizerischer Herkunft) führten den Laden und waren sehr sachkundig. Man konnte mit ihnen darüber diskutieren, was in anderen Ländern vorging und wenn einer der beiden im Geschäft war, würde der andere die Studios besuchen, bestückt mit einer Tasche voll mit den neuesten Büchern über Grafikdesign. Um ganz ehrlich zu sein glaube ich, dass man ihnen den Großteil des Einflusses, den das schweizerische Design hatte, zuschreiben kann - und natürlich Castiglionis Studio.

Wirklich viele von uns arbeiteten dort: Max an einigen Sachen, Heinz Waibl, der zu der Zeit Max' Assistent war, an anderen Sachen, als auch Tovaglia, Munari und Bianconi. Es war ein Ort, an dem wir Ideen austauschten, also sahen wir uns auch an, woran die anderen im Studio arbeiteten. Wir standen nicht miteinander im Wettbewerb und die Atmosphäre war freundlich und

gemeinschaftlich, was in der puren und steifen Philosophie der verschiedenen Müller-Brockmanns nie möglich gewesen wäre.

Eine weitere Schlüsselrolle in der Italien-Schweiz-Beziehung spielte der Grafikdesign-Kurs für Assistenten an der Humanitaria Schule, die 1961 von Michael Provinciali gegründet und während der acht Jahre ihrer Bestehenszeit erst von Bauer und später von Melino geleitet wurde. Und was entscheidende Erfahrungen angeht, dürfen wir auch nicht Rinascente vergessen, ein Warenhaus, dessen fantastische Ausstellungen über Japan, Indien und Mittelamerika den Mailändern die Existenz anderer Kulturen näherbrachte. Dies beeinflusste von 1955 an alles.

Rinascente hat schon immer als Impulsgeber für den Austausch zwischen Leuten, Designern, Musikern, Grafikdesignern, Schriftstellern und seiner Direktion gedient. Es gab zwei Familien, die sich mit den Rollen der Geschäftsführung und des Vorsitzes abwechselten, die Borlettis und die Bruschis, und beide spielten eine entscheidende Rolle. Sie behielten immer andere Warenhäuser in London und Paris im Auge und hatten eine Wissbegierde und Offenheit, die in vieler Hinsicht ertragreich war und eine ideale Kombination zur Prägung durch schweizerische Einflüsse, aus Zürich und Basel, darstellte.

Max Huber hatte eine begabte Hand und ein gütiges Auge; er wusste die Arbeit von allen zu schätzen und es war faszinierend, ihm bei seiner Arbeit an großen Displays zuzusehen. Er legte mit riesigen Zellophanbögen eine Farbschicht über eine andere. Dann bepinselte er sie mit Wasser (in das er etwas Leim gemischt hatte) und

Ein interview mit Giancarlo Iliprandi.

breitete sie mit einer Spachtel aus. Wir waren alle davon entzückt, wie schnell er dieses oder jenes in Ordnung bringen konnte. Steiner allerdings kritisierte oft andere. Seiner Meinung nach musste Kommunikation einen sozialen Wert mit sich bringen, und wenn dem nicht so war, dann betrachtete er es als Zeitverschwendung. Er war viel schweizerischer als Huber, obwohl er Italiener war. Erst später fand ich heraus, dass mich alle „kleiner Steiner" nannten, weil ich so wählerisch wie er war.

Abgesehen von Max und Steiner bewunderte ich Gfeller, aber insbesondere Serge Libiszewski, ein wahrer Wegbereiter der Fotografie. Er war ein Stillleben- und Modefotograf und hatte die unglaubliche Fähigkeit, Menschen so zu fotografieren, als ob auch sie Stillleben wären. Er war sehr auf Komposition und Beleuchtung bedacht und wenn etwas in einem seiner Fotos beiläufig aussah, dann war das bei weitem kein Zufall.

Wir lernten uns alle kennen als Frau Latis, Rinascentes künstlerische Leiterin, mich anstelle von Steiner wählte, um an einem Design Display zu arbeiten. Vielleicht tat sie es, weil ich es gewohnt war, an Kulissen zu arbeiten. Tatsächlich war die Arbeit in einem Warenhaus wie eine Kulisse für mich, mit Farben und großen Pinseln. Ich erinnere mich, dass ich einmal den ganzen Laden für Weihnachten

gestaltete, einschließlich des Eingangs. Lamm kümmerte sich um das Design der kleinen Schönheitsläden. Sie wurde als Ersatz für Max gewählt, hauptsächlich weil ihre feminine Herangehensweise besser mit Latis' Vorstellung übereinstimmte. Latis wurde von einer neuen, jungen künstlerischen Leiterin namens Adriana Botti abgelöst, die begann, mit vielen anderen jungen Leuten wie Massimo Vignelli und Salvatore Gregorietti, Vignellis Assistent vor der Gründung Unimarks, zu arbeiten.

Der Wandel des Grafikdesigns wurde in der nächsten Designer-Generation ersichtlich: die gegenseitigen schweizerischen/italienischen Einflüsse hatten ihre Spuren hinterlassen. Auf jeden Fall in Vignelli, der wahrscheinlich der stärkste Befürworter des Schriftzuges Helvetica der Haas Gießerei war; im Gegensatz dazu verwendete Max die Schriftzüge Futura und Bodoni sobald er in Italien angekommen war. Dann gab es noch die Gruppe, die von Cappelli, Bonini und Calabrese ins Leben gerufen wurde, oder die CNTP Gruppe - Confalonieri, Negri, Provinciali und Tovaglia – die sich durch Kursivschrift auf eine Art und Weise ausdrückte, die humanistischer und weniger schweizerisch war.

Zu der Zeit war ich ein Gegner der Sans Serif Schriftzüge, denn ich war davon überzeugt, dass viele sie einfach in der Annahme verwendeten, das sei genug, um ein Design modisch und modern aussehen zu lassen. Ich mochte Trends noch nie und glaubte fest daran, dass Designer ihren Stil dem Kunden und dem Produkt anpassen sollten. Aber Massimo setzte Helvetica geschickt ein. Er beauftragte Nava, in die Schweiz zu reisen und dort die Bleiblöcke für diesen Schriftzug zu kaufen. Beim zweiten Mal klappte es, aber Nava war nicht der Einzige mit Helvetica in Mailand. Tipocromo, die später Cromotipo

wurden, führten den Schriftzug auch in ihrem Katalog.

Ein Schriftzug, der uns viele Schwierigkeiten bereitete, war Times New Roman. Ich mochte ihn sehr, besonders als er in Italien noch nicht erhältlich war. Er war zu der Zeit urheberrechtlich geschützt, also schnitten wir die Buchstaben aus einer The Times Zeitung, setzten sie zusammen und fotografierten sie dann alle.

Damals gab es auch keine Manager in Italien. Wir unterhielten eine direkte Beziehung mit dem Padrun (Chef): wir kümmerten uns um die Idee, schrieben den Text und im Falle einiger großer Firmen sprachen wir sogar direkt mit dem Kunden. Franco Fortini von Pirelli, Siniscaldi und Volponi von Olivetti und Vittorio Sereni waren alle Intellektuelle und man konnte Sachen mit ihnen diskutieren und erklären, warum Dinge auf eine bestimmte Art geschrieben waren oder warum ein einzelnes Foto nicht genug war. Nun ja, sagen wir mal so, eine Zeit lang gaben wir in manchen Unternehmen ein wenig „Unterricht".

Doch nachdem die Padruns nicht mehr da waren, begann das Zeitalter der multinationalen Agenturen, die den Markt völlig in Anspruch nahmen. Es gab eine Zeit, in der wir ein gutes Verhältnis zu diesen Agenturen hatten – Mailands Art Directors Club wurde 1967 von Leuten aus verschiedenen Disziplinen gegründet: Pino Tovaglia, Blachian von Young & Rubicam, Flavio Lucchini (Vogues künstlerischer Leiter) und mir – aber es hielt nicht lange an. Langsam welkte alles dahin, auch das Experimentieren, was zum Entstehen unserer kleinen Bewegung geführt hatte. Wir hatten einfach versucht, Dinge auf neue Art zu machen mit Leuten, die wir trafen und mit denen wir arbeiteten und dabei einige Verbindungen, vielleicht einige Freundschaften, zu schließen.

Giancarlo Iliprandi, Ricorda Hiroshima, 1967

Ein interview mit Felix Humm.

Schweizer Designer arbeiten in der Schweiz und Italien seit den 1960er Jahren.

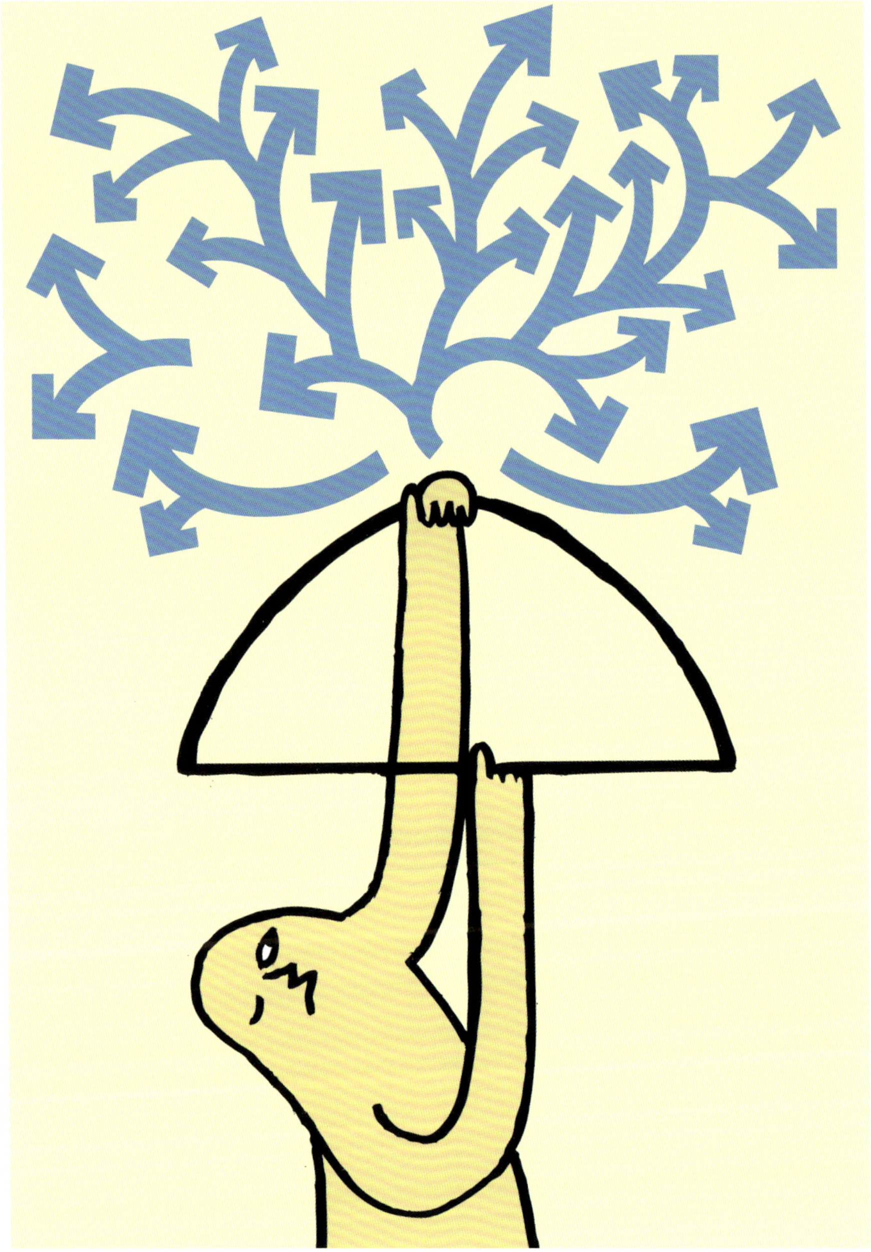

Elena Xausa, after Giovanni Pintori

Grafikdesign spielte eine Hauptrolle im Mailand der Jahre 1945 bis 1970. Viele schweizerische Designer zogen in diesen Jahren aus Basel und Zürich in die Stadt. Andere kamen aus Deutschland (inspiriert durch die Bauhaus Schule), aber was auch immer ihr Herkunftsland, viele von ihnen kamen zu Studio Boggeri, wo ich die Ehre hatte, als sehr junger Mann zu arbeiten.

Nach meinem Studium ging ich allerdings nicht direkt nach Mailand, sondern nach Turin. Als ich noch in der Schweiz lebte, arbeitete ich für eine Werbeagentur namens Reiwald, in Basel. Ich gehörte zu dem Team, das sich um den Kunden Fiat Schweiz kümmerte. Nach einer kurzen Zeit gewann die Agentur auch den Kunden Fiat Italien, und ich wurde deswegen nach Turin versetzt. Ich war damals 21 Jahre alt. Aus einem geplanten Aufenthalt von drei Tagen wurden letztendlich vierzig Jahre, die ich zuerst in Turin und anschließend in Mailand verbrachte. Zu der Zeit herrschte eine gewisse kulturelle Renaissance in Italien vor, hauptsächlich von Firmen wie Olivetti, La Rinascente und Pirelli angeführt, die alle eine aufgeklärte Firmenphilosophie teilten.

Die Auswirkungen dieser Aufklärungsepoche waren auch bei Fiat in Turin spürbar, was zum Großteil dem Leiter von Fiats Kommunikationsabteilung, Odone Camerena, zu verdanken ist. Er war mit der Olivetti Familie verwandt und studierte an der Oxford Universität in England. Eine neue Atmosphäre entwickelte sich, die man überall fühlen konnte. In Turin und Mailand manifestierte sie sich in unternehmerischen Initlativen (selbstverständlich) und neuen Möglichkeiten auf sozialem Niveau. Es wäre heute unmöglich, Projekte vorzuschlagen, die so extravagant sind und die gleiche Ausdrucksfreiheit besitzen wie in dieser Zeit. Zum Beispiel wurden die fotografischen Kollagen, die ich für ein Buch namens *70 Jahre Fiat* zusammenstellte, im Großformat gedruckt und im Büro Gianni Agnellis (Fiats Vorsitzendem) neben Werken von anderen Malern wie Rauschenberg und Lichtenstein angebracht.

Während meiner Zeit in Turin fand ich besondere Inspiration in dem Ideenaustausch mit einem jungen Produktdesigner namens Pio Manzù. Er war der Sohn des berühmten Bildhauers Giacomo Manzù und ich mochte ihn sehr. Er kam nach seinem Studium an der Hochschule für Gestaltung Ulm (in der Schweiz) zu Fiat und unsere Beziehung wurde erleichtert, weil wir beide miteinander deutsch sprechen konnten. Ich war zudem von Typografen begeistert – von ihren Maschinen, dem Geruch ihrer Ateliers und dem Zusammenspiel unserer Berufe.

Aber um etwas tiefer in die Szene des Grafikdesigns einzudringen, ich glaube, dass die Beziehung zwischen dem Avantgardismus (sowohl künstlerisch als auch intellektuell) und der Arbeit einiger Grafikdesigner, die versuchten, eine Symbiose zwischen Kunst und visueller Kommunikation zu schaffen, grundlegend für die Entwicklung eines neuen Stils waren.

Was meinen eigenen Stil angeht, denke ich, dass ich hauptsächlich durch mein Studium in Basel beeinflusst wurde. In Italien selbst inspirierten mich die Schönheit der Grabsteine des Forum Romanum in Rom und die Eleganz der römischen Architektur, die mir den Goldenen Schnitt näherbrachte. Aber jede Region Italiens war einfach so wunderschön, dass man Gefahr lief, unter dem Stockholm-Syndrom zu leiden!

Sicher hatte ich in einem Land (Schweiz) studiert, in dem Grafikdesign

fest als Beruf etabliert war und nicht als „Kunst" angesehen wurde, wie es oft in Italien der Fall war. Aber ich glaube dennoch nicht, dass es so etwas wie „Schweizer" Grafikdesign gibt. Schweizerisches Grafikdesign ist aus einer Mischung von El Lissitzkys russischem Konstruktivismus mit Moholy-Nagys Bauhaus, Piet Zwarts *de Stijl*, Jan Tschicholds *Neue Grafik* und Max Bills erster Hochschule für Gestaltung Ulm entstanden.

Die Schweizer Schulen und Institute, die Grafikdesign lehrten, übermittelten die Prinzipien dieser Bewegungen und aus dieser Bildung entwickelten sich Designer wie Max Huber, Hans Neuberg, Armin Hoffmann, Emil Ruder, Josef Müller-Brockmann und viele andere. Ich traf Huber erst, als er schon ein alter Mann war, genauso mit Castiglioni. Als ich in Mailand ankam, war es üblich, sich mit anderen Ausländern zusammenzuschließen; obwohl ich auch viele anregende Italiener kennenlernte, insbesondere A.G. Fronzoni, dessen Arbeit im Bereich Typografie wirklich innovativ war und viele Grenzen sprengte. In dieser Zeit wurden Experimente und Intuition sehr hoch geschätzt - so eine Situation ist heute undenkbar. Mit der Ankunft von Marketing änderte sich alles auf drastische Weise. Marketing folgte einem Motto, das jeglicher Form von Kreativität und Innovation widersprach, beherrscht von der Angst, ein paar Produkte weniger zu verkaufen. Intuition wurde langsam aber sicher zu einem Tabu. Aber ohne Intuition besteht keine Chance auf zukünftige Änderung.

Design Italien et Suisse expliqué aux débutants.

William Georgi

Même en tant que rédacteur anglais travaillant à Amsterdam, certes avec un directeur artistique italien, j'ai l'avantage de pouvoir me prononcer sur le design italien et suisse. En effet, si je suis capable de comprendre son incroyable complexité et son impact, alors vous le pourrez vous aussi, chers lecteurs. Surtout après avoir lu les dissertations qui suivent celle-ci. Des dissertations écrites par des personnes qui connaissent bien le sujet: d'une part Bettina Richter (suisse) et Maurizio Vitta (italien) deux académiciens qui apportent un point de vue perspicace sur ce qui s'est passé dans les deux pays après la Seconde Guerre Mondiale ; d'autre part Giancarlo Iliprandi et Felix Humm deux designers qui ont vécu pendant cette période et qui apportent un point de vue personnel.

Mais au cours des prochaines pages vous serez en ma compagnie. Hourra! Parce qu'en tant que rédacteur, je voulais que ce livre soit à la portée de tous : pas seulement à celle des designers ou des personnes qui connaissent la différence entre un graphiste et un directeur artistique sans avoir à vérifier dans un dictionnaire ou à demander à l'un de ses amis designers comme je l'ai fait.

Alors j'aimerais vous demander d'être patients pendant que j'explique pourquoi nous sommes ici et ce que nous allons célébrer. Parce que tout le monde, j'entends bien tout le monde, sait que le design italien et suisse sont absolument fabuleux, mais peu de gens savent à quel point ils sont proches, ou même ce que le design suisse et italien sont. Pour être clair, il s'agit ici de graphisme. L'art, ou plutôt l'utilisation de la communication visuelle pour faire passer un message aussi clairement, efficacement et de façon attrayante que possible. Il pourrait s'agir d'un poster, d'un logo, d'un emballage, d'une devanture de magasin, d'un oiseau, d'un avion ou quelque autre support. Tant qu'il est possible d'imprimer ou de dessiner dessus, alors il s'agit de graphisme. Et comme vous le verrez, qu'il s'agisse de promouvoir une machine à écrire, un supermarché ou un pneu, on peut créer quelque chose de beau.

Et ce que l'on veut célébrer, c'est l'influence énorme qu'un groupe de designers et d'artistes Suisses et Italiens, qui ont travaillé ensemble à Milan après la Seconde Guerre Mondiale, a eu sur le monde entier.

En bref, deux mondes sont entrés en collision – les Suisses qui sont techniques et les Italiens qui sont artistiques (qui n'apprécie pas un bon vieux stéréotype). Mais dans le cas présent, c'était vrai : les Suisses ont longtemps mis de l'importance sur le design et avaient même des écoles de design, chose qui nous parait banale aujourd'hui – mais à l'époque c'est une chose qu'il n'y avait pas en Italie, entre autres. Soyons donc un tant soit peu technique : les Suisses étaient plutôt des graphistes puisqu'ils se basaient sur un système de quadrillage et les Italiens étaient plutôt artistiques puisqu'ils apprenaient leur discipline à l'école des Beaux Arts.

« Qu'est ce que le système de quadrillage ? » me demandez vous. C'est une façon de créer un design à partir d'un quadrillage. Tout ce qui fait partie du design (texte, photos, images, etc. …) doit être conforme aux lignes de ce quadrillage.

Cela parait simple. Sauf que ça ne l'est pas vraiment. Dépendant du point de vue, c'est soit indispensable, soit une façon d'assassiner la créativité. Dans les deux cas, pour l'utiliser correctement, il faut apprendre

comment. Et cela prends du temps. Et des études. C'est pourquoi les Suisses, et son plus célèbre partisan, Josef Müller-Brockmann, étaient si doués. C'est pour cette raison précise que les Italiens, qui avaient fait l'école des Beaux Arts (ou étaient simplement artistiques), étaient si doués pour travailler avec eux ou à leur encontre. Nous le savons tous, les règles sont là pour être remises en cause.

Mais après la Seconde Guerre Mondiale, c'était l'Italie, et surtout Milan, qui était comme un aimant pour les personnes créatives. Les designers Suisses venait à Milan parce que a) on avait besoin d'eux et b) c'était là où se trouvaient les travaux les plus palpitants.

Les clients vous donnaient carte blanche pour faire ce que vous vouliez. Vous pouviez avoir des débats avec des collègues designers et des

intellectuels au cours du déjeuner.

Ce qui devient apparent lorsque l'ont lit les dissertations qui vont suivre, c'est que les gens comme Iliprandi avaient la chance d'être présents à l'un de ces moments clé ou toutes les conditions sont réunies afin de créer quelque chose de vraiment remarquable. Les bonnes personnes – de bas en haut, des illustrateurs aux musiciens, de Zurich à Milan – étaient au bon endroit. Dcs idées ont été échangées et les barrières ont été à peine éliminées, elles n'existaient simplement pas.

Les créatifs et les clients étaient à pied d'égalité et il s'agissait d'échanger des idées et non de l'argent. John Steinbeck a une fois dit que les gens créatifs vont toujours là où ils sont appréciés. Et Milan de 1945 aux années soixante faisait partie des ces endroits. Le monde du design ne serait plus jamais le même.

L'inspiration Italienne dans le graphisme Suisse de l'après-guerre.

Bettina Richter

Conservatrice de la collection d'affiches du Museum für Gestaltung à Zurich.

Zürich et Milan, env.1945: des mondes à part.

Peu de temps après la Seconde Guerre Mondiale la Suisse traversa une vague de prospérité économique qui créa un besoin immédiat de main d'œuvre pour la soutenir. Un nombre incalculable de personnes – beaucoup du sud de l'Italie – affluait vers la Suisse à la recherche de travail et d'une vie meilleure. Pour poursuivre ce rêve ils devaient endurer le dur labeur et le racisme politique Suisse, pendant que les conditions de travail et le besoin pour le nombre de travailleurs demandait des changements constants, rendant impossible pour les Italiens de se sentir chez soi.

Mais pour un groupe de graphistes Suisses qui faisaient le trajet en sens inverse vers Milan au même moment, c'était une histoire complètement différente. L'atmosphère *Dolce Vita* qui embaumait la ville promis un nouveau départ pour les immigrants, qui étaient tous les bienvenus, malgré les différences entre l'Italie et la Suisse à cette époque.

La Suisse (neutre pendant la 2nde Guerre Mondiale) était devenue de plus en plus conformiste depuis 1939 et isolée politiquement et culturellement du reste de l'Europe. Le travail intellectuel s'était arrêté net et le pays fut enveloppé dans un déclin créatif qui allait à l'encontre de l'essor économique.

Mais dans les années 1950 le Modernisme de l'avant-guerre recommença à prospérer au sein du graphisme. A Zürich, Josef Müller-Brockmann développa son mélange d'Art Concret et de typographie, tandis qu'à Bâle Armin Hofmann et Emil Ruder offrait une vision du graphisme Suisse plus sensuelle et joueuse.

Ils étaient les principaux protagonistes du « Style Suisse » qui deviendrait célèbre dans le monde entier. Ses fondations étaient celles d'un quadrillage où les lignes horizontales et verticales dans lesquelles la composition d'une image et du texte étaient considérées comme plus importantes que le contenu créatif lui-même.

Cependant ces principes étaient souvent appliqués de façon trop rigide, donnant naissance à des graphismes assez mous et conventionnels. C'était une tendance qui imprègnerait même le travail futur d'un tel pionnier que Müller-Brockmann.

Le Milan de 1945, en revanche, se réjouissait du flamboiement d'une atmosphère ouverte nouvelle et progressive rendue d'autant plus riche par la même vague de prospérité économique dont profitait la Suisse.

Et comme la Suisse, le mouvement Avant Garde reprenait ses activités où il les avait laissés avant la guerre. De plus, il y avait beaucoup de discussions au sujet de ce qui c'était passé pendant la guerre, surtout au sein des intellectuels, ce qui mena à des changements radicaux au sein de la société et de la politique. Bien entendu, cela toucha le monde des affaires, au sein duquel le principal avant-coureur du changement était Adriano Olivetti.

Les graphistes artistiques Suisses à Milan

Xanti Schawinsky et Max Huber étaient les premiers ambassadeurs du design Suisse qui étaient allés s'installer en Italie. Schawinsky était un homme doué qui avait étudié la musique et la peinture en Allemagne et qui était enthousiaste à expérimenter de nouvelles techniques et reformer les arts et la société.

Il fuit l'Allemagne pour aller en Suisse en 1933 avant de s'installer en Italie plus tard dans la même année où il fit la connaissance avec Antonio Boggeri. Boggeri est un autre morceau vital du puzzle de l'histoire Suisse-Italienne. Il était un musicien passionné et un photographe profondément influencé par le travail d'artiste avant-gardistes tels qu'El Lissitzky et Jan Tschichold.

Inspiré par le mélange sensible de typographie, illustration, graphisme et photographie, Boggeri ouvra son propre studio en 1933. Schawinsky était l'un de ses premiers employés, tandis que Huber vint le rejoindre en 1940. Une multitude de designers Suisses suivirent dans leurs pas comme Bruno Monguzzi, Walter Ballmer, Serge Libiszewski, Lora Lamm et Bruno Monguzzi. Beaucoup utilisèrent leur situation au sein du Studio Boggeri pour rebondir et faire avancer leur carrière ou pour ouvrir leur propre studio, beaucoup des employés chez Boggeri ne restèrent donc pas très longtemps. Mais ils partageaient tous une curiosité créative et une ouverture qui devint la marque du studio.

Le seul réel compétiteur de Boggeri à Milan était le studio de graphistes de Franco Grignani, où la plupart des employés étaient Suisses aussi. Ensemble ils formaient un groupe intime de jeunes designers qui se retrouvaient pour déjeuner à midi dans de petites Trattorias, où ils tenaient d'intense discours avec des auteurs et autres artistes sur la valeur sociale du design, l'art et la responsabilité sociale du designer.

Pendant ce temps, Max Huber, qui avait été forcé de retourner en Suisse pendant la guerre, trouva à nouveau son inspiration en Italie après 1945. Il collabora avec le graphiste Albe Steiner de 1950 à 1954 dans la section publicitaire du célèbre magasin La Rinascente.

Dans les années 1950 La Rinascente représentait la renaissance culturelle et économique d'Italie. La mode et les meubles devinrent synonymes de design et de qualité et les produits de La Rinascente étaient un mélange d'esthétique et d'innovation que l'on pouvait se permettre. L'architecte et designer Giò Ponti a tenu ses expositions à La Rinascente dès 1953 et le prestigieux prix du design, le *Compasso d'Oro*, était une autre initiative de La Rinascente. Huber créa le logo de l'entreprise ainsi que l'entier concept de communication.

Lora Lamm était l'une des seules femmes Suisses qui travaillaient à Milan dans les années 1950. Elle travailla au Studio Boggeri de 1953 à 1954, quand Max Huber la fit rentrer dans le secteur de la publicité à La Rinascente. En 1956 elle créa le matériel promotionnel pour une exposition de produits Japonais à La Rinascente qui l'établi en tant que l'un des designers majeurs. Après le départ d'Hubert de La Rinascente, elle devint responsable du secteur publicitaire de 1958 à 1962.

Le photographe Serge Libiszewski était l'une des autres personnes à être invité par Max Huber pour travailler à La Rinascente. Libiszewski avait étudié à la Kunstgewerbschule à Zürich avant de travailler au studio Müller-

Olivetti commença à travailler dans l'entreprise crée par son père en 1926 et commença à construire son utopie concrète de *città degli uomini*, où les profits étaient d'importance secondaire par rapport au bien-être des employés. Olivetti fut exilé en Suisse en 1944 à cause de ses affaires, mais après son retour après la guerre il développa son concept de communication visuelle en fusionnant l'éthique et l'esthétique; faisant de ces deux principes les piliers de son entreprise. La création d'un secteur publicitaire et de communication à Olivetti en 1933 fut un des développements majeurs.

L'engagement socioculturel d'Olivetti a servi d'exemple à d'autres entreprises telles que La Rinascente, Pirelli et Montecatini qui ont toutes suivies Olivetti en créant leur propre secteur publicitaire. Ainsi, les artistes et photographes professionnels devinrent de plus en plus en demande, mais jusque dans les années 1950 il n'y avait pas d'école de design en Italie et donc pas de graphistes ayant suivi une formation classique.

Les quelques agences et studios de publicité qui existaient étaient principalement pourvus de peintres ou d'architectes, une situation qui était très avantageuse pour les graphistes et photographes Suisses qui avaient suivis une formation dans le domaine du design.

L'inspiration Italienne dans le graphisme Suisse de l'après-guerre.

Brockmann. À cause du manque de photographes commerciaux dans le nord de l'Italie, Libiszewski était enthousiaste d'accepter l'invitation de Huber. Toutefois leur collaboration pris un mauvais départ : il n'y avait pas de commandes alors Libiszewski fut réduit à aider Huber dans son studio.

Le succès arriva enfin quand Libiszewski ouvrit son propre studio en 1962. Les commandes affluaient de La Rinascente, Studio Boggeri, Olivetti et Pirelli. À cette époque la photographie évoluait en une forme artistique nouvelle et indépendante au sein du graphisme publicitaire. Ensemble, avec Salvatore Gregorietti, Giancarlo Iliprandi (à La Rinascente) et Walter Ballmer (à Olivetti), il travailla sur de nombreuses campagnes de posters innovatrices.

Tous les graphistes et photographes qui arrivaient à Milan après 1950 partageaient la même soif pour de nouveaux challenges qu'ils ne trouvaient pas dans les cercles artistiques conservateurs et orthodoxes en Suisse. Ils voulaient être créatifs, outre les limites entre les différentes formes artistiques. Toutefois, ces périodes intenses et innovatrices ne malheureusement durent jamais longtemps.

Au début des années 1970 cette utopie sociale disparait peu à peu. Des concepts marketing basé sur l'efficacité, avec moins d'art et de plus gros logos, commencèrent à dominer les campagnes de communication. Les comptes furent confiés aux agences de publicité dominantes plutôt qu'à des designers individuels. La relation entre le management d'une grande entreprise et les designers et photographes individuels arriva à sa fin.

Le graphisme contemporain Suisse

Le graphisme Suisse doit sa réputation d'aujourd'hui à l'influence absorbée d'Italie durant les années 1950 et 1960. L'éducation solide des designers Suisse encra des fondations, mais ce fut leur interaction inspirante avec leurs homologues Italiens qui permit à Max Huber, Lora Lamm, Walter Ballmer et bien d'autres de s'épanouir.

Cela et de bien meilleures conditions à Milan pendant cette période : la vague de prospérité économique, des studios ambitieux et des clients enthousiastes contribuaient à la richesse du style du graphisme. Une tradition formelle et sévère avec une curiosité expérimentale, de la couleur, un esprit poétique et une soif de vie créa une combinaison excitante qui fut hautement fructueuse pour les deux parties et continue d'inspirer le graphisme Suisse d'aujourd'hui.

Sa variété esthétique montre que même pendant une période politique turbulente comme dans les années 1980, la tradition du design de l'*Aufbruch* (départ) peut encore survivre. L'application stricte du Helvetica est encore remise en question de façon provocante par les designers.

Et le graphisme en Suisse continue de prospérer à travers les échanges culturels avec d'autres formes artistiques telles que la musique, la littérature qui s'enrichissent toutes mutuellement. Ces tendances, qui ont commencé dans l'après-guerre, sont encore présentes aujourd'hui et mènent encore à des expériences fabuleuses et excitantes, du moins en ce qui concerne le design.

Il est encore plus encourageant de voir qu'il a émergé dans les années 1990 une génération de graphistes qui ne se restreint pas aux graphismes de synthèse ; mais qui, tout comme ses prédécesseurs retournent aux bases et se servent de leurs mains.

Lorsque l'on touche et apprécie des matériaux, des solutions différentes et plus créatives émergent donnant lieu à des résultats plus personnels, subjectifs et moins orthodoxes. Tout ce qui n'est pas parfait, de coïncidence et spontané peut influencer la pratique du design de tous les jours de façon positive.

Des illustrations à main levée, l'écriture, la création de nouveaux types de lettres et un mélange inhabituel de lettres ont tous leurs échos dans les posters contemporains. Jouer avec le média de masse, comme la photographie et les beaux-arts, reflète les nombreux moyens existants d'aborder les images et les textes d'aujourd'hui.

En ce qui concerne le contenu, les posters contemporains culturels dénotent une compréhension différente du poster médiatique de masse. Les anciennes règles comme quoi le poster est un moyen de communication (comme sa lisibilité et une compréhension immédiate du message) ne sont plus en application.

Une fois de plus, les gens sont requis d'évaluer la façon traditionnelle d'interpréter des textes, des messages et des images.

Le design Italien après 1945.

Maurizio Vitta

Professeur d'histoire du design et de culture du design à la faculté de design du Politecnico di Milano.

L'histoire du design Italien dans la seconde partie du 20ème siècle ne commence pas en 1950 mais pendant la première partie de ce siècle.

C'est plus précisément en 1933 que le Studio Boggeri a ouvert ses portes, que la première édition de *Campo Grafico* (Champ Graphique) a été publiée et que la cinquième *Triennale di Milano* a été tenue, où la section du graphisme Allemand désigné par Paul Renner a suscité beaucoup d'intérêt. Donc, du début ; le graphisme Italien ne s'est pas développé de façon linéaire mais à partir d'une série d'échanges culturels établis à partir de réseaux formés au sein de deux centres urbains.

A travers ses liens étroits avec le design industriel, champs d'expérience mutuels avec l'architecture moderne et comparaisons constantes avec l'art contemporain, le graphisme Italien a profité d'une approche approfondie et du savoir professionnel, ainsi qu'un sens de l'internationalisme aigu qui s'est développé avec des échanges vivants entre designers Européens, particulièrement Suisses.

Ceci était le creuset dans le lequel le graphisme Italien moderne s'est formé: un chaudron bouillant dans lequel l'âge moderne longtemps attendu commencerait enfin. Ce n'était pas le résultat de la recherche pour de nouveaux moyens d'expression, mais un essai pour construire des fondations que l'on pourrait mieux définir comme culture visuelle. Cette culture visuelle a été établie au sein du monde intellectuel de cette époque, tout en étant liée au classicisme et au principe de l'équilibre formel; de la section dorée de Luca Pacioli et de la révolution dans le domaine de l'imprimerie de Aldus Manutius, aux innovations sans précédent de la première phase du mouvement Futuriste et aux expériences raffinées de sa seconde phase principalement menées par Fortunato Depero.

Après la désolation de l'après guerre, le besoin impératif pour le développement économique et social de l'Italie nécessitait la création de nouveaux moyens de communication et d'information capables de faire face aux demandes d'une société de masse démocratique et industrialisée. Ce n'est pas par hasard si le réseau du graphisme s'est concentré dans les capitales de l'édition de l'Italie, Milan et Turin, deux villes qui avaient la capacité industrielle et culturelle de mettre en route la propagation rapide du consumérisme à travers le pays.

Malgré leur polarité évidente, les deux mondes entrepreneurs et culturels partageaient une idéologie qui les unissait : un désir de communication claire et logique. Un message simple exprimé aussi directement que possible.

L'œuvre d'Albe Steiner est la plus caractéristique de cette approche. Il a débuté en 1945 avec le poster désigné pour la *Mostra della ricostruzione* (Exposition pour la Reconstruction) et a continué avec le design du *Politecnico*, un magasine crée par Elio Vittorini qui avait pour but d'être un véhicule pour la nouvelle culture visuelle.

Ce désir pour la rationalité avait commencé avec les expériences, réflexions et contacts au niveau international faits pendant les décennies précédentes. La brève vie de *Campo Grafico* a survécu au sein de la mémoire de ses protagonistes, alors que le Musée Triennal de Milan s'est immédiatement encré comme endroit pour de nouvelles expériences et initiatives. Le groupe important de graphistes Suisses au Studio Boggeri avant la guerre (Schawinski, Ballmer, Huber, Calabresi, Vivarelli, Monguzzi) n'a pas seulement transmis un héritage riche qui sera devenu le point de référence de ses successeurs italiens mais assureras aussi sa possible continuité en restant à Milan. En plus du contingent Suisse Boggeri, Bauhaus a été une influence clé, tout comme l'école Hollandaise (Bob Noorda est venu s'installer à Milan au début des années cinquante) et les enseignements de Max Bill. Une comparaison de l'histoire du graphisme Italien avec les 'vedettes' de cette période) - design industriel et

Le design Italien après 1945.

Elena Xausa, after Walter Ballmer

architecture (ensemble avec le cinéma) – révèle comme il est étroitement lié au développement en général de la culture du design.

L'homme qui a le plus incarné cette approche holistique du design était Olivetti. Ses valeurs industrielles se reflétaient directement dans les travaux qu'il commandait pour son entreprise: l'architecture de Gabetti et Isola, le design de Sottsass, le travail de consultant fait par des intellectuels tels que Giudici ou Volponi, et en dernier, mais non par ordre d'importance, la légendaire identité graphique pour Olivetti conduite par Giovanni Pintori.

D'autres grandes entreprises suivirent Olivetti en mettant en place des stratégies de marketing, bien que pas à la même échelle : Pirelli, par exemple, s'est concentré pour construire un studio de graphisme interne (aidé par des designers tel que Pino Tovaglia) et a communiqué à travers un magasine appelé tout simplement *Pirelli*, qui exprimait l'esprit dynamique de l'entreprise à travers style graphique rigoureux – amplifié par la construction de la Tour Pirelli gratte-ciel désigné par Gio Ponti – et son intérêt pour les arts.

L'expansion rapide de l'industrie de la télévision a donné beaucoup de sa production graphique à Erberto

Carboni, qui a interprété le nouveau moyen de masse en traduisant sa complexité technologique en un simple et attrayant langage visuel pour Rai, présageant le travail culte qu'il créera pour Barilla.

Par conséquent, dès les années 1960, l'âge moderne entra dans la première partie du siècle arrivant enfin à maturité et le graphisme Italien était fermement encré dans le monde professionnel – sa position étant assurée par la prolifération d'écoles, de publications et de la popularité au sein du publique.

Cela prépara le terrain pour une nouvelle génération de designers qui s'élèvera au top de l'industrie de la communication visuelle : A .G. Fronzoni avec sa maîtrise absolue de *Gestaltung* et une utilisation raffinée du noir et blanc ; Franco Grignani qui a mené des expériences optiques sophistiquées recherchant un nouveau langage visuel ; Pino Tovaglia, un interprète excellent du nouveau monde des affaires ; Giancarlo Iliprandi, un savant du langage visuel; Michele Provinciali, Ilio Negri, Giulio Confalonieri et beaucoup d'autres, tout comme Armando Testa à Turin, dont le nom commençait à être remarqué dès ces premiers jours.

Chacun de ces noms rappelle un style différent, mais ils partagent tous une influence culturelle commune. Sous ces différences subjectives il y avait une couche de concept homogène qui rendait le graphisme le dominant de la logique Carthésienne, supporté par une série de règles claires : chaque image était fabriquée dans un ordre logique à travers un modèle géométrique calculé. Ce modèle garantissait que chaque image produite soit minimaliste; un résultat obtenu à travers un processus métonymique adroit. D'où le désir commun de réduire le discours visuel au strict minimum en enlevant constamment le contenu surplus. Cette technique fit émerger le message comme si de rien, du silence qui était aussi fort que le message lui-même.

Partant de cette perspective il est possible d'identifier des tendances personnelles : l'obsession de Fronzoni avec les formes de communication les plus simples, la recherche de Iliprandi pour les outils afin de construire une rhétorique visuelle, Grignani qui jouait de la perception et de la géométrie pour créer un tourbillon d'ensembles de langues.

Les développements en art moderne contemporain, de la rigueur du Pop Art aux esthétiques technologiques de l'art programmé ont aussi trouvé un écho dans le monde du graphisme bourgeonnant. Comme l'ont fait les dialectiques en architecture, qui sont encore déchirés entre leurs sentiments pour Wright et ceux pour les enseignements de Giuseppe Terragini. Ou bien le design industriel, au sein duquel chaque édition de la remise des prix du *Compasso d'Oro* marquait un progrès significatif dans ce domaine.

Il n'est pas difficile de discerner un fil rouge au sein de ce processus; une nouvelle tradition de design qui a ses origines dans la culture du design du Nord de l'Europe dans la première partie du 20ème siècle. Le progrès de cette nouvelle tradition a été temporairement suspendu par la fermeture de l'Ecole de Design de Ulm, un évènement marqué par le débat animé entre Max Bill et Tomas Maldonado, qui a créé des doutes pour beaucoup au sujet du processus du design.

Mais il y avait déjà du changement à l'horizon annoncé par l'apparition de nouvelles formes et moyens de communication. Ce n'était pas un accident si la publicité à la télévision, par exemple, était mieux comprise par des gens comme Armando Testa, un génie créatif et vivant qui pouvait transformer un signe en personnage, un personnage en héros de communication, transformé en poster avec une imagerie vivante, allant de la métamorphose (le pneu éléphant de Pirelli) à un concept abstrait (le logo Punt e Mes). L'énergie du Pop Art était dans l'air, mais au delà il y avait un nouveau monde de la communication, décidé à changer les rituels de la consommation et donc les modèles de communication.

Pendant ce temps, le graphisme éditorial était en train de subir une évolution lente mais fondamentale – comme ce media en avait besoin – parfaitement mis à l'évidence dans le travail que Unimark (Massimo Vignelli et Bob Noorda) a fait pour Mondadori et Feltrinelli.

Entre la fin du 20ème siècle et le début du 21ème siècle, le graphisme fit face à un monde encore plus changeant et instable (marqué par des changements structurels importants et une conscience plus aiguë d'autres modèles esthétiques de l'Est à l'Ouest) et il le fit en adoptant une politique de renouvellement continue sans couper les liens avec la tradition. En fait, dans le travail de Massimo Dolcini, Armando et Maurizio Milani, Italo Lupi et Pierluigi Cerri, on peut voir une continuité indéniable ; des antécédents classiques, discrets, implicites, tenaces auquel le schéma du design fait encore référence, y compris en adressant des nouvelles questions. Cette même approche classique est assez flexible pour permettre aux designers de garder un lien fort avec les cultures régionales (Franco Balan) et d'adresser des questions liées au nouveau climat sociopolitique (Michele Spera, Ettore Vitale) tout comme d'aller au-delà du déclin du poster comme forme de média dû aux changements sismiques qui opèrent dans le paysage urbain (malgré une renaissance temporaire grâce à un photographe, et non un graphiste, appelé Oliviero Toscani).

D'une façon ou d'une autre, cette formation classique permet au graphisme Italien de garder ses caractéristiques exceptionnelles dans un monde ou les différences culturelles ont tendance à se dissoudre dans le nuage de la globalisation et l'avancement sans arrêt des allusions à la technologie digitale au commencement d'un nouveau monde, qui reste encore à être exploré.

Cela révèle un autre aspect de la tradition culturelle de l'Italie: son cosmopolitanisme intellectuel. Il a soutenu la créativité nationale de ce pays pendant des siècles et aide encore à résoudre des problèmes aujourd'hui; problèmes qui sont de plus en plus européens que nationaux.

Un Entretien avec Giancarlo Iliprandi.

Designer italien travaillant à Milan depuis les années 50s.

Giancarlo Iliprandi, NO MORE WAR, 2003

La fin des années 1950 et 1960 était une période particulièrement fertile en Italie. Tout arriva au même moment : le design prospéra, les entreprises étaient innovatrices et, bien sûr, beaucoup de gens étaient attirés par cette situation, y compris les Suisses.

Naturellement, quand ils arrivèrent, nous ne savions pas que leur influence changerait l'histoire du graphisme Italien. Les Italiens qui s'intéressaient au design avaient pour la plupart une formation artistique comme Bigani, Carboni et Italo Lupi, qui étaient tous architectes. En revanche, de l'autre côté des Alpes tout était plus rigoureux, formel et technique.

En Suisse le graphisme était

déjà considéré comme étant une profession, alors qu'ici nous étions tous considérés en tant qu' « artistes publicitaires ». Beaucoup de gens avaient déjà essayé (et essayaient encore) de se détacher du concept « d'art graphique », comme Munari qui, comme beaucoup d'autres, trouvait que ce terme dévalorisait sa profession. Le début du vrai changement dans ce domaine se fit seulement quand les Suisses arrivèrent, ou après que leur manière de faire devint plus répandue. Pour des gens comme moi qui voulaient devenir graphiste, une méthode, un ensemble de règles était essentiel. Nous pensions que le processus du design était indispensable et qu'il devait être établit à partir d'une méthode qui engloberait forme et fonctionnalité à travers le design dans sa globalité, et enfin nous avons trouvé quelqu'un ou plusieurs personnes qui pensaient comme nous et qui y avaient même pensé avant nous!

Quand à moi, je commençais à penser sérieusement au graphisme pendant que je travaillais dans l'entreprise d'architecture de Castiglioni. C'est là que j'ai découvert cette chose appelé communication visuelle et graphisme et où j'ai rencontré Max Huber pour la première fois. Avant cela j'avais fais des études de médecine, quatre ans de peinture et quatre ans de scénographie à l'Académie des Beaux-arts de Brera, mais je n'avais toujours pas trouvé quelque

chose qui m'intéressait réellement. J'étais profondément insatisfait. Bien sûr, la scénographie était mieux que la peinture puisque cela me donnait l'opportunité de travailler avec la musique mais finalement un scénographe travaille toujours pour un directeur, alors à moins que vous soyez quelqu'un comme Zefirelli, qui passait d'un rôle à l'autre avec succès, c'était restreignant. Du moins pour moi.

Mes rapports avec Max étaient inspirants. Non pas que nous nous entretenions toujours au sujet du graphisme, nous allions aussi beaucoup dans des clubs de jazz et des concerts. Durant ces années, alors que j'étais toujours au studio, j'ai eu l'opportunité de faire la connaissance de Steiner et Boggeri et je me souviens de m'être dit un jour « oui, ça c'est quelque chose d'intéressant ». C'est là que j'ai vraiment commencé à m'y mettre. Observer Max travailler sur des display design m'a donné l'envie d'apprendre, j'ai donc commencer à expérimenter avec ce « graphisme Suisse », acheter des livres et des magasines tels que *Neue Grafik* écrits entièrement en police Helvetica. Je les achetais à la librairie Salto, un endroit très significatif, pas seulement pour moi. Les deux frères Salto (d'origine Suisse) tenaient le magasin et étaient très bien informés. Vous pouviez leur parler de ce qui se passait dans d'autres pays, et quand l'un d'eux était au magasin, l'autre venait au studio avec un sac plein des derniers livres sur le graphisme. En toute honnêteté, je suis convaincu que beaucoup de l'influence du design Suisse leur est due, ainsi qu'au studio de Castiglioni bien sûr.

Nous étions beaucoup à travailler là bas, tous sur beaucoup de projets différents de design display : Max sur certaines choses, Heinz Waibl, qui était l'assistant de Max à l'époque, sur

d'autres, Tovaglia, Munari et Bianconi aussi. C'était un endroit où nous pouvions échanger des idées, et nous avions ainsi aussi la possibilité de voir ce sur quoi les autres travaillaient. L'atmosphère n'était pas compétitive, mais amicale et collaborative, ce qui n'aurait pas été possible dans les nombreux studios Müller-Brockmann où la philosophie était pure et rigide.

Le cours de graphisme pour assistants à L'Humanitaria joua aussi un rôle clé dans la relation Italo Suisse, l'école fut fondée en 1961 par Michael Provinciali et d'abord dirigée par Bauer pendant ses huit premières années puis par Melino. En parlant d'expériences cruciales, il est aussi juste de mentionner Rinascente, un grand magasin qui apprit aux Milanais que différentes cultures existaient en tenant des expositions au Japon, en Inde et en Amérique Centrale. Cela eu un effet sur tout à partir de 1955.

Rinascente a toujours été un stimulant pour rendre les échanges possible entre les gens, designers, musiciens, graphistes, auteurs et sa direction. Il y avait deux familles qui se relayaient entre les places de Directeur Général et Président, les Borletti et les Bruschi – et toutes deux avaient un rôle important dans tout cela. Ils gardaient toujours un œil sur ce que d'autres grand magasins faisaient à Londres et à Paris, et ils avaient une curiosité et une ouverture qui était fructueuse en de nombreux aspects et présentait une combinaison idéale pour que les influences Suisses, de Zürich à Bâle, laissent une emprunte.

Max Huber avait une main douée et un œil bienveillant, il appréciait le travail de tous et il était fascinant de le voir travailler sur de grands displays. Il mettait une couche de couleur sur l'autre en utilisant d'énormes feuilles de cellophanes. Ensuite il brossait chacune d'elles avec de l'eau (dans

Un Entretien avec Giancarlo Iliprandi.

laquelle il avait dilué de la colle) et les étirait avec une spatule. Nous étions tous ravis de voir à quelle rapidité il arrivait à s'occuper de ceci et cela. Steiner, en revanche, critiquait souvent les autres. Pour lui, la communication devait avoir une valeur sociale, et si elle ne l'avait pas ce n'était qu'une perte de temps. Il était certainement plus Suisse que Huber, malgré qu'il soit Italien. C'est seulement après que j'appris que tout le monde m'appelait « petit Steiner », parce qu'ils pensaient que j'étais aussi difficile que lui.

En dehors de Max et Steiner, j'admirais Gfeller, et plus particulièrement Serge Libiszewski, un réel innovateur en photographie. Il était photographe de nature morte et de mode et avait cette façon incroyable de prendre en photo les gens comme s'ils étaient des modèles de nature morte aussi. Il se souciait beaucoup de la composition et de la lumière, et toute chose qui semblait arriver par hasard était loin d'être accidentelle. Ceci était sa grande aptitude.

Nous nous sommes tous connus quand Madame Latis, directeur artistique chez Rinascente, m'a choisi plutôt que Steiner pour travailler sur un display design. Peut être qu'elle l'a fait parce que j'avais l'habitude de travailler sur des décors. En effet, travailler dans un grand magasin était comme travailler sur des décors pour moi, avec de la peinture et de gros pinceaux. Je

me souviens avoir mis en place tout le magasin pour Noël une fois, y compris l'entrée. Lamm s'occupa du design des petits magasins de beauté. Elle fut choisie pour remplacer Max, surtout parce que sa façon féminine de faire les choses convenait plus à la vision de Latis. Après Latis il y a eu un nouveau, jeune directeur artistique, Adriana Botti, et elle commença à travailler avec beaucoup d'autres gens jeunes comme Massimo Vignelli et Salvatore Gregorietti, qui était l'assistant de Vignelli avant la création de Unimark.

Le changement au sein du graphisme devint apparent avec la génération de designers suivante : les influences mutuelles Suisses/Italiennes avaient laissé leur trace.

Certainement avec Vignelli qui était probablement le plus grand partisan de la police Helvetica de la fonderie Haas ; réciproquement Max commença à utiliser Futura et Bodoni dès qu'il arriva en Italie. Ensuite il y a eu le groupe formé par Capelli, Bonini et Calabrese ou le groupe CNTP – Confalonieri, Negri, Provinciali et Tovaglia – qui avaient une façon de s'exprimer au travers des italiques qui était plus humaine et moins Suisse.

À l'époque j'étais contre les polices Sans Serif parce que j'étais convaincu que beaucoup l'utilisaient pensant que c'était assez pour que leur travail ai l'air plus à la mode et contemporain. J'ai toujours été opposé aux tendances et convaincu qu'il était du devoir des designers d'adapter leur style à celui de leur client et produit, mais Massimo l'utilisait Helvetica bien. Il demanda à Nava d'aller en Suisse et d'acheter les blocs de plomb pour cette police. Cela fonctionna la deuxième fois, mais Nava n'était pas le seul à avoir Helvetica à Milan. Tipocromo, qui devint ensuite Cromotipo, l'avait aussi dans son catalogue.

Times New Roman était une police qui nous causa beaucoup d'ennuis. Je l'aimais beaucoup, surtout du temps où elle n'était pas encore disponible en Italie. Elle était protégée par des droits d'auteurs à l'époque, alors nous devions découper les lettres du journal The Times, assembler le texte et tout photographier pour l'utiliser.

A l'époque il n'y avait pas de managers en Italie non plus. Nous avions une relation directe avec le *Padrun* (directeur) : nous prenions soin de l'idée, écrivions un exemplaire et pour de plus larges entreprises, nous étions même en relation directe avec le client. Franco Fortini chez Pirelli, Siniscaldi et Volponi chez Olivetti ou Vittorio Sereni étaient tous des intellectuels et vous pouviez discuter de choses avec eux, expliquer pourquoi les choses étaient écrites dans un certain sens ou pourquoi une seule photo n'était pas suffisante. Disons donc que pendant une courte période nous donnions des « leçons » à quelques entreprises.

Par contre lorsque les *Padruns* étaient partis, les agences multinationales arrivèrent et contrôlèrent tout le marché. Il y a eu une période pendant laquelle nous avions de bonnes relations avec elles – le Club des Directeurs Artistiques de Milan a été fondé en 1967 par des gens venant de différents horizons : Pino Tovaglia, Blachian de Young & Rubicam, Flavio Lucchini (directeur artistique chez Vogue) et moi-même – mais cela ne marcha pas longtemps. Tout disparu peu à peu, y compris l'expérimentation qui donna naissance à notre petit mouvement. Nous voulions juste trouver un nouveau moyen de faire les choses avec les gens que nous rencontrions et avec qui nous travaillions alors que nous créions des liens, peut être même nous faisions des amis en cours de route.

Giancarlo Iliprandi, Basta una pillola, 1967

Un Entretien avec Felix Humm.

Designer suisse travaillant en Suisse et en Italie depuis les années 60s.

Felix Humm, FIAT corporate advertisements, 1970

Le graphisme avait un rôle de vedette dans le Milan des années 1945-1970. Pendant ces années, beaucoup de designers Suisses avaient migré vers la ville de Bâle et Zurich. D'autres venaient d'Allemagne (inspirés par l'école Bauhaus), mais qu'importe leur origine, beaucoup passaient au studio Boggeri, où j'ai eu l'honneur de travailler en tant que très jeune homme.

En revanche, après avoir été diplômé, je ne suis pas allé tout de suite à Milan mais à Turin. Pendant que j'étais encore en Suisse, j'ai travaillé pour une agence de publicité Suisse appelé Reiwald, à Bâle. Je faisais partie de l'équipe qui avait Fiat en Suisse en tant que client. Après un petit moment, l'équipe a aussi obtenu Fiat en Italie comme client, alors ils m'ont transféré à Turin. J'avais 21 ans. J'étais censé rester en Italie pour trois jours, mais j'ai fini par rester quarante ans, d'abord à Turin puis à Milan. À cette époque il y avait comme une renaissance culturelle en Italie, essentiellement menée par des entreprises comme Olivetti, La Rinascente et Pirelli qui partageaient toutes une philosophie d'entreprise éclairée.

Les effets de cet éclaircissement s'étendirent aussi à nous chez Fiat à Turin, surtout grâce à la personne qui était chargée du secteur de communication chez Fiat à cette époque, Odone Camerena. Il était parent de la famille Olivetti et avait étudié à l'université d'Oxford, Angleterre. Cela créa une nouvelle atmosphère que l'ont pouvait ressentir partout. À Turin et à Milan, elle se manifesta au travers d'initiatives d'entrepreneur (bien sûr) et de nouvelles opportunités au niveau social. Aujourd'hui il serait impossible de mettre en avant un travail aussi extravagant et avec la même liberté d'expression comme je l'ai fait à cette époque. Les collages photographiques que j'ai réalisés pour un livre appelé *70 Ans de Fiat* par exemple, ont été agrandis pour être placardés sur les murs du bureau de Gianni Agnelli (président de Fiat) à côté d'autres peintures de Rauschenberg et Lichtenstein.

Pendant que j'étais à Turin j'ai été personnellement particulièrement inspiré par un échange d'idées que j'ai

eu avec un jeune designer de produits appelé Pio Manzù. Il était le fils du célèbre sculpteur Giacomo Manzù et je l'aimais beaucoup. Il est arrivé chez Fiat après avoir été diplômé de la Ulm School of Design (en Suisse) et nos rapports ont été facilités par le fait que nous parlions tous les deux allemand. J'étais également fasciné par les typographes, par leurs machines, l'odeur de leurs ateliers et la façon dont nos professions dialoguaient.

Mais pour approfondir ma vision du monde du graphisme, je pense que la relation entre l'avant-garde (artistique et intellectuelle) et le travail de quelques graphistes qui essayaient de produire une symbiose entre l'art et la communication visuelle, était fondamentale pour le développement d'un nouveau style.

En ce qui concerne mon propre style, je trouve qu'il a été principalement influencé par mes études à Bâle. Une fois en Italie, j'étais inspiré par la beauté des tombes dans le Forum Romain à Rome et l'élégance de l'architecture romaine, qui m'a enseigné le Nombre d'Or. Mais toutes les parties d'Italie que vous visitiez étaient si belles que vous risquiez d'être accablé par le syndrome de Stockholm !

Bien sûr mes études avaient leurs origines dans un pays (la Suisse) où le graphisme était fermement établi en tant qu'une profession et n'était pas considéré comme de « l'art », comme

il en était souvent le cas en Italie. Mais je ne crois pas au fait qu'il y ai une chose appelée le style de graphisme « Suisse ». Le graphisme Suisse est dérivé d'un mélange de construction Russe de El Lissitzky, du Bauhaus de Moholy-Nagy, du *de Stijl* de Piet Zwart, de la *Neue Graphik* de Jan Tschichold et de la première école de design de Ulm de Max Bill.

Les écoles et institutions suisses qui enseignaient le graphisme passaient outre les principes de ces mouvements, et de cette éducation en sortait des designers comme Max Huber, Hans Neuberg, Armin Hoffmann, Emil Ruder et Josef Müller-Brockmann et beaucoup d'autres. J'ai seulement rencontré Huber alors qu'il était un vieil homme, la même chose vaut pour Castiglioni. Quand je suis arrivé à Milan, la tendance était de s'associer surtout avec des étrangers, mais j'ai eu rencontré beaucoup d'Italiens stimulants, surtout A.G. Fronzoni, dont le travail en typographie était réellement innovateur et dépassait bien des limites. À celle époque l'expérimentation et l'intuition avaient une grande valeur et il est impossible d'imaginer qu'une même situation soit possible aujourd'hui. Quand le marketing arriva sur la scène, tout changea de façon radicale. Le marketing avait une vision contraire à toutes les formes créatives et innovatrices, dominée par la peur de vendre quelques produits de moins. L'intuition devint peu à peu tabou. Mais sans intuition, il n'y a aucune chance de changer le futur.

Guida al design svizzero e italiano per principianti.

William Georgi

Essere un copywriter inglese che lavora ad Amsterdam, sebbene con un art director italiano, mi mette in una posizione unica per parlare del design svizzero e di quello italiano. Perché, se sono riuscito io a capire la sua meravigliosa complessità e importanza, allora caro lettore, ce la puoi fare anche tu, soprattutto dopo aver letto i brani che seguiranno. Questi sono infatti alcuni saggi di persone che sanno realmente il fatto loro. Bettina Richter e Maurizio Vitta sono accademici provenienti rispettivamente dalla Svizzera e dall'Italia, e forniscono una prospettiva intelligente su ciò che è accaduto in entrambi i paesi dopo la Seconda Guerra Mondiale, mentre Giancarlo Iliprandi e Felix Humm sono due designer che erano proprio lì in quel periodo e che hanno operato nel campo del design.

Tuttavia, per le prossime pagine, sarò io la tua guida. Evviva. Perché in quanto copywriter, volevo che questo libro fosse per tutti, non solo per designer, e nemmeno per persone che sanno la differenza fra un grafico e un art director senza dover consultare un dizionario o chiederlo a un amico designer, come ho dovuto fare io.

Ti vorrei chiedere dunque un po' di pazienza mentre ti spiego il motivo per cui siamo qui e cosa stiamo celebrando. Tutti ma proprio tutti, infatti, sanno che il design italiano e quello svizzero sono fantastici, ma non tutti sanno quanto questi siano simili o addirittura cosa siano realmente.

Per essere chiaro, stiamo parlando del design grafico, l'arte di creare, beh... arte, dalla comunicazione visiva, per trasmettere un messaggio nel modo più chiaro, efficace e attraente possibile. Potrebbe essere un manifesto, un logo, un packaging, l'allestimento di un negozio, un uccello, un aeroplano, quello che vuoi. Qualsiasi cosa su cui puoi dipingere o disegnare, quello è design grafico. E come vedrai, non importa se è destinato a promuovere una macchina da scrivere, un supermercato o uno pneumatico: da qualunque cosa si può creare qualcosa di bello.

Quello che siamo qui a celebrare, è l'enorme influenza che avrebbe avuto sul mondo un gruppo di designer e artisti svizzeri e italiani, che a Milano lavorarono insieme dopo la Seconda Guerra Mondiale.

Fondamentalmente si scontrarono due mondi - la tecnica degli svizzeri e l'arte degli italiani (giusto per citare un paio di stereotipi nazionali). In questo caso però era proprio così; gli svizzeri, infatti, valorizzavano già da tempo la disciplina del design e disponevano perfino di scuole dedicate, cosa che ora per noi è scontata, ma che a quel tempo, almeno l'Italia, non aveva.

Volendo quindi andare almeno un minimo sul tecnico, gli svizzeri erano più grafici perché si basavano su una gabbia tipografica, mentre gli italiani erano più artisti perché imparavano il loro mestiere nelle scuole d'arte.

Ti chiederai cosa sia una gabbia tipografica. Bene, è un sistema per organizzare i contenuti di una pagina basandosi su una gabbia. Tutti gli elementi che inserisci nel progetto (testi, fotografie, immagini, ecc.) devono conformarsi alle linee della gabbia. Semplice. Solo che in realtà non lo è affatto. A seconda del tuo punto di vista può essere una pratica indispensabile oppure qualcosa che uccide la creatività. In entrambi i casi però, per usarla correttamente è necessario imparare come farlo, e per questo ci vogliono tempo e studio. È per questo motivo che gli svizzeri, e soprattutto il loro principale esponente, Josef Müller-Brockmann, erano così bravi, ed è proprio per questo che gli italiani, formatisi nelle scuole d'arte (o che erano semplicemente artisti) erano così bravi a lavorare insieme a (o contro di) loro. Come tutti sappiamo, infatti, tutte le regole sono fatte per essere rotte.

Ma quello che l'Italia, e soprattutto Milano, aveva dopo la Seconda Guerra Mondiale, era una grande attrattiva nei confronti dei creativi. Gli svizzeri vennero a Milano perché a) erano richiesti e b) lì c'erano i lavori più stimolanti; c'erano clienti che ti offrivano carta bianca per fare quello che volevi e colleghi designer e intellettuali con cui fare quattro chiacchiere durante un pranzo.

Quello che risalta più chiaramente quando si leggono i saggi che seguono, è che persone come Iliprandi erano fortunate a essere presenti in uno di quei periodi storici in cui tutto si fonde per creare qualcosa di veramente formidabile. C'era la gente giusta a tutti i livelli, dagli illustratori ai musicisti, da Zurigo a Milano, nel posto giusto. Le idee venivano scambiate e i confini non erano semplicemente abbattuti: non esistevano affatto. Creativi e clienti erano alla pari e commerciavano idee invece di denaro. John Steinbeck disse una volta che i creativi vanno sempre dove sono apprezzati e Milano, fra il 1945 e il 1960 circa, era uno di quei luoghi speciali. Il mondo del design non sarebbe mai più stato lo stesso.

L'ispirazione italiana nel design grafico svizzero del dopoguerra.

Bettina Richter

Curatrice della collezione di Manifesti del Museum für Gestaltung di Zurigo.

Zurigo e Milano, c.1945: mondi lontani

Poco dopo la fine della Seconda Guerra Mondiale, la Svizzera visse un periodo di boom economico che necessitava nell'immediato di forza lavoro che potesse sostenerlo. Innumerevoli persone - molte provenienti dal sud Italia - si trasferirono in Svizzera alla ricerca di un impiego e di una vita migliore. Per inseguire questo sogno dovettero però sopportare il peso del duro lavoro e il razzismo politico degli svizzeri, mentre le condizioni lavorative e il numero degli impiegati richiesti cambiavano in continuazione, facendo sì che fosse impossibile per gli Italiani sentirsi ben accolti nel loro nuovo paese.

Fu invece tutta un'altra storia per un gruppo di grafici svizzeri che nello stesso periodo, a Milano, fece il percorso inverso. L'atmosfera della *Dolce Vita* che pervadeva la città, prometteva un nuovo inizio per gli immigrati, che furono ben accolti nonostante le differenze fra Svizzera e Italia in quel periodo.

La Svizzera (che era rimasta neutrale durante la Seconda Guerra Mondiale)

era diventata sempre più conservatrice a partire dal 1939, ed era politicamente e culturalmente isolata dal resto dell'Europa. Si era cristallizzata a tal punto da raggiungere la paralisi intellettuale, ed era avvolta da una crisi creativa che andava in senso contrario al boom economico.

Negli anni '50 comunque, il Modernismo degli anni precedenti alla guerra ricominciò a prosperare nel design grafico. A Zurigo, Josef Müller-Brockmann sviluppò una sua unione fra Arte Concreta e tipografia, mentre a Basilea, Armin Hofmann ed Emil Ruder proposero una visione più sensuale e ludica delle grafiche svizzere.

Essi furono i principali esponenti dello "Stile Svizzero" che sarebbe diventato famoso in tutto il mondo. Questo si basava sull'utilizzo di una gabbia tipografica composta da linee orizzontali e verticali, nel quale la composizione delle immagini e dei testi era considerata più importante del contenuto creativo in sé.

Tuttavia, questi principi furono spesso applicati in modo troppo rigoroso, producendo grafiche piuttosto deboli e convenzionali; era questa una tendenza che avrebbe pervaso anche i lavori di un pioniere quale Müller-Brockmann.

La Milano del 1945 invece, si crogiolava nella freschezza di un ambiente nuovo,

aperto e progressista, reso ancor più ricco dallo stesso boom economico del quale stava godendo anche la Svizzera.

Ed esattamente come in Svizzera, l'avanguardia ricominciò da dove si era fermata prima dalla guerra. Inoltre, in particolare fra l'intellighenzia, era molto sentito il dibattito su che cosa fosse accaduto durante la guerra. Queste discussioni portarono a cambiamenti radicali nella società, nella politica e conseguentemente nel mondo del business, dove il maggior portatore di cambiamento fu Adriano Olivetti.

Olivetti cominciò a lavorare nel 1926 nella ditta fondata da suo padre, e iniziò a costruire la sua concreta utopia di una città degli uomini, dove il profitto aveva importanza secondaria rispetto al benessere degli impiegati. Olivetti fu esiliato in Svizzera nel 1944 per causa dei suoi ideali, ma quando ritornò dopo la guerra, estese il concetto di comunicazione visiva, fondendo l'etica con l'estetica e rendendo questi due principi i caposaldi della sua azienda. Uno sviluppo significativo fu la creazione di un reparto di pubblicità e comunicazione per Olivetti nel 1933.

L'impegno sociale e culturale di Olivetti fu ispirazione per altre aziende come La Rinascente, Pirelli e Montecatini, che presero Olivetti come esempio quando crearono i propri reparti di pubblicità. Artisti e fotografi professionisti divennero dunque sempre più richiesti, ma in Italia, fino agli anni '50, non c'erano scuole di design e dunque neppure designer di formazione classica.

Le poche agenzie e studi di pubblicità che esistevano, vedevano per lo più impiegati pittori o architetti, situazione questa molto vantaggiosa per i grafici e fotografi svizzeri che disponevano già di un'educazione al design.

I designer artistici svizzeri a Milano

Xanti Schawinsky e Max Huber furono i primi ambasciatori del design svizzero a intraprendere l'avventura italiana. Schawinsky era un uomo di talento che in Germania aveva studiato musica e pittura e aveva una gran voglia di sperimentare e riformare le arti e la società.

Fuggì dalla Germania verso la Svizzera nel 1933, prima di trasferirsi più tardi nello stesso anno, in Italia, dove conobbe Antonio Boggeri. Boggeri è un altro pezzo indispensabile del puzzle della storia svizzera-italiana. Era un musicista e fotografo appassionato, profondamente influenzato dalle opere dei maggiori artisti dell'avanguardia come El Lissitzky e Jan Tschichold.

Ispirato dal loro sapiente mix fra tipografia, illustrazione, design grafico e fotografia, Boggeri aprì il proprio studio nel 1933. Schawinsky fu uno dei suoi primi impiegati, mentre Huber arrivò nel 1940. Una moltitudine di designer svizzeri seguì i loro passi, e fra questi Carlo Vivareli, Walter Ballmer, Serge Libiszewski, Lora Lamm e Bruno Monguzzi. Molti di loro utilizzarono l'esperienza allo studio Boggeri come trampolino di lancio per progredire nella carriera o per aprire un proprio studio, e nessuno degli impiegati di Boggeri rimase a lungo alle sue dipendenze. Tutti comunque condividevano una forte curiosità, un'apertura creativa che sarebbe diventata una caratteristica saliente dello studio.

L'unico vero concorrente di Boggeri a Milano era lo studio del grafico Franco Grignani, e anche lì la maggior parte degli impiegati era svizzera. Insieme formarono un gruppo intimo di giovani designer che si riuniva a mezzogiorno per pranzare nelle piccole trattorie e discutere intensamente con scrittori e altri artisti sul valore sociale del design, dell'arte e sulla responsabilità del designer.

Nello stesso momento Max Huber, dopo essere stato forzato a tornare in Svizzera durante la guerra, stava cercando ancora una volta ispirazione in Italia dopo il 1945. Lavorò insieme al grafico Albe Steiner dal 1950 al 1954 nel reparto di pubblicità del rinomato grande magazzino La Rinascente.

Negli anni '50 La Rinascente rappresentava il rinascimento culturale ed economico dell'Italia. La moda e i mobili divennero sinonimi di design e qualità, con i prodotti de La Rinascente che univano estetica, innovazione e accessibilità. L'architetto e designer Giò Ponti teneva le sue mostre a La Rinascente a partire dal 1953 e il prestigioso premio per il design, il Compasso d'oro, fu un'altra iniziativa de La Rinascente.

Huber progettò il logo dell'azienda insieme alla sua immagine coordinata.

Lora Lamm fu una delle prime donne svizzere a lavorare a Milano negli anni '50. Lavorò presso lo Studio Boggeri dal 1953 fino al 1954, quando Max Huber la collocò nel reparto pubblicitario de La Rinascente. Nel 1956 progettò il materiale promozionale per una mostra di prodotti giapponesi a La Rinascente, che l'avrebbe consacrata come designer di grande rilievo. Dopo la partenza di Huber da La Rinascente, diventò infatti direttrice del reparto pubblicitario, carica che ricoprì dal 1958 al 1962.

Il fotografo Serge Libiszewski fu un altro personaggio che fu invitato da Huber a lavorare a La Rinascente. Libiszewski aveva studiato presso il Kunstgewerbeschule a Zurigo prima di lavorare allo Studio Müller-Brockmann. A causa della mancanza di fotografi commerciali nel nord Italia, Libiszewski fu entusiasta nell'accettare l'invito di Huber. Tuttavia il loro rapporto lavorativo cominciò in modo infausto: non c'erano commissioni e Libiszewski si ridusse ad aiutare Huber nel suo studio.

Il successo finalmente arrivò quando nel 1962 Libiszewski avviò il proprio studio. Un diluvio di ordini arrivò da La Rinascente, Studio Boggeri, Olivetti e Pirelli. In questo periodo la fotografia stava evolvendo in una forma artistica nuova e indipendente, all'interno della grafica pubblicitaria. Con Salvatore Gregorietti e Giancarlo Iliprandi (per La Rinascente) e Walter Ballmer (per Olivetti) lavorò a tante campagne pubblicitarie innovative.

Tutti i grafici e fotografi che vennero a Milano dopo il 1950 condividevano la stessa sete di nuove sfide, che non riuscivano a soddisfare nella conservatrice e ortodossa scena artistica della Svizzera. Volevano essere creativi, a prescindere dal confine tra le diverse forme d'arte. Purtroppo però, periodi di tale intensità e innovazione non durano mai molto tempo.

All'inizio del 1970 quest'utopia sociale scomparì gradualmente. Il concetto di marketing basato sull'efficacia, con meno arte e loghi più grandi, cominciò a dominare le campagne di comunicazione. Si cominciarono a indirizzare le commesse alle maggiori agenzie pubblicitarie invece che ai singoli designer: finiva così il rapporto fra il direttivo di grandi aziende, singoli designer e fotografi indipendenti.

L'ispirazione italiana nel design grafico svizzero del dopoguerra.

Il design grafico svizzero contemporaneo

La fama che oggi gode il design grafico svizzero deve molto all'influenza che l'Italia ha avuto nei suoi confronti durante gli anni 50 e '60. La solida formazione dei designer svizzeri pose le basi, ma fu la loro ispirata collaborazione con la controparte italiana che permise a Max Huber, Lora Lamm, Walter Ballmer e ad altri di avere successo.

Questo scambio virtuoso, unitamente alle condizioni favorevoli che si presentavano a Milano durante lo stesso periodo (boom economico, studi ambiziosi e clienti entusiasti), contribuì alla ricchezza stilistica del design grafico. Una tradizione di rigore formale unita alla curiosità per la sperimentazione, il colore, lo spirito poetico e l'entusiasmo per la vita, formò una combinazione esaltante, altamente fruttuosa per entrambe le parti e che continua a ispirare il design grafico svizzero di oggi.

La sua varietà estetica dimostra che persino durante un periodo di turbolenza politica come gli anni '80, la tradizione del design *Aufbruch* (partenza) può comunque sopravvivere. L'impiego stretto del carattere Helvetica viene tuttora messo in discussione in modo provocatorio dai designer.

Il design grafico svizzero continua a fiorire attraverso gli scambi culturali con altre forme d'arte come la musica e la letteratura, le quali si arricchiscono a loro volta. Queste tendenze, che cominciarono nel dopoguerra, continuano oggi e portano ancora a delle esperienze meravigliose ed esaltanti, almeno per quanto riguarda il design.

Ancora più incoraggiante è il fatto che sia emersa a partire dagli anni '90, una giovane generazione di grafici che non si limita a soluzioni grafiche generate dal computer ma, esattamente come i loro predecessori, usa le mani, tornando così alla base e alle origini della disciplina.

Quando si toccano e si sentono i materiali, vengono alla luce soluzioni diverse e creative, che portano a un risultato più personale, soggettivo

e meno ortodosso. Tutte le cose imperfette, casuali e spontanee, possono influenzare in modo positivo la pratica giornaliera del design.

Le scrittura e le illustrazioni a mano libera, lo sviluppo di nuovi tipi di carattere e la loro unione insolita, sono tutti elementi che risuonano nei manifesti contemporanei. Giocare con altri mass media, come la fotografia e le belle arti, riflette i vari modi di affrontare le immagini e i testi di oggi.

Per quanto riguarda il contenuto, i manifesti culturali contemporanei, dimostrano un'interpretazione diversa del manifesto come strumento di comunicazione di massa. Le vecchie regole del manifesto come mezzo di comunicazione (per esempio la leggibilità e una comprensione immediata del messaggio) non si applicano più.

Le persone sono nuovamente stimolate a mettere in discussione il tradizionale modo di interpretare testi, messaggi e immagini.

Il Design Italiano Dopo il 1945.

Maurizio Vitta

Professore di Storia e Cultura della Progettazione presso la facoltà di Design del Politecnico di Milano.

La storia della grafica italiana della seconda metà del XX secolo comincia nella prima metà, con una data di nascita fissata nel 1933, quando apre lo studio Boggeri, viene pubblicato il primo numero di "Campo grafico" e si inaugura la V Triennale di Milano, dove la sezione grafica tedesca allestita da Paul Renner suscitò un vivo interesse. Già nelle sue origini essa appare dunque disegnata non secondo uno sviluppo lineare, ma attraverso una serie di triangolazioni, di incroci, di nodi culturali: le tangenze con le parallele ricerche dell'architettura moderna, lo stretto legame con il nascente disegno industriale, gli insistiti confronti con l'arte contemporanea trovarono la loro espressione più immediata in una professionalità rigorosa e consapevole, oltre che in un vivace senso della internazionalità, reso vivace dallo scambio di esperienze con i grafici europei, in particolare con quelli svizzeri. Sarà questo il crogiolo nel quale si formerà la grafica italiana contemporanea: un calderone ribollente, nel quale la modernità annunciata, perseguita, progettata,

avrebbe infine trovato la sua definizione conclusiva. Non si trattava di mettere a punto nuove tecniche espressive, ma di fondare una vera e propria cultura visiva ispirata a una ragione all'altezza dei nuovi scenari, e che oltretutto poteva ricollegarsi a un'antica tradizione di classicità e di equilibrio formale, spaziante dal De divina proportione di Luca Pacioli alla editoria di Aldo Manuzio, oltre che alle dirompenti innovazioni del primo Futurismo e al loro approfondimento nella sua seconda fase, grazie soprattutto all'opera di Fortunato Depero.

Dopo la devastazione del dopoguerra, l'imperativo della ricostruzione economica e sociale impose all'Italia la messa a punto di protocolli di comunicazione e informazione capaci di fronteggiare le esigenze della nuova società industriale, democratica e di massa. Non a caso la struttura professionale e disciplinare della grafica italiana si concentrò lungo l'asse Milano-Torino, capitali dell'editoria e poli

di uno sviluppo neocapitalistico fondato sull'industria leggera e sulla sua capacità di diffusione capillare attraverso accorte strategie di immagine. Questa polarità si manifestò in un pluralismo di proposte formali, che però riconducevano tutte a un'unica matrice ideologica, quella di una razionalità limpida e ferma, espressa in un linguaggio essenziale, i cui geometrici equilibri dovevano garantire chiarezza e verità. In questo senso resta emblematico il lavoro di Albe Steiner, inaugurato dal manifesto disegnato nel 1945 per la "Mostra della ricostruzione" e proseguito con il progetto grafico del "Politecnico", la rivista creata da Elio Vittorini come veicolo di una nuova cultura.

Fu quello il punto di snodo di una vicenda avviata con le ricerche, le riflessioni e i contatti internazionali dei decenni precedenti. La breve stagione di "Campo grafico" era tuttora viva nella memoria dei suoi protagonisti, e la Triennale milanese seppe subito imporsi come luogo di sperimentazione e proposta. Inoltre

Il Design Italiano Dopo il 1945.

la presenza di un nutrito gruppo di grafici elvetici dello studio Boggeri (Schawinski, Ballmer, Huber, Calabresi, Vivarelli, Monguzzi) non solo aveva lasciato in eredità un intreccio di esperienze che offrivano materiale esemplare in vista dei nuovi compiti, ma ne consentiva anche una sicura continuità grazie alla permanenza di alcuni di essi nella Milano del dopoguerra. Il punto di riferimento privilegiato restava naturalmente il Bauhaus di Gropius; ma una sicura influenza esercitarono anche la scuola olandese (Bob Noorda si trasferì a Milano nei primi anni Cinquanta) e la lezione magistrale di Max Bill.

Situata su questo orizzonte, la vicenda della grafica italiana si innestò quindi al più generale sviluppo della cultura progettuale, attraverso un serrato confronto con il disegno industriale e l'architettura, protagonisti (insieme al cinema) di quel periodo. Il caso più evidente resta in tal senso quello della Olivetti, il cui valore industriale trovò riscontro diretto nell'architettura di Gabetti e Isola, nel design di Sottsass, nella consulenza di letterati come Giudici o Volponi, e, non ultimo, in

una ricchezza grafica imperniata sul lavoro di Giovanni Pintori, proseguito poi da un nutrito gruppo di designer. Altre grandi società misero in atto strategie dell'immagine altrettanto raffinate, sebbene più sottili: l'industria Pirelli, per esempio, puntò su una progettazione grafica interna (ma con la collaborazione di grafici come Pino Tovaglia), e dilatò la sua comunicazione attraverso la rivista omonima, che espresse nel rigore della sua veste grafica il dinamismo dell'azienda – esaltato dalla costruzione del grattacielo progettato da Gio Ponti – e la sua attenzione alla cultura umanistica; l'industria televisiva, in rapidissima crescita, affidò invece molta parte della sua produzione grafica a Erberto Carboni, che interpretò il nuovo mass medium traducendone la complessità tecnologica in un linguaggio visivo semplice e accattivante, lo stesso adottato per la campagna pubblicitaria della Barilla.

La modernità annunciata nella prima parte del Novecento giunse a maturazione negli anni Sessanta, quando la grafica italiana si attestò su posizioni disciplinari e professionali ormai garantite dal proliferare di scuole, pubblicazioni e risonanza culturale. Una nuova generazione di progettisti si affacciò allora alla ribalta della comunicazione visiva: A.G. Fronzoni, con le sue assolutezze gestaltiche e un raffinatissimo uso del bianco e nero; Franco Grignani, impegnato in sofisticate ricerche ottiche su cui basare una nuova grammatica dell'immagine; Pino Tovaglia, finissimo interprete della nuova realtà industriale; Giancarlo Iliprandi, studioso del linguaggio visivo;

Michele Provinciali, Ilio Negri, Giulio Confalonieri e molti altri, tra i quali prese a spiccare allora, a Torino, la figura di Armando Testa.

Ciascun nome rinvia a uno stile individuale, ma ogni stile denuncia ascendenze culturali comuni, che in vari casi finiscono col coincidere. Al di sotto dei caratteri soggettivi, si distendeva una griglia concettuale omogenea, che faceva dello spazio grafico il dominio di una ragione cartesiana, sorretta da regole nitidamente enunciabili: ogni figurazione si inscriveva in un ordine logico, in un modello geometrico accuratamente calcolato, che imponeva a ogni immagine una misura minimale, ottenuta attraverso un sapiente processo metonimico. Di qui la comune volontà di ridurre il discorso visivo alla sua struttura essenziale, di farsi carico di un processo di implacabile sottrazione di materia che ricordava il "levare" michelangiolesco e che faceva emergere il messaggio in un vuoto, un silenzio altrettanto carico di significati. Solo a partire da queste premesse condivise è possibile districare le inclinazioni personali: l'ossessiva tendenza di Fronzoni verso un grado della comunicazione prossimo allo zero, gli schemi grafici di Iliprandi alla ricerca di formule per una nuova retorica visiva, l'assunzione da parte di Grignani della geometria della percezione come scaturigine di turbinose concrezioni linguistiche. Non sfugge, in questo panorama, l'eco delle contemporanee ricerche artistiche, dai rigori della Op Art all'estetica tecnologica dell'Arte programmata, o quella della dialettica architettonica, ancora nutrita di umori wrightiani e memore della lezione di Terragni,

Elena Xausa, after Franco Grignani

oppure quella proveniente dall'area del disegno industriale, i cui sviluppi erano ormai scanditi dalle edizioni del Compasso d'Oro.

Non è difficile scorgere in questo processo il filo rosso di una tradizione moderna che affondava le sue radici nella cultura progettuale nordica e nelle esperienze ancestrali della prima metà del Novecento, provvisoriamente concluse con la chiusura della scuola di Ulm, segnata dall'acceso dibattito tra Max Bill e Tomás Maldonado, che non mancò di far riflettere. Ma già allora altri mutamenti incalzavano, reclamando la nascita di nuovi paradigmi espressivi. La pubblicità televisiva, per esempio, fu non a caso interpretata al meglio da un autore come Armando Testa, sanguigno, creativo e geniale, capace di fare di un segno un personaggio e di un personaggio un'icona comunicativa, condensata nei manifesti in immagini icastiche, oscillanti tra la tecnica della metamorfosi (l'elefante-pneumatico) e l'astrazione concettuale (il Punt e Mes). C'era nell'aria l'energia dirompente della Pop Art, ma al di là di essa si distendeva un nuovo panorama produttivo destinato a mutare i rituali del consumo e, di conseguenza, i modelli della comunicazione. Nel frattempo, la grafica editoriale denunciava una evoluzione lenta – come il tema richiedeva – eppure approfondita, perfettamente esemplificata nei lavori dell'Unimark (Bob Noorda e Massimo Vignelli) per Mondadori e Feltrinelli.

Tra la fine del XX secolo e l'inizio del XXI la grafica italiana ha dovuto affrontare scenari ancora più mutevoli e instabili (segnati da grandi trasformazioni strutturali e da un serrato confronto con modelli estetici diversi, occidentali e orientali), ma lo ha fatto adottando una tattica di progressivo aggiornamento senza tuttavia rinunciare ai legami con la propria tradizione. In effetti nei lavori di Massimo Dolcini, Armando e Maurizio Milani, Italo Lupi, Pierluigi Cerri, si coglie una indiscussa continuità rispetto a una classicità di fondo, discreta, sottintesa, tenace, alla quale gli schemi progettuali fanno comunque riferimento, anche in presenza di tematiche nuove. La stessa classicità ha consentito di conservare un forte legame con la cultura regionale (Franco Balan), di affrontare le tematiche connesse al nuovo clima politico e sociale (Michele Spera, Ettore Vitale), oltre che di superare il declino del manifesto dovuto alle trasformazioni radicali del tessuto urbano (e confermato dalla sua provvisoria rinascita dovuta non a un grafico, ma a un fotografo come Oliviero Toscani).

In un modo o nell'altro, proprio questa classicità fondativa consente ancora alla grafica italiana di esaltare i propri caratteri identitari, in un mondo in cui le differenze culturali tendono a dissolversi nella nebulosa della globalizzazione e l'avanzata inarrestabile delle tecnologie digitali fa sorgere all'orizzonte un mondo nuovo, ancora tutto da esplorare. In ciò soccorre un altro aspetto della tradizione culturale dell'Italia, quello del cosmopolitismo intellettuale, che nei secoli ha tenuta viva la creatività nazionale e che oggi può ancora contribuire a risolvere i problemi, i quali del resto, a questo punto, non sono più nemmeno nazionali, bensì europei.

Una Intervista con Giancarlo Iliprandi.

Designer italiano che ha lavorato a Milano sin dagli anni '50.

Giancarlo Iliprandi, PAX, 1980

A cavallo tra gli anni '50 e '60 l'Italia visse un periodo di gran fermento. Tutto prendeva forma, il design iniziava a fiorire, le aziende erano particolarmente ricettive e, ovviamente, molti ne furono attratti. Svizzeri compresi.

Quando arrivarono, comprensibilmente, ancora non sapevamo che le loro influenze avrebbero cambiato la storia della grafica italiana. Chi si occupava di grafica in Italia, aveva una formazione prevalentemente artistica come Bigani, Carboni o Italo Lupi che arrivavano dall'architettura. Dall'altra parte delle Alpi era invece tutto più rigoroso, formale, tecnico.

La grafica in Svizzera era già percepita

come una professione vera e propria, noi invece eravamo ancora considerati artisti pubblicitari e il nostro mestiere puramente basato sul talento. Erano in molti quelli che avevano cercato e stavano cercando di staccarsi dal concetto d'arte grafica, Munari ad esempio. Come molti altri, anche lui pensava che questa posizione sminuisse il lavoro, ma a dare inizio al vero cambiamento fu l'incontro con gli svizzeri, o meglio, con il loro metodo. Per quelli come me che volevano essere designer, il metodo era fondamentale. Pensavamo che il progetto fosse importante, che dovesse essere basato su un metodo e che in tutto il design ci fossero una forma e una funzione che dovevano combaciare e, finalmente, trovammo qualcuno che la pensava come noi, anzi prima di noi.

Per quanto mi riguarda iniziai a pensare seriamente alla grafica frequentando lo Studio degli Architetti Castiglioni. È lì che scoprii questa cosa chiamata comunicazione visiva e grafica, ed è lì che incontrai per la prima volta Max Huber. Prima di quel giorno avevo studiato medicina, avevo fatto quattro anni di pittura e quattro di scenografia all'Accademia delle Belle Arti di Brera, ma non ero ancora riuscito a trovare qualcosa che m'interessasse veramente. Vivevo una profonda insoddisfazione. Certo, la scenografia era meglio della pittura, almeno dava la possibilità di avvicinarsi ai testi, alla musica, ma alla fine lo scenografo esiste pur sempre in funzione di un regista, quindi se non si è Zeffirelli, che passò da un ruolo

all'altro con successo, era limitante. Almeno per me.

L'incontro con Max fu ispirante invece. Non che Max ed io parlassimo propriamente di grafica, ma avevamo una vita notturna fatta di locali e concerti decisamente interessante. Negli stessi anni, sempre presso lo Studio, ebbi l'occasione di conoscere anche Steiner, Boggeri e ricordo che un giorno iniziai a dirmi "sì, questa è una cosa interessante". Fu lì che iniziai ad applicarmi veramente. Guardare Max lavorare agli allestimenti mi faceva venire voglia di imparare e così cominciai a sperimentare questa grafica svizzera, a comprare libri, riviste come *Neue Grafik*, tutta fatta in Helvetica. Li compravo alla libreria Salto, un luogo molto importante, e non solo per me. I due fratelli Salto che la gestivano, d'origine svizzera, erano molto informati. Con loro si poteva parlare di ciò che succedeva negli altri paesi e, mentre uno stava in negozio, l'altro andava negli studi con una borsa colma degli ultimi libri usciti sulla grafica. Sinceramente credo che molta dell'influenza svizzera sia dovuta a loro, oltre che allo studio Castiglioni ovviamente.

Per loro abbiamo lavorato veramente in tanti e su diversi allestimenti: Max per certe cose, Heinz Waibl, che al tempo era assistente di Max, su altre, e poi Tovaglia, Munari, Bianconi. Ci andavamo anche per vedere quello che facevano gli altri, era un posto dove ci si scambiavano idee senza mettersi in concorrenza l'uno con l'altro, ma piuttosto in un clima d'amicizia e

complicità che è lo stesso che ha reso possibili quelle contaminazioni che altrimenti nella purezza e nel rigore del pensiero dei vari Müller-Brockmann sarebbero state impensabili.

Altro ruolo fondamentale in questo rapporto Italia-Svizzera lo giocò il corso per assistenti grafici dell'Humanitaria, la scuola media fondata nel 1961 da Michele Provinciani e diretta per i suoi otto anni d'attività da Bauer prima e da Melino poi. E se si parla d'esperienze fondanti, non si può non parlare della Rinascente che, con le sue grandi mostre sul Giappone, l'India, il Centro America, insegnò ai milanesi una cultura diversa che avrebbe influenzato tutte le attività dal 1955 in poi.

Ha sempre fornito stimoli che rendevano possibile lo scambio tra persone, designer, musicisti, grafici, letterati e la sua conduzione, due erano le famiglie che si alternavano alla direzione generale e alla presidenza, quella dei Borletti e quella dei Bruschi, ha giocato un ruolo fondamentale in tutto questo. Il loro, era uno sguardo sempre orientato verso quello che facevano i grandi magazzini di Londra e di Parigi, avevano una curiosità e un'apertura mentale che si rivelò proficua per molti aspetti tanto da rappresentare il binomio ideale perché le influenze svizzere, sia quelle di Zurigo che di Basilea, lasciassero il segno.

Max Huber aveva non solo una mano felice ma anche un occhio benevolo, apprezzava il lavoro di tutti, e nei

Una Intervista con Giancarlo Iliprandi.

grandi allestimenti poi era davvero interessante. Riusciva a sovrapporre i colori mettendo uno sopra l'altro dei grandi fogli di cellophane. Li spennellava con acqua in cui aveva diluito la colla e poi li tirava con la spatola. Eravamo tutti incantati nel vedere con quale rapidità metteva a posto questo e quello. Steiner invece, era uno che gli altri li criticava eccome. Per lui la comunicazione doveva essere d'utilità sociale e quando non lo era, non era altro che tempo sprecato. Era di certo più svizzero di Huber, pur essendo italiano.

Oltre Max e Steiner, ho ammirato Gfeller, ma soprattutto Serge Libiszewski, un vero innovatore nel campo della fotografia. Faceva still life e moda e aveva questo modo incredibile di trattare le persone come fossero una natura morta. Curava moltissimo la composizione, le luci e anche quello che nelle sue opere sembrava accidentale non lo era affatto. Era questa la sua grande capacità.

Ormai ci conoscevamo quasi tutti quando l'art director della Rinascente, la signora Latis, mi scelse per lavorare agli allestimenti al posto di Steiner. Forse lo fece perché ero abituato a lavorare sulle grandi dimensioni e, in effetti, lavorare su un grande magazzino è stato per me come lavorare su un palcoscenico, con le tempere e i pennelli grossi. Ricordo che l'allestimento di tutto il negozio, compreso il portico esterno, che feci per Natale. Dei piccoli Beauty Shop se né occupò

invece la Lamm, scelta per sostituire Max e, soprattutto, per quel suo modo di fare femminile che meglio si addiceva alla visione delle cose della Latis. Scoprii solo in un secondo momento che tutti mi chiamavano piccolo Steiner, dicevano che ero pignolo come lui. Poi, al posto della Latis, arrivò un nuovo e giovane art director, Adriana Botti, e con lei iniziarono a lavorare molti altri giovani come Massimo Vignelli, Salvatore Gregorietti, che ai tempi, ancora prima della fondazione di Unimark, era il suo assistente.

Il cambiamento grafico era ormai evidente: le reciproche influenze avevano lasciato una traccia. Di sicuro in Vignelli, che rimase probabilmente il più forte sostenitore dell'Helvetica della fonderia Haas; in modo diverso in Max che invece, appena arrivato in Italia, si mise ad usare il Futura e il Bodoni. Poi c'era il gruppo formato da Cappelli, Bonini e Calabrese o il gruppo CNTP – Confalonieri, Negri, Provinciali, Tovaglia - che aveva un modo di esprimersi legato al corsivo, più umanistico e meno svizzero.

Ai tempi anche io sono stato critico con i caratteri bastoni, perché ero convinto che molti lo usassero pensando che fosse sufficiente a rendere il lavoro attuale e alla moda. Io sono sempre stato contrario alle mode e convinto che si dovesse adattare il proprio stile al cliente e al prodotto, ma Massimo lo usava bene. Fu lui a chiedere a Nava di andare in Svizzera a comprare i piombi. L'operazione andò bene solo la seconda volta e, in ogni modo, Nava non era l'unico ad avere l'Helvetica Haas a Milano. Anche la Tipocromo, diventata poi

Cromotipo, l'aveva in catalogo. Un carattere che invece creava problemi era il Times New Roman. Era coperto dai diritti d'autore quindi per usarlo ritagliavamo le lettere dal giornale, assemblavamo il testo e poi fotografavamo il tutto. A me il Times New Roman è piaciuto parecchio, quando in Italia ancora non esisteva soprattutto. Come non esistevano i manager.

In quegli anni si aveva un rapporto diretto con il *padrùn*, ci si occupava anche dell'idea, si mettevano i testi e nel caso d'aziende più grandi c'erano i portavoce con cui parlare. Ma Franco Fortini di Pirelli, Siniscaldi, Volponi di Olivetti, Vittorio Sereni erano anche degli intellettuali, con loro c'era modo di discutere le cose, di spiegare perché le cose fossero scritte in un certo ordine o perché una sola fotografia non era sufficiente. Insomma, diciamo che per un periodo abbiamo fatto un po' di scuola a certe industrie.

Finiti i grandi proprietari però sono arrivate le agenzie, le multinazionali e si sono mangiate tutto il mercato. E anche se con le agenzie c'è stato un periodo in cui abbiamo avuto un buon rapporto - nel '67 l'Art Directors Club è stato fondato da personaggi provenienti da diverse discipline, Pino Tovaglia, io, poi Blachian di Young&Rubicam e ancora Flavio Lucchini che era l'art director di Vogue – le cose non hanno funzionato a lungo. Tutto è andato a spegnersi lentamente, compresa la sperimentazione che ai tempi aveva creato un piccolo movimento, il nostro, il cui unico interesse era che da questi incontri-scontri nascesse qualcosa di nuovo.

Una Intervista con Felix Humm.

Designer svizzero attivo in Svizzera ed in Italia dagli anni '60.

A Milano, tra il 1945 e il 1970, la grafica giocò un ruolo molto importante. Molti furono i grafici svizzeri che da Basilea e Zurigo arrivarono in città in quegli anni. Altri arrivarono dalla Germania, dal Bauhaus, e molti di loro passarono per lo Studio Boggeri, dove anche io, giovanissimo, ebbi l'onore d lavorare.

Subito dopo il diploma però non approdai direttamente a Milano, bensì a Torino. Lavoravo presso l'agenzia di pubblicità Reiwald di Basilea e fui inserito nel gruppo che si occupava di Fiat Suisse. Poco dopo la stessa agenzia ottenne anche Fiat Italia come cliente e quindi mi trasferirono. Avevo 21 anni, dovevo fermarmi tre giorni e alla fine in Italia ci sono rimasto per 40 anni, prima a Torino e poi a Milano. In quel periodo c'era un fermento culturale importante in Italia e molte aziende ne furono protagoniste dirette: l'Olivetti, la Rinascente, Pirelli erano accumulate da una filosofia aziendale illuminata, ma anche in Fiat a Torino nel settore della comunicazione visiva si percepiva questo fermento.

Di questo il merito è da attribuire sicuramente all'ora responsabile della comunicazione, Odone Camerana, legato alla famiglia Olivetti da vincoli di parentela e con alle spalle studi a Oxford. Questo clima di apertura, di internazionalità che si respirava un po' ovunque, si traduceva a Torino come a Milano, sia in iniziative imprenditoriali che in aperture a livello sociale. Sarebbe impensabile oggi proporre lavori tanto stravaganti con la stessa libertà espressiva di un tempo. I collage fotografici che realizzai per la monografia "70 anni Fiat", per esempio,

finirono come gigantografie sui muri dell'ufficio di Gianni Agnelli, insieme ai quadri di Rauschenberg e Lichtenstein.

Ci fu poi, sempre a Torino, e decisamente agevolato dalla reciproca conoscenza del tedesco da parte di entrambi, uno scambio di idee anche con il giovane product designer Pio Manzù, figlio dello scultore Giacomo che era appena arrivato alla Fiat da Ulm. Lo stimavo molto, così come ero profondamente affascinato dai tipografi, dai loro apparecchi, dagli odori che si respiravano in quei luoghi, dal rapporto professionale che si creava fra di noi.

Entrando però più approfonditamente nel discorso grafico, credo che anche il dialogo con le avanguardie, artistiche e intellettuali, e il tentativo di produrre una simbiosi tra arte e comunicazione visiva siano stati fondamentali per lo sviluppo stilistico.

Per quello che riguarda il mio di stile penso che sia influenzato sicuramente dalla scuola di Basilea come base, ma una volta in Italia, mi sono ispirato molto alla bellezza delle lapidi del Foro Romano e all'eleganza dell'architettura romanica, dove ho incontrato la divina proporzione. Si rischiava di prendersi la "Sindrome di Stoccolma" tanta era la bellezza che in ogni angolo d'Italia di poteva incontrare.

Di certo, la mia era una formazione consolidata in un paese in cui la grafica era decisamente un mestiere, non veniva considerato arte come spesso accadeva in Italia, ma non credo di possa parlare di una specifica grafica svizzera. È più

un derivato dal costruttivismo russo con El Lissitzky, Moholy-Nagy del Bauhaus e "de Stijl" con Piet Zwart, la "Neue Graphik" con Jan Tschichold, Max Bill alla prima scuola di Ulm.

Le scuole svizzere si orientarono verso questi movimenti e così uscirono personaggi come Max Huber, Hans Neuburg, Armin Hoffmann, Emil Ruder e Josef Müller-Brockmann e tanti altri ancora. Huber lo conobbi però che era già anziano così come Castiglioni. Quando arrivai a Milano, la tendenza era quella di stare tra stranieri, anche se a stimolarmi furono in molti, sicuramente i lavori di A.G. Fronzoni che, nella tipografia, portava un discorso davvero innovativo e capace di rompere le regole. In quegli anni la sperimentazione e l'intuito erano decisamente protagonisti, oggi sembra impensabile poter fare altrettanto. Quando arrivò il marketing cambiò tutto prepotentemente: con quella visione contraria a qualsiasi forma di creatività e innovazione per paura che si possano vendere tre prodotti in meno, l'intuito è diventato sempre più un tabù. Ma senza intuito non c'è e non ci può essere futuro.

Celebrate The Present.

To bring the story of Swiss and Italian design full circle, 22 of the best designers and design studios from both countries were invited to collaborate on posters celebrating the shared design heritage of their two countries. These are the results.

CCRZ

ENG

CCRZ specialises in visual communication, design and architecture, with particular expertise in graphic design, photography, illustration and exhibition design. The studio has completed projects ranging from graphic art to packaging, corporate identity to advertising, signs to interior design, web design to planning and managing communication strategies and production. The members of CCRZ have more than ten years experience in these areas at both national and international level. Thanks to its multidisciplinary approach CCRZ is able to manage even complex projects by effectively combining communicative and aesthetic values without ever losing sight of practicalities or value for money.

DE

CCRZ ist auf visuelle Kommunikation, Design und Architektur spezialisiert, mit besonderer Expertise in Grafikdesign, Fotografie, Illustration und Messedesign. Das Studio beschäftigt sich mit einem breiten Spektrum an Projekten, von Grafikdesign bis zu Verpackung, von Corporate Identity bis zu Werbung, von Bildzeichen bis zu Innenarchitektur, von Webdesign bis hin zur Planung und Verwaltung von Kommunikationsstrategien und Produktion. CCRZs Mitglieder haben in diesen Bereichen über zehn Jahre Erfahrung, sowohl auf nationalem als auch internationalem Niveau. Dank seiner fachübergreifenden Fähigkeiten kann CCRZ auch sehr komplexe Projekte verwalten und dabei effektiv kommunikative und ästhetische Werte miteinander kombinieren, ohne jemals die praktische Anwendbarkeit oder das Preisleistungsverhältnis aus den Augen zu verlieren.

FR

CCRZ est spécialisé en communication visuelle, design et architecture avec un savoir-faire particulier en graphisme, photographie, illustration et design d'expositions. Le studio a bouclé des projets allant de l'art graphique à l'emballage, de l'image de marque à la publicité, d'enseignes au design d'intérieur, du design de sites web à planifier et organiser des stratégies de communication et de production. Les membres de CCRZ ont plus de dix ans d'expérience dans ces domaines au niveau national comme au niveau international. Grâce à son approche pluridisciplinaire CCRZ est capable de mener des projets complexes en combinant communication et esthétique sans jamais perdre de vue les détails pratiques ou le rapport qualité / prix.

ITA

CCRZ si occupa di comunicazione visiva, design e architettura, con una competenza particolare nel design grafico, la fotografia, l'illustrazione e gli allestimenti. Lo studio ha realizzato progetti che vanno dall'arte grafica al packaging, dalla corporate identity alla pubblicità, dalla segnaletica alla progettazione d'interni, dal web design alla pianificazione e gestione di strategie comunicative e di produzione. Gli associati di CCRZ possono vantare oltre dieci anni d'esperienza in questi ambiti, sia a livello nazionale che internazionale. Grazie al suo approccio multidisciplinare CCRZ è in grado di gestire progetti anche complessi, unendo in modo efficace valori comunicativi ed estetici, senza mai perdere di vista i risvolti pratici ed economici del lavoro.

Studio FM

ENG

Studio FM Milano is a Milan based graphic design studio. It was founded in 1996 by Barbara Forni and Sergio Menichelli, who were subsequently joined in 2000 by Cristiano Bottino. Today Studio FM specializes in graphic design, specifically art direction, corporate identity, books, exhibition/installation design and web design.

Studio FM projects have received several awards and been published internationally on various occasions.

FR

Studio FM Milano est un studio de graphisme basé à Milan. Il a été fondé en 1996 par Barbara Forni et Sergio Menichelli, qui ont ensuite été rejoints par Cristiano Bottino en 2000. Aujourd'hui Studio FM se spécialise en graphisme, spécifiquement dans le domaine de l'art, de l'image de marque, des livres, du design d'installations et d'expositions et du design de sites web.

Les projets de Studio FM ont reçus de nombreux prix et ont été publiés à l'international à de nombreuses reprises.

ITA

Studio FM Milano è uno studio di design grafico con sede a Milano. È stato fondato nel 1996 da Barbara Forni e Sergio Menichelli, ai quali si è unito in seguito Cristiano Bottino nel 2000. Studio FM oggi è specializzato nel design grafico, e in particolare art direction, immagine coordinata, libri, progettazione di mostre/installazioni e web design.

Alcuni dei progetti di Studio FM hanno vinto vari premi e sono stati pubblicati a livello internazionale in varie occasioni.

DE

Studio FM Milano ist ein Grafikdesign Studio in Mailand. Es wurde 1996 von Barbara Forni und Sergio Menichelli gegründet, denen Cristiano Bottino im Jahr 2000 beitrat. Studio FM spezialisiert sich heute auf Grafikdesign, insbesondere künstlerische Leitung, Corporate Identity, Bücher, Messe-/Installationsdesign und Webdesign.

Studio FMs Projekte wurden mehrmals ausgezeichnet und wurden international mehrfach veröffentlicht.

CCRZ

Ufficio Cultura Comune di Chiasso Visual Identity (2009)

Ufficio Cultura Comune di Chiasso Visual Identity (2009)

Ufficio Cultura Comune di Chiasso Visual Identity (2009)

Flora Ferroviria book design (2010)

Flora Ferroviria book design (2010)

Flora Ferroviria book design (2010)

Studio FM

Arclinea is a top-end furniture firm that produces kitchens designed by Antonio Citterio. Studio FM Milano developed an illustrative language for the brand based on common kitchen items.

Trienalle Design Musuem, Milan. Studio FM worked with architecture studio Antonio Citterio Patricia Viel & Partners to create the graphic design for the second edition Serie Fuori Serie of the Triennale Design Museum in 2009.

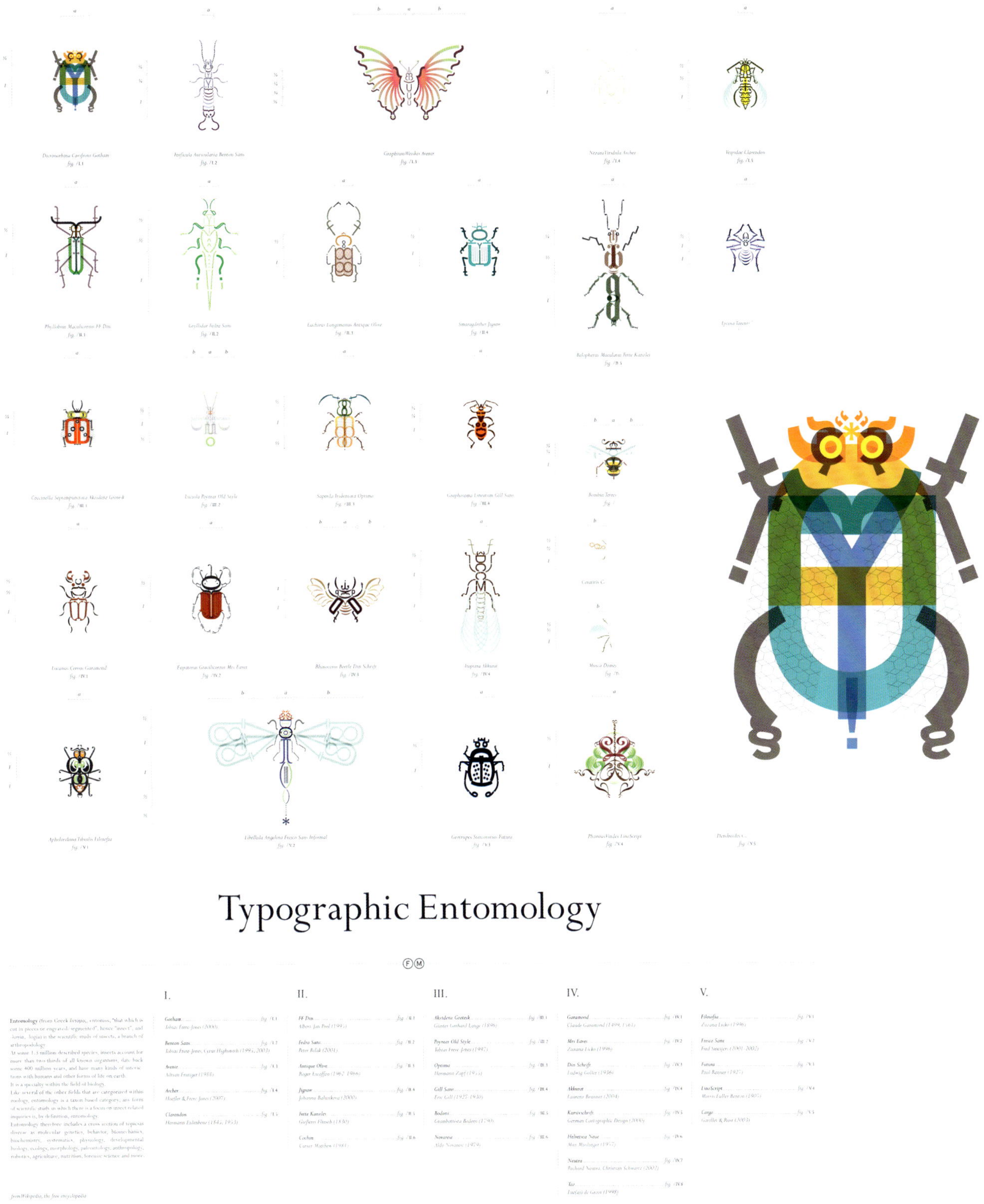

Typographic Entomology

F M

Figure captions (left to right, top to bottom):

- *Dicronorhina Carifrons* Gotham — fig. /I.1
- *Forficula Auricularia* Benton Sans — fig. /I.2
- *Graphium Weiskei* Avenir — fig. /I.3
- *Nezara Viridula* Archer — fig. /I.4
- *Vespidae* Clarendon — fig. /I.5
- *Phyllobius Maculicornis* FF Din — fig. /II.1
- *Gryllidae* Fedra Sans — fig. /II.2
- *Euchirus Longimanus* Antique Olive — fig. /II.3
- *Smaragdesthes* Jigsaw — fig. /II.4
- *Belopherus Maculatus* Fette Kanzlei — fig. /II.5
- *Coccinella Septempunctata* Akzidenz Grotesk — fig. /III.1
- *Luciola* Poynter Old Style — fig. /III.2
- *Sagenella* Optima — fig. /III.3
- *Graphosoma Lineatum* Gill Sans — fig. /III.4
- *Bombus Terres* — fig.
- *Lucanus Cervus* Garamond — fig. /IV.1
- *Eupatorus Gracilicornis* Mrs Eaves — fig. /IV.2
- *Rhinoceros Beetle* Din Schrift — fig. /IV.3
- *Isoptera* Akkurat — fig. /IV.4
- *Aphelocheirus Tibialis* Filosofia — fig. /V.1
- *Libellula Angelina* Fresco Sans Informal — fig. /V.2
- *Geotrupes Stercorosus* Futura — fig. /V.3
- *Phanaeus Vindex* LinoScript — fig. /V.4

Entomology (from Greek ἔντομον, entomon, "that which is cut in pieces or engraved/segmented", hence "insect", and -λογία, logia) is the scientific study of insects, a branch of arthropodology.

At some 1.3 million described species, insects account for more than two-thirds of all known organisms, date back some 400 million years, and have many kinds of interactions with humans and other forms of life on earth.

It is a specialty within the field of biology.

Like several of the other fields that are categorized within zoology, entomology is a taxon-based category; any form of scientific study in which there is a focus on insect-related inquiries is, by definition, entomology.

Entomology therefore includes a cross section of topics as diverse as molecular genetics, behavior, biomechanics, biochemistry, systematics, physiology, developmental biology, ecology, morphology, paleontology, anthropology, robotics, agriculture, nutrition, forensic science and more.

from Wikipedia, the free encyclopedia

I.

Gotham	fig. /I.1	*Tobias Frere-Jones (2000)*
Benton Sans	fig. /I.2	*Tobias Frere-Jones, Cyrus Highsmith (1995, 2003)*
Avenir	fig. /I.3	*Adrian Frutiger (1988)*
Archer	fig. /I.4	*Hoefler & Frere-Jones (2001)*
Clarendon	fig. /I.5	*Hermann Eidenbenz (1845, 1953)*

II.

FF Din	fig. /II.1	*Albert-Jan Pool (1995)*
Fedra Sans	fig. /II.2	*Peter Bilak (2001)*
Antique Olive	fig. /II.3	*Roger Excoffon (1962-1966)*
Jigsaw	fig. /II.4	*Johanna Balusikova (2000)*
Fette Kanzlei	fig. /II.5	*Gießerei Flinsch (1830)*
Cochin	fig. /II.6	*Matthew Carter (1981)*

III.

Akzidenz Grotesk	fig. /III.1	*Günter Gerhard Lange (1896)*
Poynter Old Style	fig. /III.2	*Tobias Frere-Jones (1997)*
Optima	fig. /III.3	*Hermann Zapf (1958)*
Gill Sans	fig. /III.4	*Eric Gill (1927-1930)*
Bodoni	fig. /III.5	*Giambattista Bodoni (1798)*
Novarese	fig. /III.6	*Aldo Novarese (1979)*

IV.

Garamond	fig. /IV.1	*Claude Garamond (1499, 1561)*
Mrs Eaves	fig. /IV.2	*Zuzana Licko (1996)*
Din Schrift	fig. /IV.3	*Ludwig Goller (1936)*
Akkurat	fig. /IV.4	*Laurenz Brunner (2004)*
Kurrentschrift	fig. /IV.5	*German Calligraphic Design (1900)*
Helvetica Neue	fig. /IV.6	*Max Miedinger (1957)*
Neutra	fig. /IV.7	*Richard Neutra, Christian Schwartz (2002)*
Taz	fig. /IV.8	*Lucas de Groot (1998)*

V.

Filosofia	fig. /V.1	*Zuzana Licko (1996)*
Fresco Sans	fig. /V.2	*Fred Smeijers (2001-2002)*
Futura	fig. /V.3	*Paul Renner (1927)*
LinoScript	fig. /V.4	*Morris Fuller Benton (1905)*
Largo	fig. /V.5	*Gottlieb & Port (1903)*

Typographic Entomology (2010)

Studio CCRZ

Studio CCRZ
"Helvetica 1960"

Studio FM
"Helvetica 1960"

According to Massimo Vignelli, the Fiat 500 had an important role in the evolution of Italian graphic design. Last year, at a conference in Milan, Vignelli told a story about Helvetica and how it came to Italy. He had seen Miedinger's new typeface, which he found extremely interesting. When he met Mr. Nava, the printer he usually worked with, he suggested that he buy this new type. Mr. Nava, with his Fiat 500 left on his journey to Switzerland. But he was unlucky: when he tried to smuggle the type past the customs, hidden in the car, he was stopped, and the type cases were confiscated. When he tried again, a few weeks later, Nava was more successful, and from the early sixties Vignelli could start working with his new beloved typeface.

Thanks to Silvia Sfligiotti who told us this story

Erich Brechbühl

ENG

Erich was born in 1977, and grew up in Sempach, Switzerland. In 1990, at the tender age of 13, he started his career with the foundation of Mix Pictures, an organisation for short film productions and cultural events.

After a typography apprenticeship near Lucerne he began an apprenticeship in graphic design at the studio of Niklaus Troxler in Willisau. He then moved to Germany for an internship at MetaDesign Berlin before returning to Lucerne to found his own graphic design studio Mixer. He has been a member of the AGI since 2007. He has won multiple national and international awards, including the Grand Prix at the 2008 Swiss Poster Awards.

DE

Erich wurde 1977 geboren und wuchs in Sempach in der Schweiz auf. 1990, im zarten Alter von 13 Jahren, begann er seine Laufbahn mit der Gründung von Mix Pictures, einer Organisation für Kurzfilmproduktionen und kulturelle Veranstaltungen.

Nach einer Ausbildung in Typografie in der Nähe von Luzern begann er seine Ausbildung zum Grafikdesigner im Studio Niklaus Troxlers in Willisau. Daraufhin zog er nach Deutschland, wo er ein Praktikum bei MetaDesign Berlin absolvierte, bevor er schließlich in die Schweiz zurückkehrte und in Luzern sein eigenes Grafikdesign Studio Mixer gründete. Brechbühl ist seit 2007 Mitglied der AGI. Er hat mehrere nationale und internationale Auszeichnungen gewonnen, unter anderem den Grand Prix bei den 2008 Swiss Poster Awards.

FR

Erich est né en 1977 et a grandi à Sempach, Suisse. En 1990, au jeune âge de 13 ans, il a commencé sa carrière en créant Mix Pictures, une organisation qui produit des courts métrages et évènements culturels.

Après un apprentissage en typographie à côté de Lucerne, il débuta un apprentissage en graphisme au studio de Niklaus Troxler à Willisau. Il s'installa ensuite en Allemagne pour faire un stage à MetaDesign Berlin avant de retourner à Lucerne pour fonder son propre studio de graphisme Mixer. Il est membre de l'AGI depuis 2007. Il a obtenu de nombreux prix nationaux et internationaux, y compris le Grand Prix à la remise des prix des Posters Suisses en 2008.

ITA

Erich nasce nel 1977 e cresce a Sempach, Svizzera. Nel 1990, alla tenera età di 13 anni, comincia la sua carriera fondando Mix Pictures, un'organizzazione di cortometraggi ed eventi culturali.

Dopo un apprendistato nel campo della tipografia vicino a Lucerna, comincia un apprendistato di design grafico nello studio di Niklaus Troxler a Willisau. Si traferisce poi in Germania per seguire uno stage presso MetaDesign a Berlino, prima di tornare a Lucerna e fondare il proprio studio grafico, Mixer. È membro di AGI dal 2007. Ha vinto diversi premi nazionali e internazionali, fra cui il Grand Prix allo Swiss Poster Awards del 2008.

Zetalab

ENG

Zetalab is a design communication studio based in Milan. Our core business is graphic design but we also enjoy exploring different fields like exhibition and product design, film and occasionally art. Zetalab believes in design that mixes and recombines different elements, styles, media and ideas.

We started in 2000 making 'pop' graphics for clients like MTV, Levi's, and Diesel, but we've grown into creating projects for Italian institutions (like the Milan City Council) and brands ranging from design (Bang&Olufsen) to stationery (Moleskine) to editorial (Italian publishers Rizzoli & Mondadori) all the way to food packaging (Ferrari).

DE

Zetalab ist ein Studio für Design-Kommunikation in Mailand. Das Herzstück unseres Unternehmens ist Grafikdesign, aber wir erkunden auch gern neue Bereiche wie Messe- und Produktdesign, Film und manchmal auch Kunst. Hier bei Zetalab glauben wir an Design, das verschiedene Elemente, Stile, Medien und Ideen miteinander vermischt und wieder verbindet.

Wir begannen unsere Arbeit im Jahr 2000 mit „Pop"-Grafiken für Kunden wie MTV, Levi's and Diesel, sind aber inzwischen zu einem Studio herangewachsen, das Projekte für italienische Organisationen (zum Beispiel dem Stadtrat Mailands) und Marken produziert, von Design (Bang&Olufsen), über Schreibwaren (Moleskine) und Editorial (italienische Verlage Rizzoli & Mondadori) bis hin zur Lebensmittelverpackung (Ferrari).

FR

Zetalab est un studio de design en communication basé à Milan. Notre cœur de métier est le graphisme mais nous aimons aussi explorer différentes avenues comme le design d'expositions et de produits, de films et parfois d'art. Zetalab croit au design q ui mélange et rassemble différents éléments, styles, médias et idées.

Nous avons commencé par créer des graphismes « pop » en 2000 pour des clients comme MTV, Levi's et Diesel mais nous créons maintenant des projets pour des institutions italiennes (comme pour la Mairie de Milan) et des marques allant du design (Bang&Olufsen) à la papèterie (Moleskine) en passant par l'édition (maison de publication italienne Rizzoli & Mondadori) jusqu'à l'emballage alimentaire (Ferrari).

ITA

Zetalab è uno studio di design della comunicazione con sede a Milano. Il nostro core business è il design grafico ma ci piace anche esplorare diversi campi come il design di mostre e prodotti, film e occasionalmente arte. Zetalab crede in un design che unisce e armonizza diversi elementi, stili, media e idee.

Abbiamo cominciato nel 2000, creando grafiche 'pop' per clienti come MTV, Levi's e Diesel, ma siamo cresciuti fino a svolgere progetti per istituzioni italiane (come il Comune di Milano) e marche che vanno dal design (Bang&Olufsen) alla cancelleria (Moleskine), dall'editoria (editori italiani Rizzoli & Mondadori) fino al packaging alimentare (Ferrari).

Erich Brechbühl

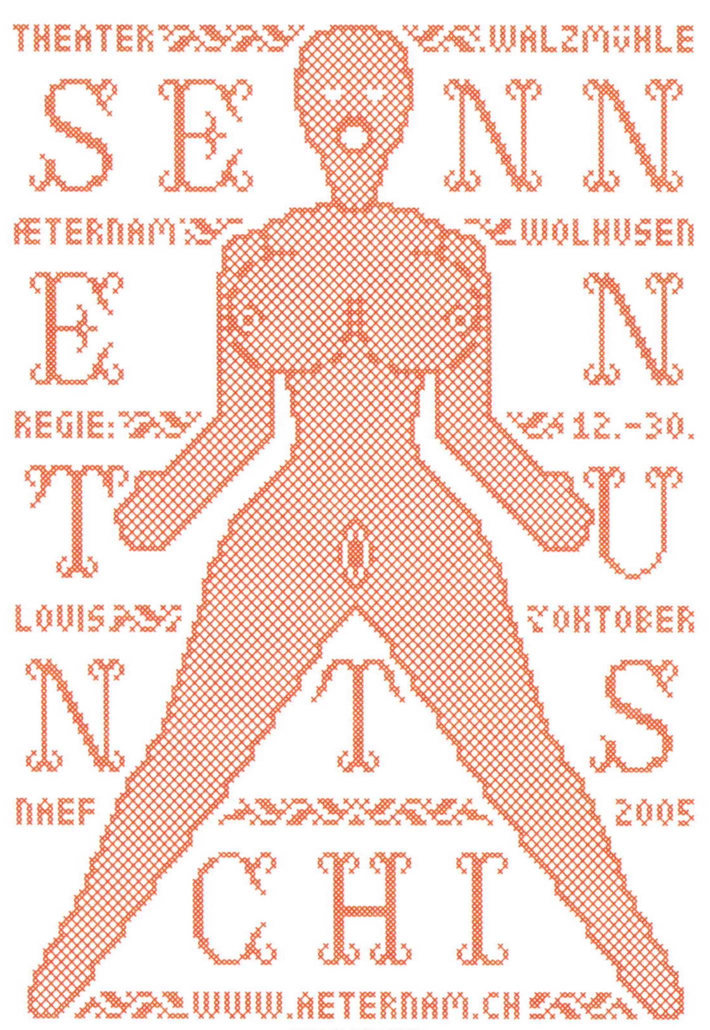

Sennentuntschi, 2005

100mal Im Schtei, 2005

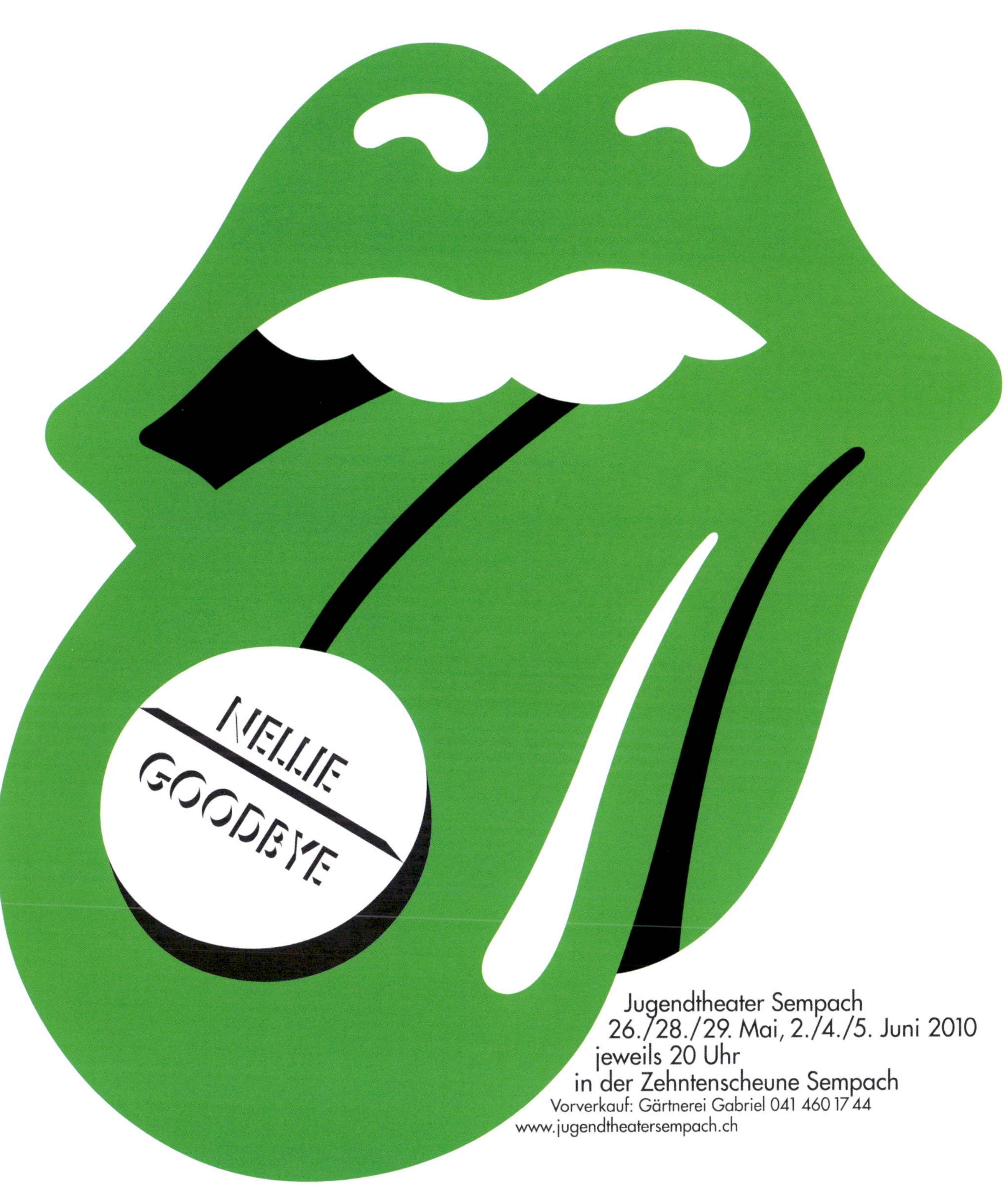

Jugendtheater Sempach
26./28./29. Mai, 2./4./5. Juni 2010
jeweils 20 Uhr
in der Zehntenscheune Sempach
Vorverkauf: Gärtnerei Gabriel 041 460 17 44
www.jugendtheatersempach.ch

Nellie Goodbye, 2010

Zetalab

Visual identity and poster campaign for Luoghi Comino (a lettera27 project) 2009

Visual Identity for Milan Film Festival 2010project) 2009

Graphic design for Pedrali publishers, 2009-2010

Graphic design for Mixa Magazine, 2010 project 2009

Erich Brechbühl

Erich Brechbühl
"Homage"

Zetalab
"Dinner"

Bureau Collective

ENG

In 2009 Rosario Florio, Larissa Kasper, Dominic Rechsteiner, Andrea Rüeger, Ollie Schaich, Lukas Schneeberger and Ruedi Zürcher came together in a studio in St. Gallen to form Bureau Collective. The great strength of their alliance lies in diversity. No matter what they make in the graphic or cultural sectors, they begin by casting out in every possible direction, before creating stimulating visuals.

Every project is founded on mutual support, a motivation to win and a healthy system of exchange, where music, opinions and even the cutting mat are shared. Besides work for clients, there's always space for your own projects and ideas at Bureau Collective; a place where both individuality and community flourish.

DE

Im Jahr 2009 trafen sich Rosario Florio, Larissa Kasper, Dominic Rechsteiner, Andrea Rüeger, Ollie Schaich, Lukas Schneeberger und Ruedi Zürcher in einem Studio in St. Gallen, um Bureau Collective zu gründen. Die große Stärke dieses Bündnisses liegt in seiner Vielfalt. Egal, woran Bureau Collective im grafischen oder kulturellen Bereich arbeiten, sie beginnen immer damit, ihre Fühler in alle möglichen Richtungen auszustrecken, bevor sie visuell anregende Werke schaffen.

Jedes Projekt ist auf gegenseitiger Unterstützung, einer gewinnorientierten Motivation und einem gesunden Austausch begründet, bei dem Musik, Meinungen und sogar die Schneidematte geteilt werden. Neben der Arbeit für Kunden ist bei Bureau Collective immer Platz für persönliche Projekte und Ideen – es ist ein Ort, an dem sowohl Individualität als auch Zusammenarbeit gedeihen.

FR

En 2009 Rosario Florio, Larissa Kasper, Dominic Rechsteiner, Andrea Rüeger, Ollie Schaich, Lukas Schneeberger et Ruedi Zürcher se réunirent dans un studio à St. Gallen pour former le Bureau Collective. Le grand atout de leur alliance est lié à leur diversité. Qu'importe ce qu'ils font dans le secteur du graphisme ou de la culture, ils commencent par explorer toutes les avenues avant de créer des supports visuels stimulants.

Chaque projet est basé sur l'entraide mutuelle, une motivation pour réussir et un système d'échanges sain, dans lequel la musique, les opinions et même le tapis de découpe sont partagés. Outre le travail pour les clients, il y a toujours du temps pour tes propres projets et tes idées au Bureau Collective, un endroit où les individus et la communauté prospèrent.

ITA

Nel 2009 Rosario Florio, Larissa Kasper, Dominic Rechsteiner, Andrea Rüeger, Ollie Schaich, Lukas Schneeberger e Ruedi Zürcher si uniscono in uno studio a San Gallo per formare Bureau Collective. La grande forza della loro alleanza è la diversità: qualsiasi cosa affrontino nel settore grafico o culturale, cominciano sempre esplorando tutte le direzioni possibili, così da creare contenuti visivi stimolanti.

Ogni progetto è fondato sul sostegno reciproco, su una tensione a vincere e su un sistema di proficua collaborazione in cui sono condivisi musica, pareri e persino il tappeto da taglio. A Bureau Collective, luogo dove prosperano sia l'individualità che la comunità, oltre ai lavori per i clienti, c'è sempre spazio per i propri progetti e le idee personali.

Jekyll & Hyde

ENG

jekyll & hyde is a Milan-based design and visual communication studio founded in 1996 by Marco Molteni and Margherita Monguzzi.

The studio's philosophy is based on teamwork: working together with great enthusiasm, an enquiring mindset and a playful outlook to develop simple yet radical products. We always focus on people's reactions to the products to discover a different perspective on the brief.

jekyll & hyde has worked with clients in fields ranging from music to contemporary art, technology to fashion, constantly refreshing their style and experimenting with graphic languages tailored to each client's individual requirements.

FR

jekyll & hyde est un studio de design et de communication visuelle basé à Milan et fondé en 1996 par Marco Molteni et Margherita Monguzzi.

La philosophie du studio est basée sur le travail d'équipe : travailler ensemble avec grand enthousiasme, une façon interrogatrice de voir les choses et une perspective joueuse afin de développer des produits simples tout en étant géniaux. Nous nous concentrons toujours sur les réactions des gens face aux produits pour découvrir une perspective différente à la mission.

jekyll & hyde a travaillé avec des clients dans des secteurs allant de la musique à l'art contemporain, de la technologie à la mode, en renouvelant leur style constamment et expérimentant avec des langages graphiques adaptés aux besoins de chaque clients.

ITA

jekyll & hyde è uno studio di design e comunicazione visiva fondato a Milano nel 1996 da Marco Molteni e Margherita Monguzzi.

Lo studio predilige il lavoro in team: insieme realizzano con passione, curiosità e voglia di divertirsi, progetti semplici e radicali allo stesso tempo. Lo studio focalizza sempre la propria attenzione su come le persone reagiranno di fronte ai prodotti, per scoprire una nuova prospettiva del brief.

jekyll & hyde ha collaborato con clienti appartenenti a settori che vanno dalla musica all'arte contemporanea, dalla tecnologia alla moda, riuscendo continuamente a cambiare stile e sperimentare linguaggi grafici adatti alle diverse esigenze di ognuno di loro.

DE

jekyll & hyde ist ein Studio für Design und Visuelle Kommunikation in Mailand, das 1996 von Marco Molteni und Margherita Monguzzi gegründet wurde.

Die Philosophie des Studios basiert auf Teamwork: mit viel Enthusiasmus, wissenshungriger Mentalität und spielerischer Perspektive zusammenarbeiten, um einfache jedoch radikale Produkte zu entwickeln. Wir konzentrieren uns immer auf die Reaktionen von Personen auf Produkte, um neue Perspektiven für einen Auftrag zu entdecken.

jekyll & hyde arbeitet mit Kunden in vielen Industrien, von Musik bis zur modernen Kunst, von Technik bis zur Mode. Ihr Stil wird permanent aufgefrischt und sie experimentieren mit grafischen Sprachen, die den individuellen Ansprüchen jedes Kunden angepasst sind.

Bureau Collective

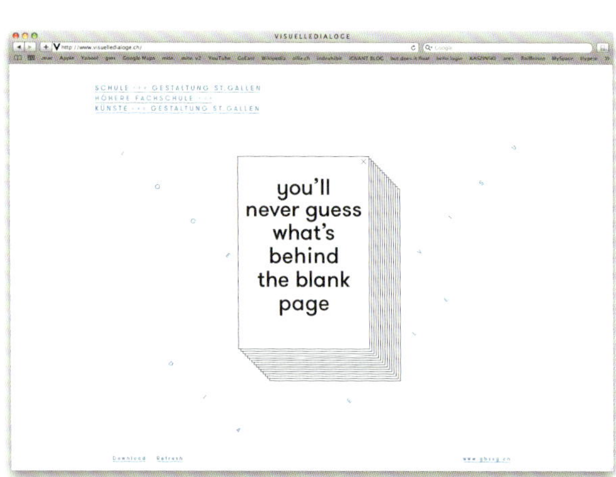

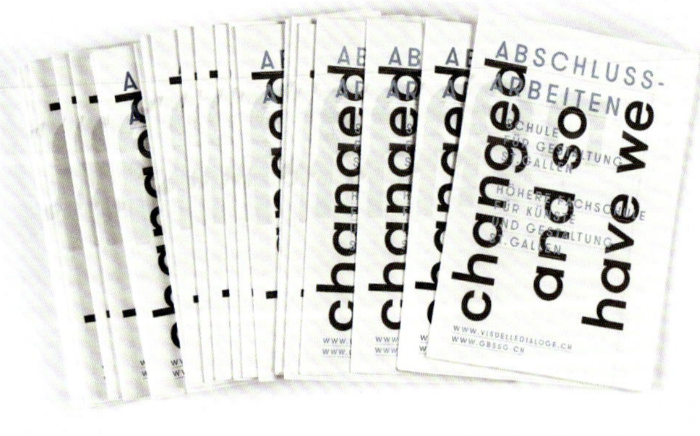

Visuelle Dialoge

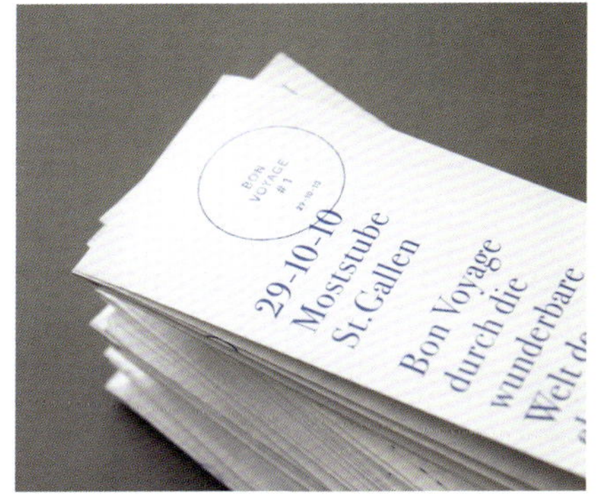

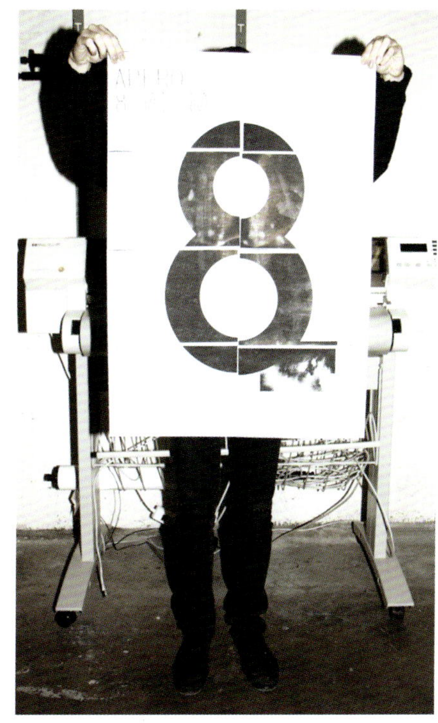

Bon Voyage

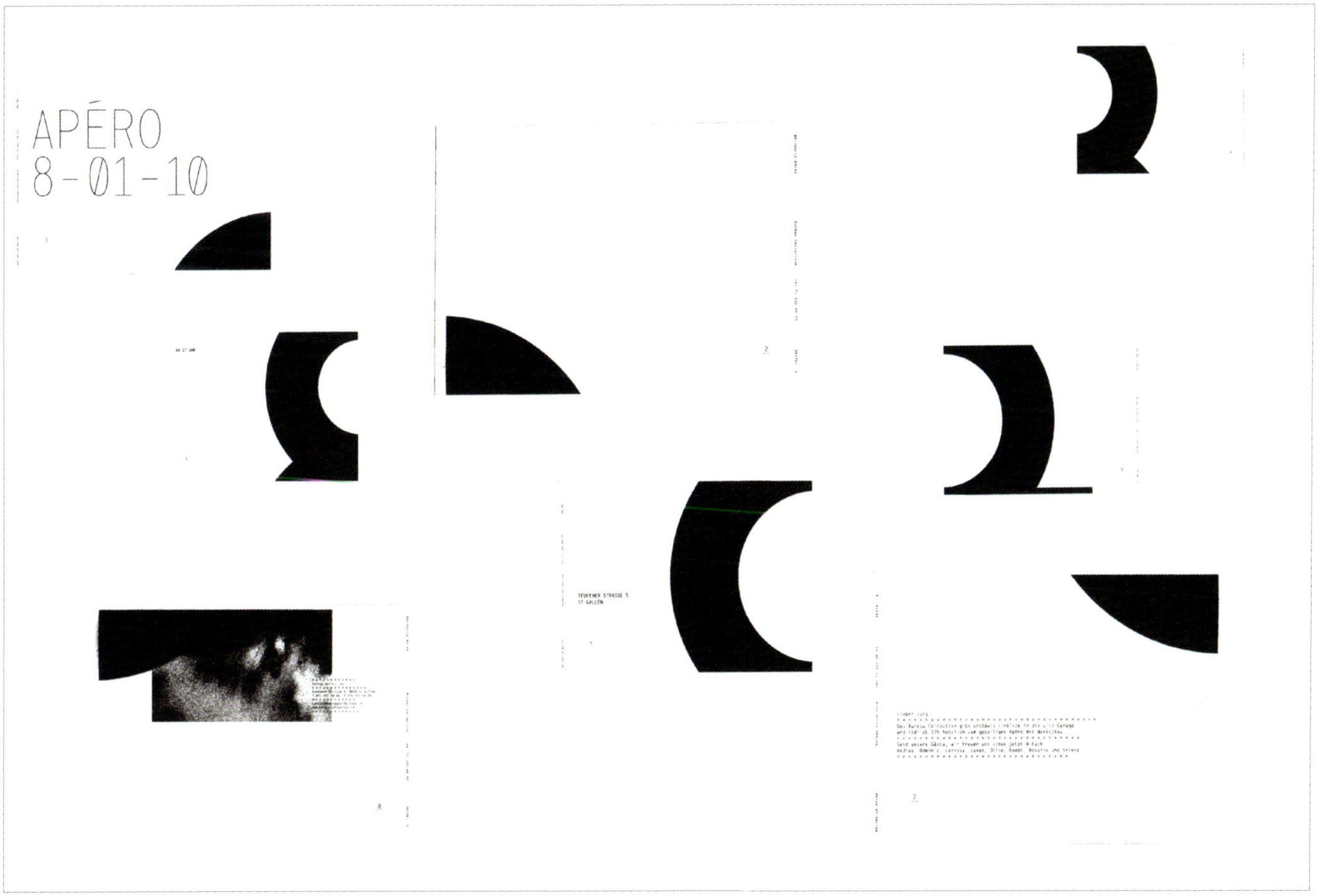

Jekyll & Hyde

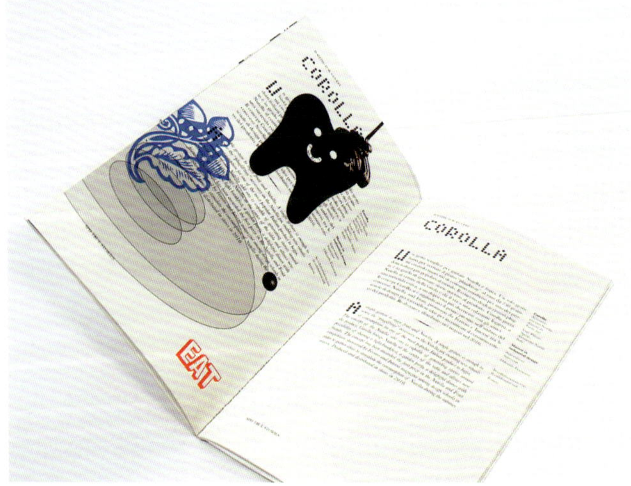

True Stories (2010). First exhibited at Salone del Mobile 2010, featuring projects by international Master's students at the Scuola Politecnica di Design, Milan. Exhibition, Graphic Identity, Typeface, Book.

Communications package for the 2008 collection of RH Milano handbags

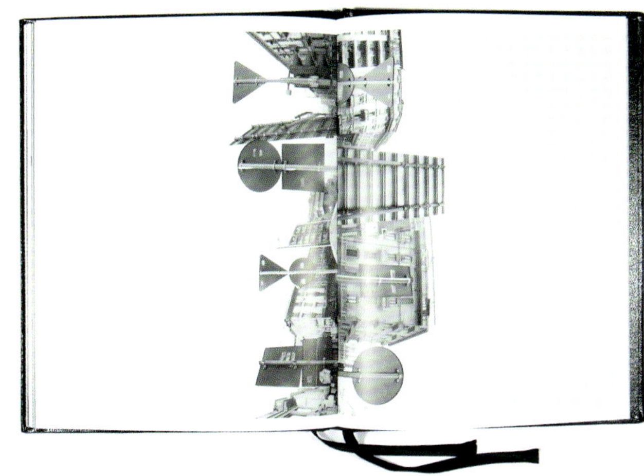

See Nothing Volume Two. It combines our experimental work with contributions from graphic designers, photographers, illustrators, professionals and young talents.

Bureau Collective + Jekyll & Hyde

ENG

Seventy years ago, the rigour of the Swiss school met the seductive fantasy of the Italians, creating a new aesthetic that would change the world of graphics forever.

We wanted to find a way to replicate the magic of that period, when different personalities worked together with a shared curiosity and desire to experiment. Thanks to a special piece of software (our 'simulator') we managed to overcome the space that separated us and join our eyes, minds and hands to work on the same document at the same time. Both studios came up with a list of seventy words (with any duplicated word deleted). Studio A chose a word from the list that Studio B had a maximum of two moves to visualize on the poster. Items could be added and changed on the board with every move, but nothing could be deleted.

The result was certainly unexpected, but we're pleased with it!

DE

Vor siebzig Jahren trafen die Exaktheit der Schweizer Schule und die verführerische Fantasie der Italiener aufeinander und schafften eine neue Ästhetik, welche die Welt der Grafiken für immer verändern würde.

Wir wollten die Magie dieser Epoche, in der Persönlichkeiten mit einer gemeinsamen Neugier und Leidenschaft fürs Experimentieren zusammenarbeiteten, wieder aufleben lassen. Dank einer besonderen Software (unserem „Simulator") konnten wir die räumliche Distanz zwischen uns überwinden und mit Augen, Gedanken und Händen zur gleichen Zeit an ein und demselben Dokument arbeiten. Beide Studios produzierten eine Liste mit siebzig Wörtern (doppelte Worte wurden entfernt). Studio A wählte ein Wort von der Liste, welches Studio B in maximal zwei Schritten auf einem Poster visualisieren sollte. Elemente konnten mit jedem Schritt auf dem Brett hinzugefügt und verändert werden, aber nichts durfte gelöscht werden.

Das Ergebnis war gewiss unerwartet, aber wir sind damit sehr zufrieden!

FR

Il y a soixante-dix ans, la rigueur de l'école Suisse rencontra la séduisante fantaisie des Italiens, ce qui créa une nouvelle esthétique qui changea le monde du graphisme pour toujours.

Nous voulions trouver un moyen de recréer la magie de cette période, pendant laquelle différentes personnalités travaillaient ensemble avec une curiosité commune et le désir d'expérimenter. Grâce à un logiciel (notre « simulateur ») nous avons réussi à franchir cet espace qui nous séparait pour faire rejoindre nos yeux, nos esprits et nos mains et pour les mettre à l'œuvre sur le même document au même moment. Les deux studios ont proposés une liste de soixante-dix mots (avec les mots doublons effacés). Le Studio A choisissait un mot de la liste et Studio B devait le visualiser en moins de deux étapes sur le poster. Les éléments pouvaient être ajoutés ou changés sur le tableau à chaque étape, mais ne pouvait être effacés.

Le résultat était certainement inattendu, mais nous en sommes certainement contents!

ITA

Settant'anni fa il rigore della scuola svizzera ha incontrato la seducente fantasia italiana e ne è nata così un'estetica nuova, che avrebbe cambiato per sempre il mondo della grafica.

Volevamo trovare il modo per far rivivere lo spirito di quel periodo, quando personalità diverse lavoravano insieme con la stessa curiosità e voglia di sperimentare. Grazie ad un software speciale (il nostro 'simulatore') siamo riusciti a superare lo spazio che ci divideva, unendo occhi, menti e mani per lavorare insieme, nello stesso tempo e sullo stesso documento. Entrambi gli studi hanno prodotto una lista di settanta parole (cancellando quelle che si ripetevano). Lo Studio A sceglieva una parola dall'elenco e lo Studio B aveva un massimo di due mosse per rappresentarla sul manifesto.

A ogni mossa si potevano modificare e aggiungere elementi, ma non si potevano eliminare.

Il risultato è stato sicuramente inaspettato ma ne siamo soddisfatti!

01. BC: distance / J&H: 1940

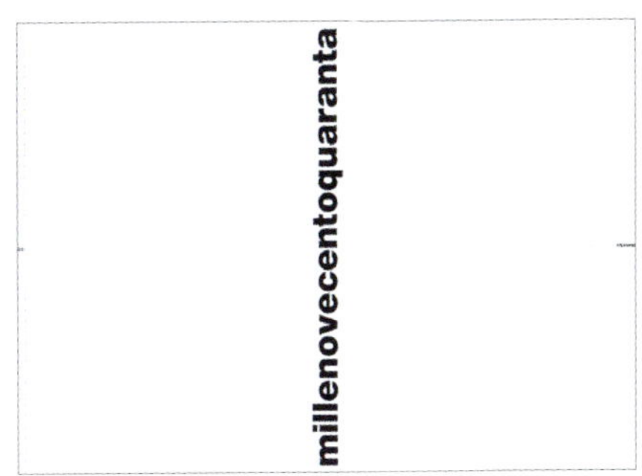

02. BC: distance / J&H: start

03. BC: piazza del duomo / J&H: start

04. BC: abstract art / J&H: meeting*

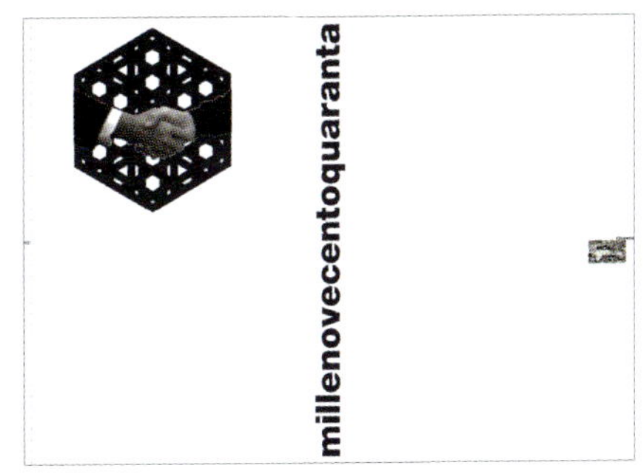

05. BC: abstract art / J&H: meeting

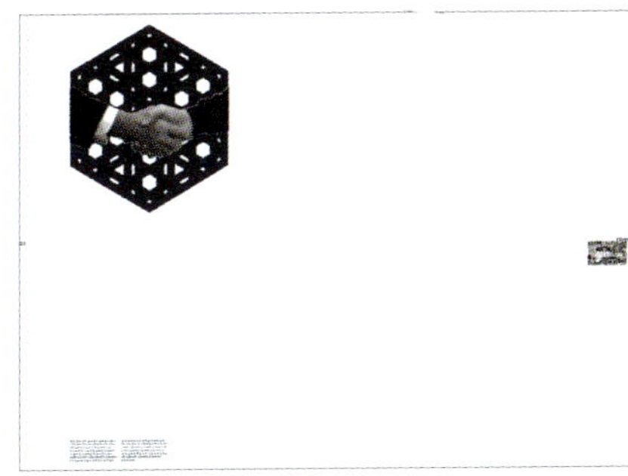

06. BC: passion / J&H: coming back

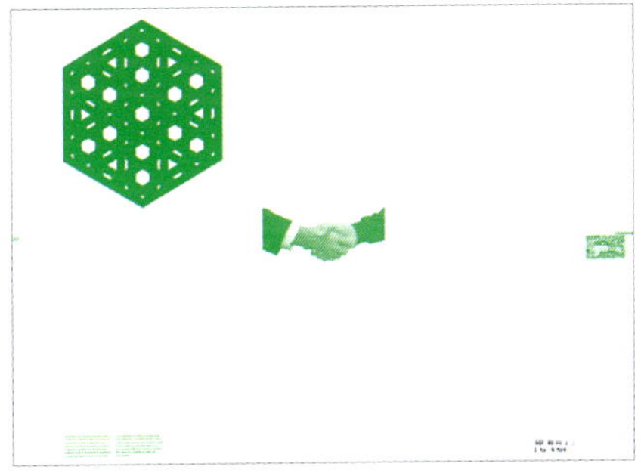

07. BC: green, white / J&H: differences

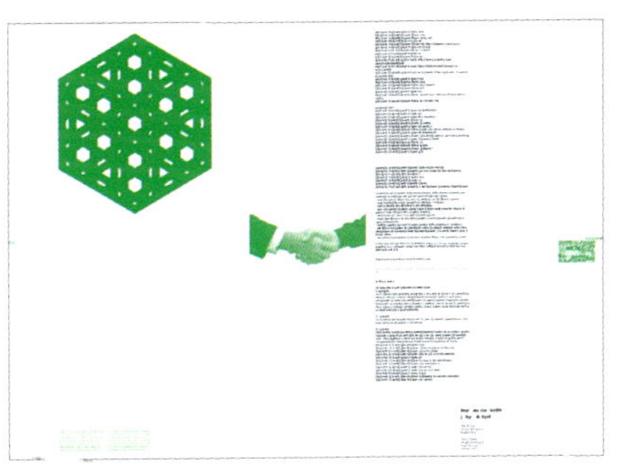

08. BC: persons / J&H: dialogue

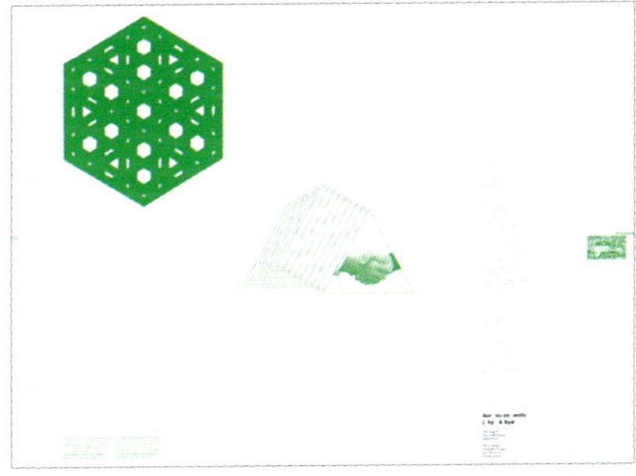

09. BC: overtake / J&H: dialogue

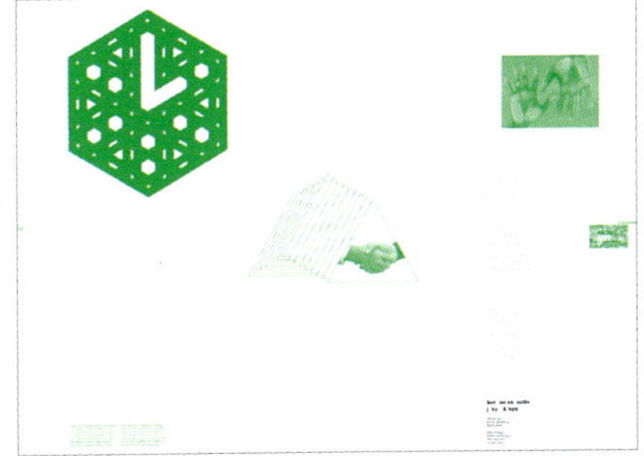

10. BC: handmade / J&H: time

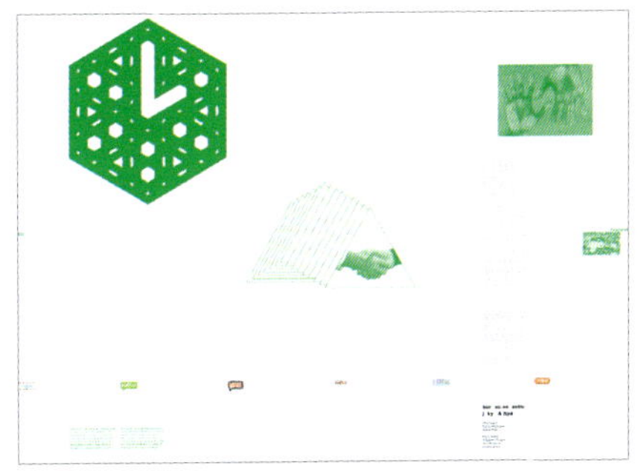

11. BC: spiral* / J&H: new

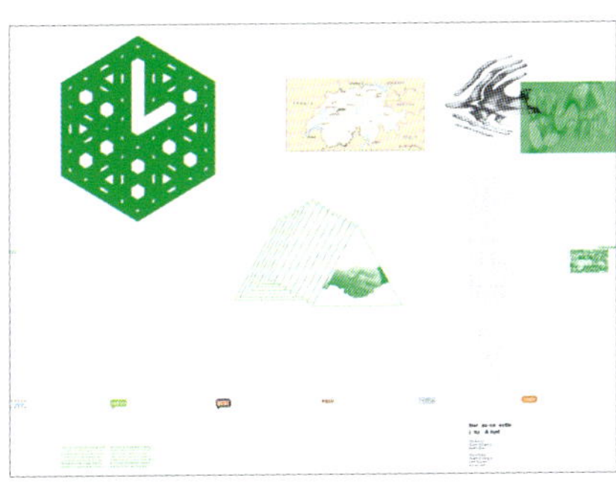

12. BC: spiral / J&H: frontier

Bureau Collective + Jekyll & Hyde

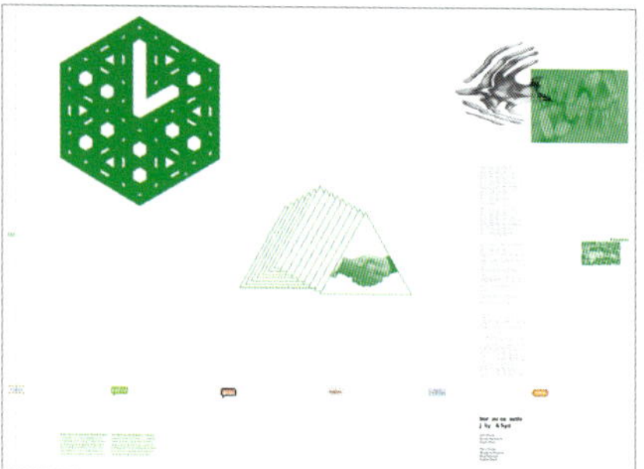

13. BC: coincidence* / J&H: frontier

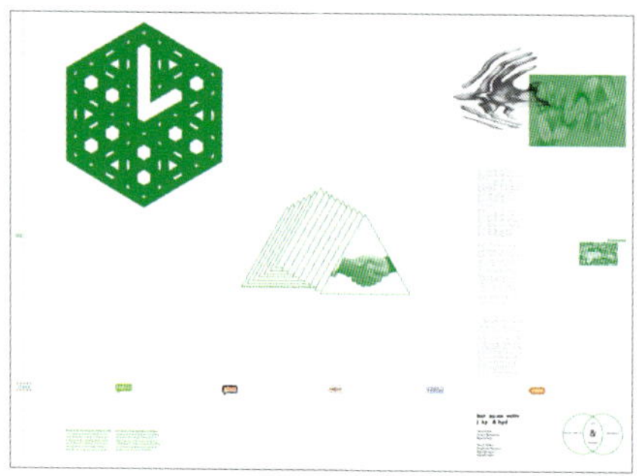

14. BC: coincidence / J&H: geometry*

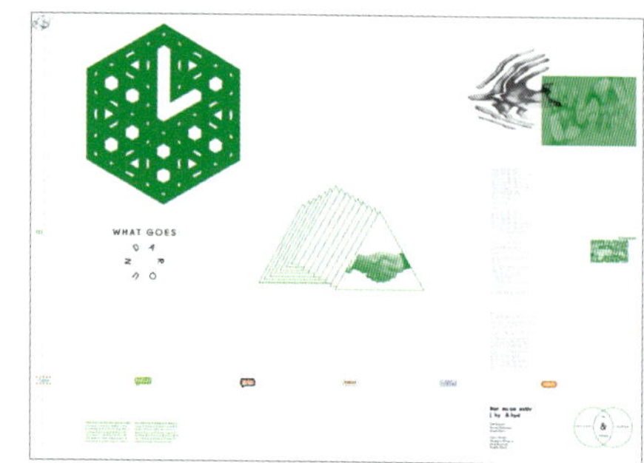

15. BC: war / J&H: geometry

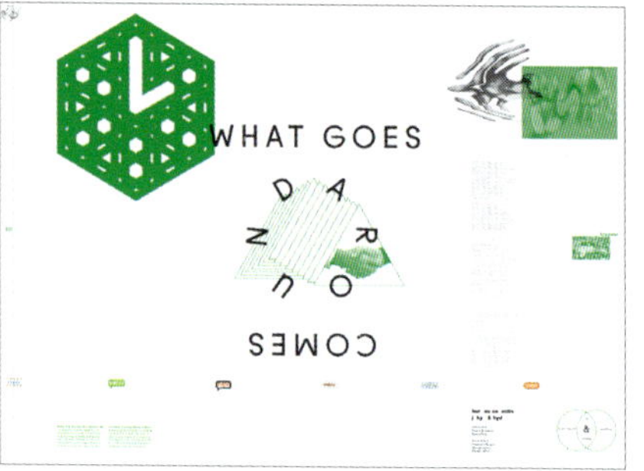

16. BC: war / J&H: geometry

17. BC: half-tone* / J&H: communication*

18. BC: half-tone / J&H: communication

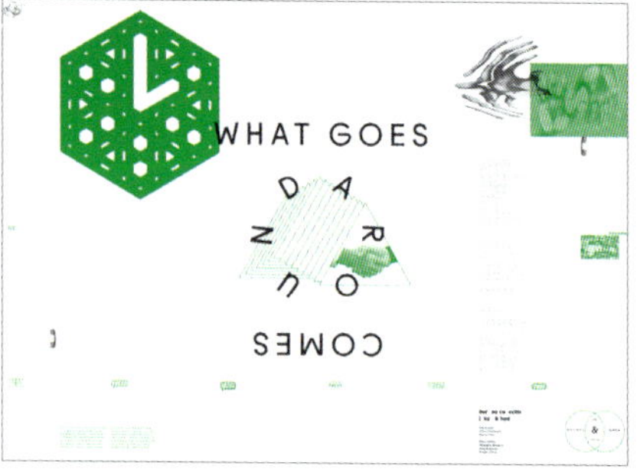

19. BC: seduction* / J&H: tradition*

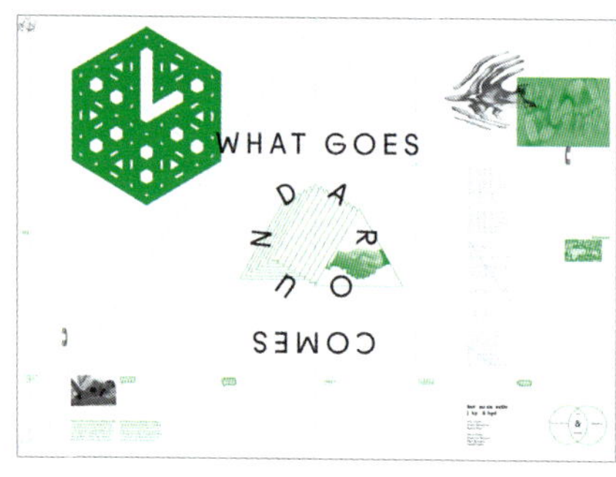

20. BC: seduction* / J&H: tradition

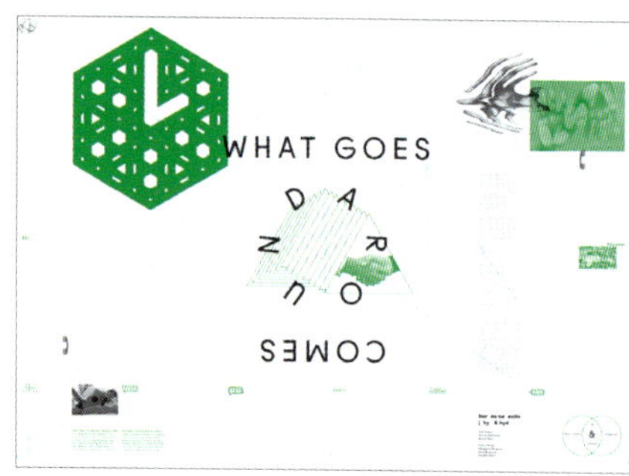

21. BC: challenge the audience* / J&H: anniversary*

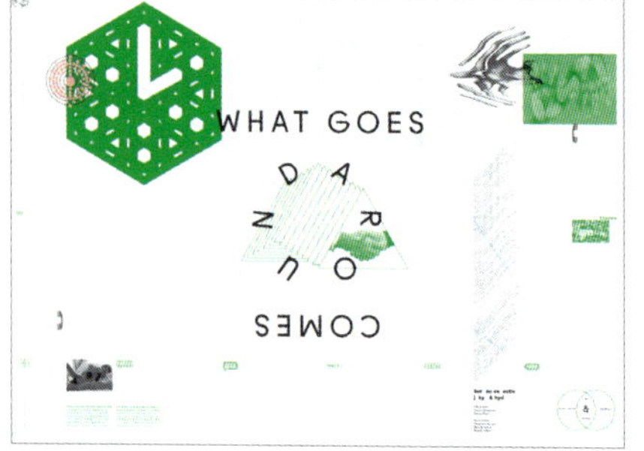

22. BC: challenge the audience / J&H: anniversary

23. BC: play / J&H: positive

24. BC: boot / J&H: cut off

 Celebrate the present: 11 collaborations between 22 of the best contemporary Swiss & Italian graphic designers.

*thinking

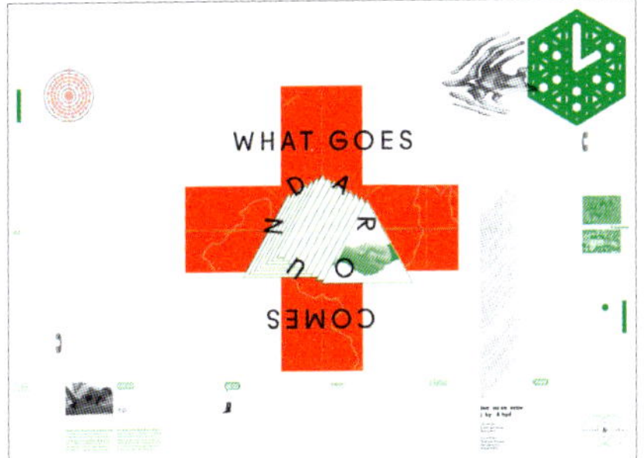

25. BC: line* / J&H: epicentre*

26. BC: line / J&H: epicentre

27. BC: modernism / J&H: permeate

28. BC: photography* / J&H: education*

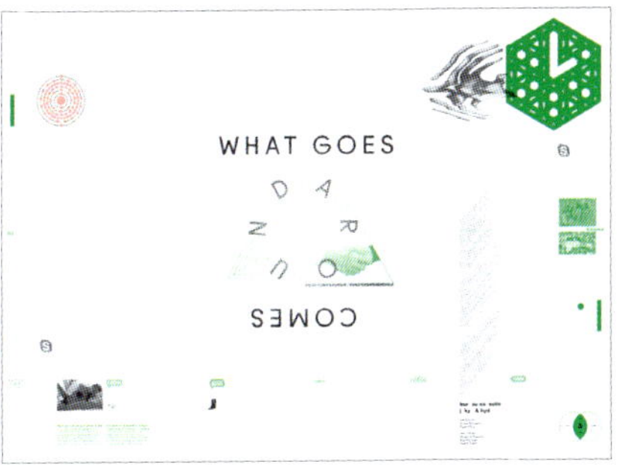

29. BC: photography / J&H: education

30. BC: overlapping* / J&H: show*

31. BC: overlapping / J&H: show

32. BC: creativity* / J&H. simplicity

33. BC: creativity / J&H: simplicity

34. BC: studio boggeri / J&H: black

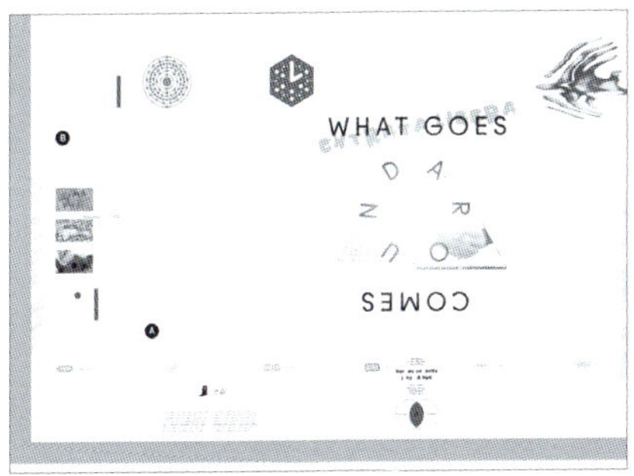

35. BC: asymmetry / J&H: radical

Bureau Collective

Bureau Collective
"What goes around comes around"

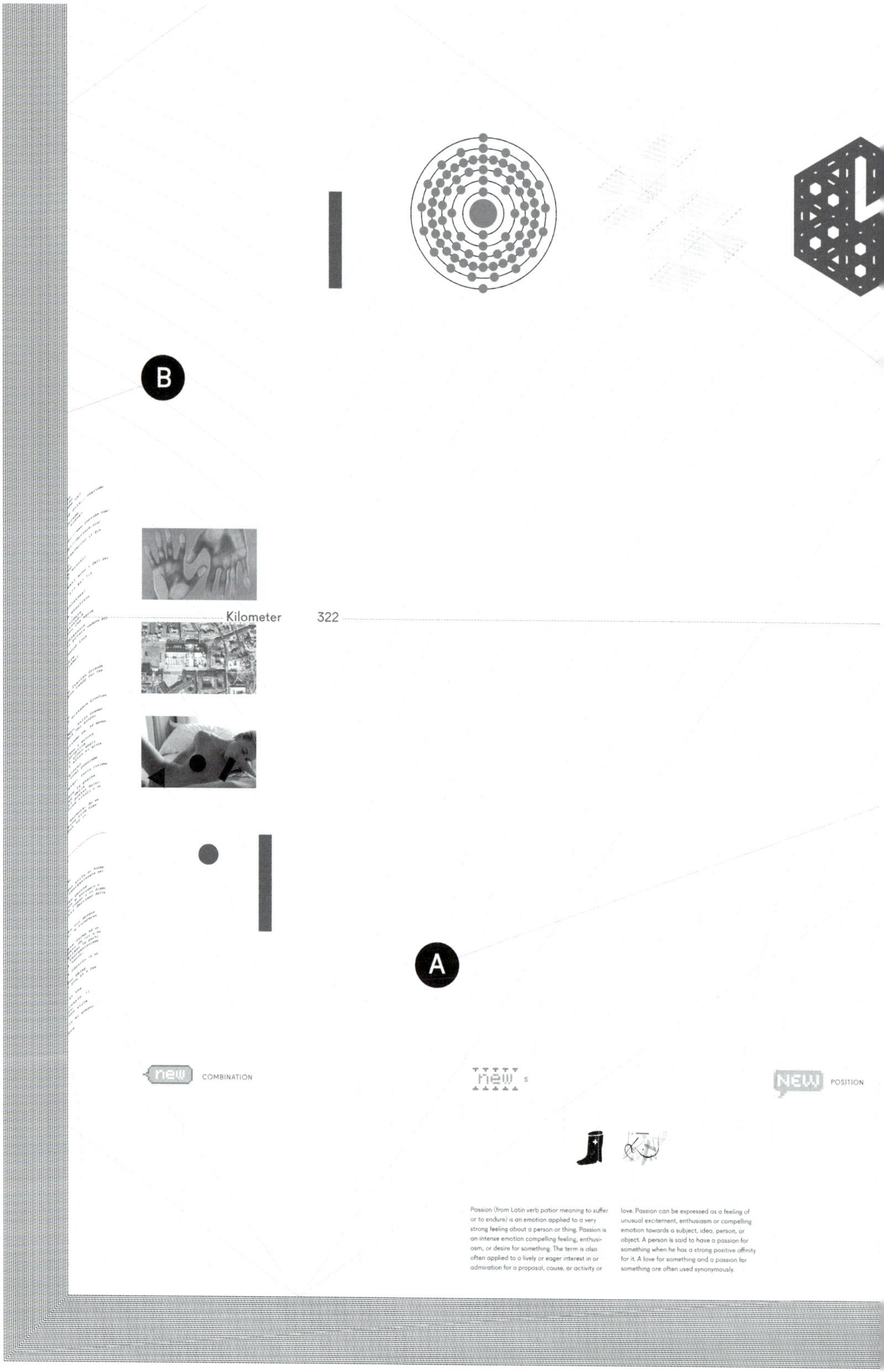

Kilometer 322

new COMBINATION

new s

NEW POSITION

Passion (from Latin verb patior meaning to suffer or to endure) is an emotion applied to a very strong feeling about a person or thing. Passion is an intense emotion compelling feeling, enthusiasm, or desire for something. The term is also often applied to a lively or eager interest in or admiration for a proposal, cause, or activity or love. Passion can be expressed as a feeling of unusual excitement, enthusiasm or compelling emotion towards a subject, idea, person, or object. A person is said to have a passion for something when he has a strong positive affinity for it. A love for something and a passion for something are often used synonymously.

Jekyll & Hyde
*"What goes around
comes around"*

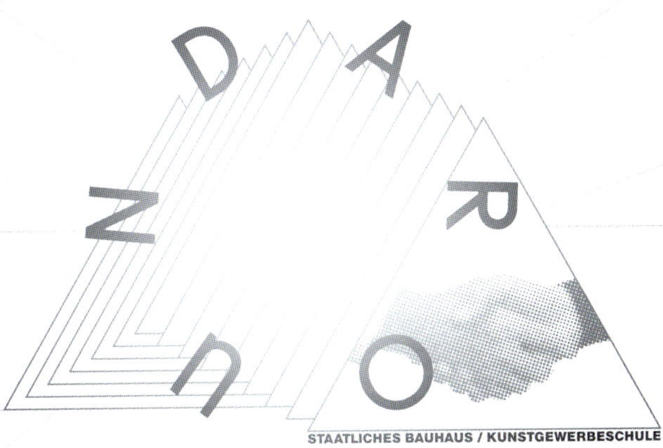

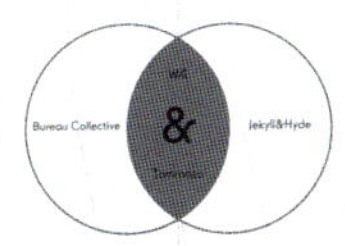

Ollie Schaich
Dominic Rechsteiner
Rosario Florio

NEW FORM

NEW DESTINATION

NEW FOCUS

**bur au co ectiv
j ky & hyd**

Marco Molteni
Margherita Monguzzi
Elena Bonanomi
Rossella Valenti

Bureau Collective & Jekyll&Hyde

Büro Destruct

ENG

Büro Destruct first appeared in 1994 as the brainchild of HGB Fideljus (Fidel Berger, 1971) and Lopetz (Lorenz Gianfreda, 1971). It grew out of "Destruct Agentur", which had been founded in 1992 to promote young artists. Over the next few years the group grew into an internationally acclaimed design studio.

Today, the four-man outfit comprises of MB (Marc Brunner, 1970), H1reber (Heinz Reber, 1971), HeiWid (Heinz Widmer, 1967) and Lopetz. Exhibitions, lectures and workshops in different countries enable Büro Destruct to exist in a state of constant renewal and widen its contacts beyond Bern (the lovely capital of Switzerland) in line with their motto: Small City - Big Design.

DE

Büro Destruct erschien zuerst in 1994 als Geistesprodukt von HGB Fideljus (Fidel Berger, 1971) und Lopetz (Lorenz Gianfreda, 1971). Es war aus der „Destruct Agentur" entstanden, die 1992 gegründet wurde, um junge Künstler zu fördern. Über die nächsten Jahre hatte sich die Gruppe in ein international gefeiertes Designstudio entwickelt.

Heute setzt sich das vier Personen starke Team aus MB (Marc Brunner, 1970), H1reber (Heinz Reber, 1971), HeiWid (Heinz Widmer, 1967) und Lopetz zusammen. Ausstellungen, Vorlesungen und Workshops ermöglichen es Büro Destruct, in einem Zustand ständiger Erneuerung zu existieren und neue Kontakte über Bern (die entzückende Hauptstadt der Schweiz) hinaus zu knüpfen – ganz nach ihrem Motto „Kleine Stadt – Großes Design".

FR

Büro Destruct est d'abord apparu en 1994 en tant que bébé de HGB Fideljus (Fidel Berger, 1971) et Lopetz (Lorenz Gianfreda, 1971). Il s'est développé au-delà de la « Destruct Agentur », qui avait été fondée en 1992 pour promouvoir les jeunes artistes. Pendant les années qui suivirent le groupe devint un studio de design reconnu à l'échelle internationale.

Aujourd'hui cette entreprise de quatre hommes comprend MB (Marc Brunner, 1970), H1reber (Heinz Reber, 1971), HeiWid (Heinz Widmer, 1967) et Lopetz. Expositions, conférences et groupes de travail dans différents pays permettent au Büro Destruct d'exister dans un état constant de renouveau et d'étendre ses relations au-delà de Berne (la charmante capitale de la Suisse) en rapport avec sa devise : Petite Ville – Grand Design.

ITA

Büro Destruct appare per la prima volta nel 1994 come intuizione di HGB Fideljus (Fidel Berger, 1971) e Lopetz (Lorenz Gianfreda, 1971) e nasce da "Destruct Agentur", che era stato fondato nel 1992 per promuovere i giovani artisti. Negli anni a seguire il gruppo diventa uno studio di design apprezzato a livello internazionale.

Oggi, questo studio di quattro persone è composto di MB (Marc Brunner, 1970), H1reber (Heinz Reber, 1971), HeiWid (Heinz Widmer, 1967) e Lopetz. Mostre, conferenze e laboratori in diversi paesi permettono a Büro Destruct di svilupparsi in uno stato di costante rinnovamento e di allargare i propri contatti oltre Berna (la bella capitale della Svizzera), in linea con il suo motto: Piccola Città – Grande design.

Andrea Rauch

ENG

Andrea Rauch (Siena, 1948) has created images for public institutions, cultural initiatives and political movements. His posters are part of the collections of the Museum of Modern Art in New York, the Louvre's Musée de la Publicité, and the Museum für Gestaltung in Zurich.

In 1993, Idea magazine named him as one of the 100 World Top Graphic Designers and he was also included in the last edition of Who's Who in Graphic Design. In 2010, he co-founded the publishing house Princes & Principles. Edition Nuages have published two extensive collections of his work: Design & Identity and Dis-continuous.

FR

Andrea Rauch (Sienne, 1948) a crée des images pour des institutions publiques, initiatives culturelles et mouvements politiques. Ses posters font partie de la collection au Museum of Modern Art à New York, au Musée de la Publicité au Louvre et au Museum für Gestaltung à Zürich.

En 1933, le magasine Idea le nomma l'un des 100 World Top Graphic Designers et il a aussi été mentionné dans la dernière édition de Who's Who in Graphic Design. En 2010 il a cofondé la maison d'édition Princes & Principles. Les Editions Nuages ont publiés deux vastes collections sur son travail : Design & Identity et Dis-continuous.

ITA

Andrea Rauch (Siena, 1948) ha disegnato e progettato immagini per enti pubblici, istituzioni culturali e movimenti politici. Alcuni suoi manifesti fanno parte delle collezioni del Museum of Modern Art di New York, del Musée de la Publicité del Louvre e del Museum für Gestaltung di Zurigo.

Nel 1993 la rivista Idea lo ha inserito tra i '100 World Top Graphic Designers' ed è presente nell'ultima edizione di Who's who in Graphic Design. È tra i fondatori, nel 2010, della casa editrice Prìncipi & Princípi. Le Edizioni Nuages hanno pubblicato i volumi Design & Identity e Dis-continuo, due vaste ricognizioni sul suo lavoro.

DE

Andrea Rauch (Siena, 1948) hat Bilder für öffentliche Einrichtungen, Kulturinitiativen und politische Bewegungen geschaffen. Seine Poster sind in dem Museum of Modern Art in New York, in Louvres Musée de la Publicité und in dem Museum für Gestaltung in Zürich zu finden.

1993 bezeichnete die Zeitschrift Idea Rauch als einen der 100 World Top Graphic Designers und er wurde auch in der letzten Ausgabe von Who's Who in Graphic Design erwähnt. Er ist ein Mitbegründer des in 2010 ins Leben gerufenen Verlagshauses Princes & Principles. Edition Nuages haben zwei umfangreiche Sammlungen seiner Werke veröffentlicht: Design & Identity und Dis-continuous.

Büro Destruct

Foundation Award. Client: Computerworks, Zurich. Offsetprint, 2010

Typedifferent Type Case Poster. 2008

Swiss Aeropolitan, Exhibition Poster, Switzerland
Design for Life, London, 2010

   Celebrate the present: 11 collaborations between 22 of the best contemporary Swiss & Italian graphic designers.

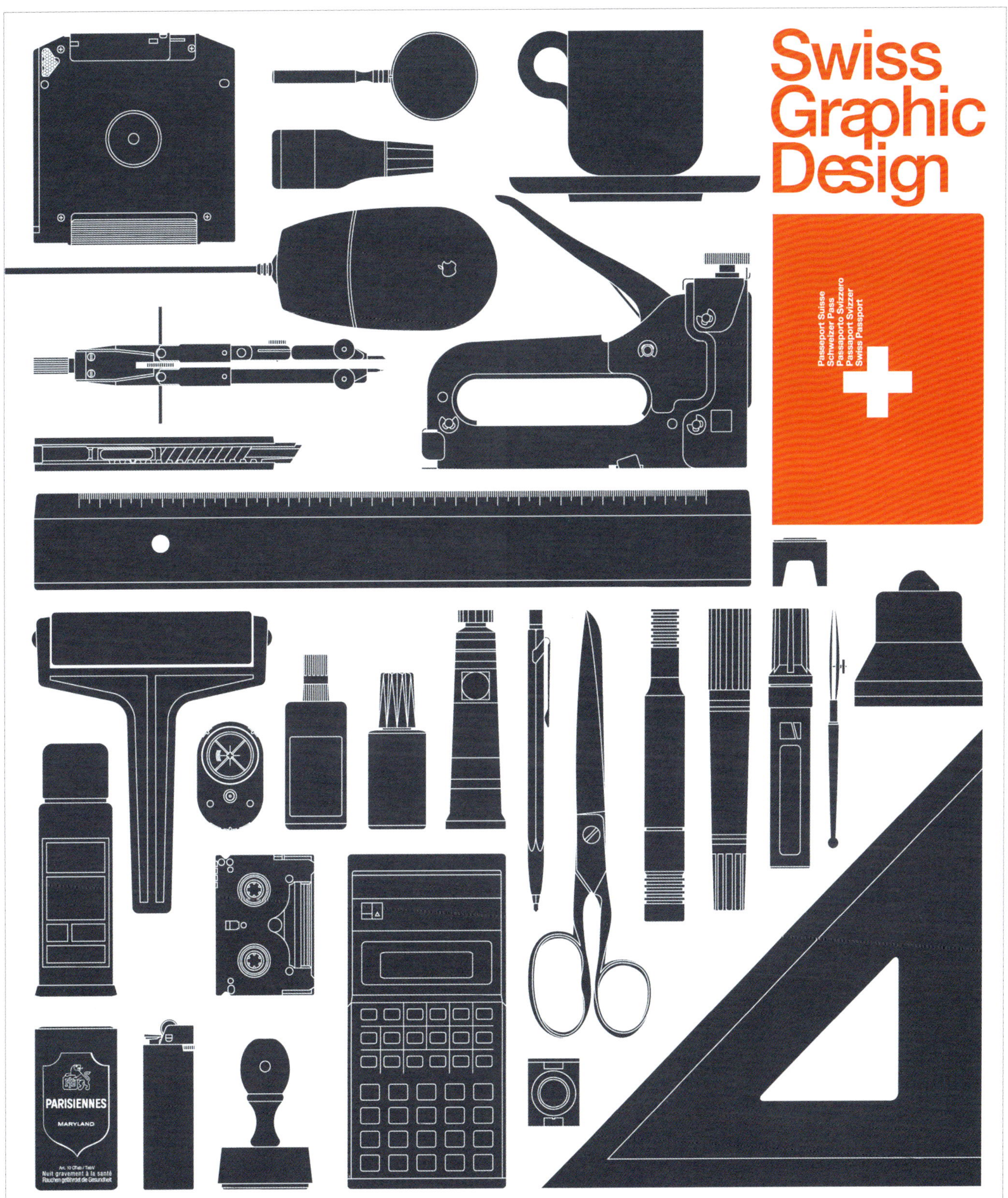

Swiss Graphic Design Book Artwork (2000)

Andrea Rauch

Basta Ya (2004) A response to the Madrid train Bombings of 2004

Poster for Teatro Stabile di Bolzano's 60th anniversary production of Molière's Le malade imaginaire

Exhibition Poster for Partito Comunista Italiano 1921-1991 at Casa dell'Architettura, Rome, 2011

Büro Destruct

Büro Destruct
"Italica"

Andrea Rauch
"Helvetica"

Chragokyberneticks

ENG

Chragokyberneticks (known as CHKY to lazy people) is a small graphic design bureau located in the heart of Berne, Switzerland. It is run by Mr. Christoph Frei and focuses on graphic storytelling, data visualisation and illustration.

Christoph founded CHKY in spring 2004 after graduating from the Hochschule der Künste, Bern. Since then CHKY has completed a heap of projects for a great variety of clients ranging from banks and universities to poets and punk rockers (all of whom have proven to be nice people). Christoph rides a DMR Switchback and a Turner RFX and plays a defective Yamaha Guitar.

DE

Chragokyberneticks (faulen Leuten auch als CHKY bekannt) ist ein kleines Grafikdesign Büro im Herzen Berns in der Schweiz. Es wird von Herrn Christoph Frei geführt und konzentriert sich auf grafisches Geschichtenerzählen, Datenvisualisierung und Illustration.

Christoph gründete CHKY im Frühjahr 2004 nach seiner Ausbildung an der Hochschule der Künste in Bern. Seitdem hat CHKY an einer ganzen Reihe Projekte für die verschiedensten Kunden gearbeitet, von Banken und Universitäten bis hin zu Poeten und Punkrockern (die sich alle als nette Leute bewährt haben). Christoph fährt ein DMR Switchback und ein Turner RFX und spielt auf einer defekten Yamaha Gitarre.

FR

Chragokyberneticks (connu sous CHKY pour les fainéants) est une petite entreprise de graphisme situé au cœur de Berne, Suisse. Elle est dirigée par M. Christoph Frei et se concentre sur le graphisme de l'art de conter, la visualisation de données et l'illustration.

Christoph a crée CHKY au printemps 2004 après avoir été diplômé de la Hochschule der Künste, Berne. Depuis CHKY a complété une montagne de projets pour une grande variété de clients allant de banques et universités, à des poètes et rockeurs punk (qui ont tous été des gens sympas). Christoph fait de la DMR Switchback et de la Turner RFX et joue de la guitare avec une Yamaha défectueuse.

ITA

Chragokyberneticks (detto CHKY dalle persone pigre) è un piccolo studio di design grafico che si trova nel cuore di Berna, in Svizzera. È gestito dal Signor Christoph Frei e si focalizza sulla narrazione grafica, la visualizzazione dei dati e l'illustrazione.

Christoph fonda CHKY nella primavera del 2004, dopo essersi laureato all'Hochschule der Künste, Berna. Da allora CHKY ha realizzato numerosissimi progetti per una varietà immensa di clienti, da banche e università a poeti e punk rocker (dei quali tutti si sono dimostrati persone simpatiche).

Christoph gira con una DMR Switchback e una Turner RFX e suona una chitarra Yamaha difettosa.

Mauro Gatti

ENG

Mauro Gatti is an Italian illustrator and designer. He loves to draw and put all the ideas swimming in his head on paper. He always tries to capture the lighter side of life and transform it into something simple but funny and memorable.

His inspiration comes from his quiet life, the sweet Giusy, their pugs Ozzy and Nena, the music of Kiss, vintage Playboy magazines, Seymour Chwast, Raymond Savignac, Alberto Sordi, Monica Vitti, Marcello Troisi and every funny thing he comes across.

In 2004 he founded Mutado, a creative studio, in Milan, and has worked for Nike, MTV, Comedy Central, Disney, Nickelodeon, Toyota and Diesel.

DE

Mauro Gatti ist ein italienischer Illustrator und Designer. Er liebt es, zu zeichnen und all die Ideen, die in seinem Kopf herumschwimmen, aufs Papier zu bringen. Er versucht immer, die Sonnenseite des Lebens zu erfassen und in etwas Einfaches jedoch Lustiges und Einprägsames zu verwandeln.

Inspiration findet er in seinem ruhigen Leben, der bezaubernden Giusy, seinen Boxern Ozzy und Nena, der Musik von Kiss, Vintage Playboy Magazinen, Seymour Chwast, Raymond Savignac, Alberto Sordi, Monica Vitti, Marcello Troisi und so ziemlich jeder lustigen Sache, auf die er stößt.

2004 gründete er Mutado, ein kreatives Studio in Milan, welches unter anderem Nike, MTV, Comedy Central, Disney, Nickelodeon, Toyota und Diesel zu seinen Kunden zählt.

FR

Mauro Gatti est un illustrateur et designer Italien. Il adore dessiner et mettre toutes les idées qui nagent dans sa tête sur papier. Il essaye toujours de saisir les moments légers de la vie et de les transformer en quelque chose de simple néanmoins drôle et mémorable à la fois.

Son inspiration viens de sa vie calme, de la mignonne Giusy, de ses carlins Ozzy et Nena, de la musique de Kiss, de magasines Playboy vintage, Seymour Chwast, Raymond Savignac, Alberto Sordi, Monica Vitti, Marcello Troisi et toutes les choses drôles sur lesquelles il tombe.

En 2004 il mit en place Mutado, un studio créatif à Milan et il a travaillé pour Nike, MTV, Comedy Central, Disney, Nickelodeon, Toyota et Diesel.

ITA

Mauro Gatti è un illustratore e designer italiano. Ama disegnare e mettere su carta tutte le idee che gli girano per la testa. Cerca sempre di catturare il lato più leggero della vita, trasformandolo in qualcosa di semplice ma allo stesso tempo divertente e memorabile.

Prende ispirazione dalla sua vita tranquilla, dalla dolce Giusy, dai loro carlini Ozzy e Nena, dalla musica dei Kiss e dalle riviste vintage di Playboy, da Seymour Chwast, Raymond Savignac, Alberto Sordi, Monica Vitti, Marcello Troisi e da tutte le cose divertenti che incontra.

Nel 2004 fonda Mutado, uno studio creativo a Milano che ha lavorato per Nike, MTV, Comedy Central, Disney, Nickelodeon, Toyota e Diesel.

CHKY

Piff Paff

Print Mag Cover

Play Patrik

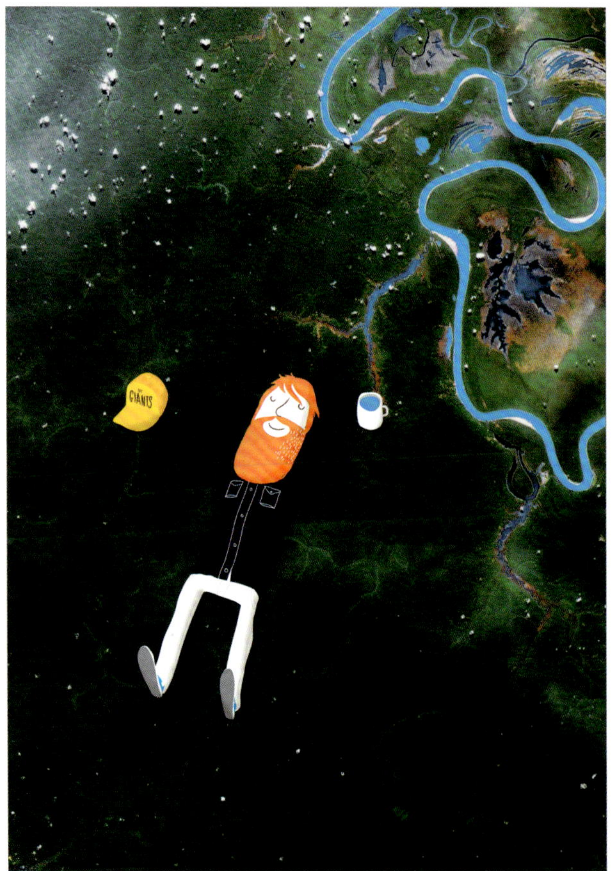

Bewegungsmelder

JE SUIS DEAD
«LIKE A POEM... EVERY MOVEMENT, TONE AND SYLLABLE IS PACKED WITH MEANING» —THE BALTIMORE SUN, USA
CONCEIVED AND DIRECTED BY
FOOL'S PROOF theatre
IN COLLABORATION WITH GEY PIN ANG

Mauro Gatti

A Small Guide To Be a Winner (Personal Project)

It's Gonna Be Rude, Funky, Hard (Jack Jaselli and the Great Vibes Foundation)

The Carrot Slayer (Very Bravo)

H.E.R.B. - Had Enough Religious Bullshit (A4God Book)

CHKY +
Mauro Gatti

The Inspiration: Carlo Vivarelli's Grid System.

1

2

The Plan

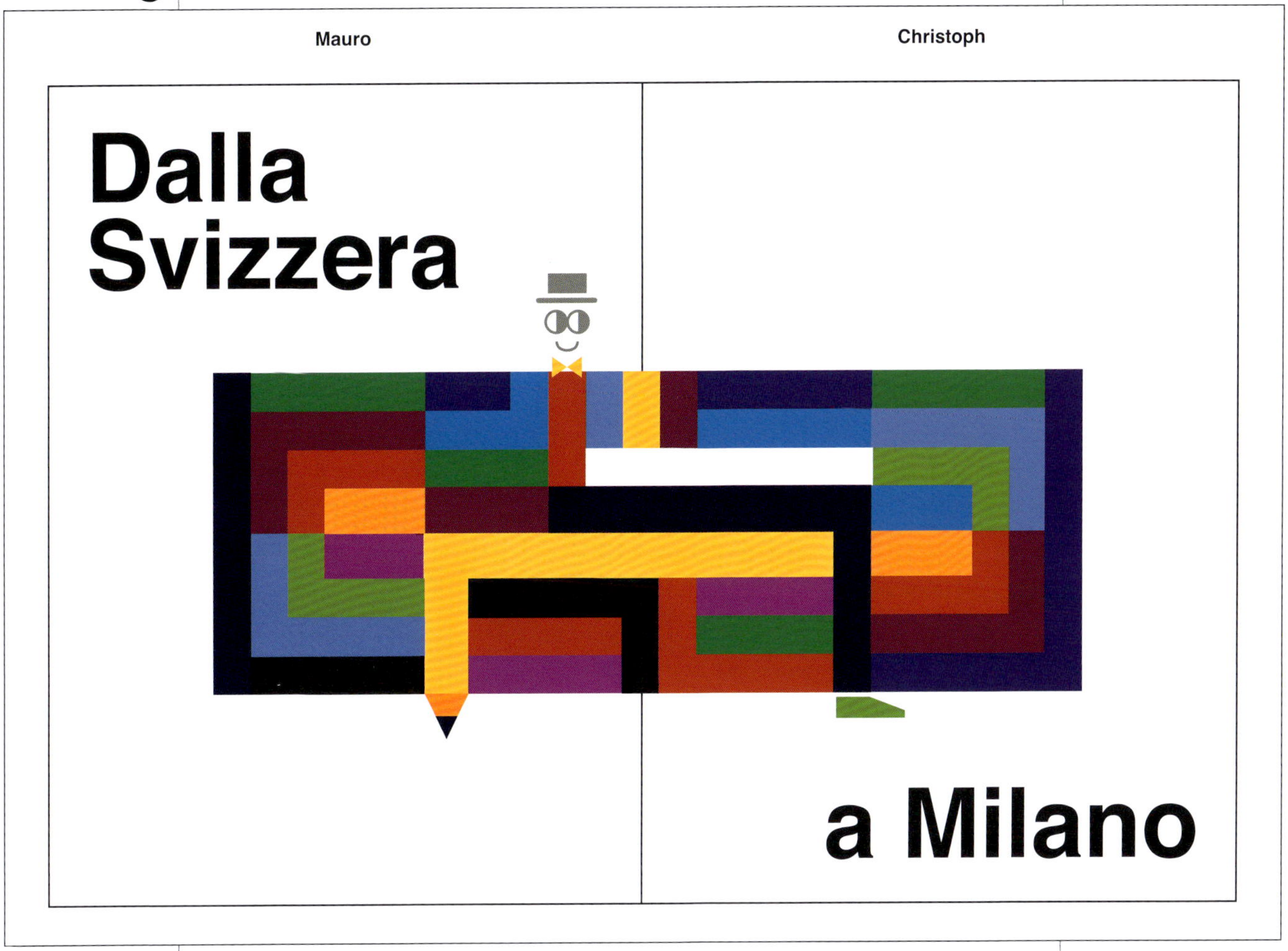

Mauro

Christoph

Dalla Svizzera

a Milano

The first steps

The preview

Chragokyberneticks

Chragokyberneticks
Christoph Frei
"Dalla Svizzera a Milano"

Mauro Gatti
"Dalla Svizzera a Milano"

GVA Studio

ENG

At GVA studio we take pleasure in letting the most basic things that surround us capture our imagination. We work without preconceived restrictions and a confidence that uncovering those things that are hidden beneath will bring us joy. Our team makes up for its small size by opening its doors to others. Our pleasure is to create: yours to enjoy.

DE

Hier bei GVS Studio finden wir Gefallen daran, unsere Fantasie durch die einfachsten Dinge um uns herum anregen zu lassen. Wir arbeiten ohne vorgefasste Einschränkungen und mit einer Überzeugung, dass uns das Entdecken versteckter Dinge Freude bringen wird. Unser Team ist zwar klein, aber unsere Türen stehen anderen offen. Unsere Freude liegt im Kreieren: Ihre Freude ist es, das Kreierte zu genießen.

FR

Chez GVA Studio nous prenons plaisir à laisser les choses les plus simples qui nous entourent interpeler notre imagination. Nous travaillons sans idées préconçues qui nous restreignent et la confiance que de découvrir ces choses qui se cachent en nous nous apportera la joie. Notre équipe se rattrape sur le fait qu'elle soit petite en ouvrant ses portes aux autres. Notre plaisir vient de la création : à vous de l'apprécier.

ITA

A GVA Studio ci piace lasciare che le cose più semplici che ci circondano, catturino la nostra fantasia. Lavoriamo senza limitazioni preconcette e con la sicurezza che svelare quello che si nasconde ci porterà gioia. Il nostro team compensa le sue piccole dimensioni aprendo le sue porte anche ad altri. Il nostro piacere è creare, il vostro è goderne.

Tomaso Marcolla

ENG

Born in Trento, Italy (1964) where he currently lives and work. Aside from his professional work as a graphic designer, he's an artist who works in watercolors, oils, photography and acrylics (and he's a published comic artist as well).

His artistic inclination is to challenge tradition in search of exploring new avenues of expression. It's part of a permanent voyage of experimentation that is difficult to capture through standard definitions of style. It's the essential characteristic of an artist who plays in many forms of media, without ever losing his originality.

DE

Geboren in Trento, Italien (1964), wo er momentan lebt und arbeitet. Neben seiner beruflichen Arbeit als Grafikdesigner ist er außerdem ein Künstler, der mit Aquarellen, Ölfarben, Fotografie und Akrylik arbeitet (und er ist ein Comic-Künstler, dessen Werke veröffentlicht wurden).

Seine künstlerischer Neigung ist es, Tradition in Frage zu stellen, um neue Ausdrucksformen zu erkunden. Es ist Bestandteil einer konstanten, durch das Experimentieren angetriebenen Reise, die man nur schwer durch übliche Stildefinitionen festhalten kann. Es ist der wesentliche Charakterzug eines Künstlers, der mit vielen Medienformen spielt, ohne dabei seine Originalität aufzugeben.

FR

Né à Trento, Italie (1964) où il vit et travaille actuellement. Outre son activité professionnelle en tant que graphiste, il est artiste et peint à l'aquarelle, à l'huile, à l'acrylique et utilise la photographie (et il est auteur de bandes dessinés qui ont été publiés).

Il a un penchant artistique pour remettre en question la tradition pour rechercher de nouvelles formes d'expression. Cela fait partie d'un voyage permanent d'expérimentation qu'il est difficile de définir à travers les définitions stylistiques standard. C'est la caractéristique essentielle d'un artiste qui aime travailler avec beaucoup de formes médiatiques différentes, sans jamais perdre son originalité.

ITA

Nasce nel 1964 a Trento, dove attualmente vive e lavora. Oltre al suo lavoro di grafico professionista, è anche artista e lavora con gli acquerelli, gli oli, la fotografia e l'acrilico (e ha anche pubblicato vignette).

La sua inclinazione artistica consiste nel confrontarsi con la tradizione, alla ricerca di nuove forme d'espressione, in una costante ricerca di cui sarebbe arduo arginare lo "stile" entro facili schemi. È questa la particolarità essenziale di un artista che sa adattarsi alle più svariate motivazioni senza mai perdere la propria originalità.

GVA Studio

Ecole de Danse de Genéve, Ballet Junior: © FEDERAL & GVA Studio These posters for the Ballet Junior are the result of a collaboration between Federal & GVA Studio.

This design examines the themes of unity and diversity through thirty chromatic variations of the Swiss flag. For no matter their origin, every citizen expresses their own way of life in Switzerland. Here the Swiss flag relates the value of collective solidarity with the personality of each citizen.

This poster was designed for the Switzerland Design For Life (A Celebration of Swiss design culture) exhibition in London. It was named one of the 100 Beste Plakate 2010.

Tomaso Marcolla

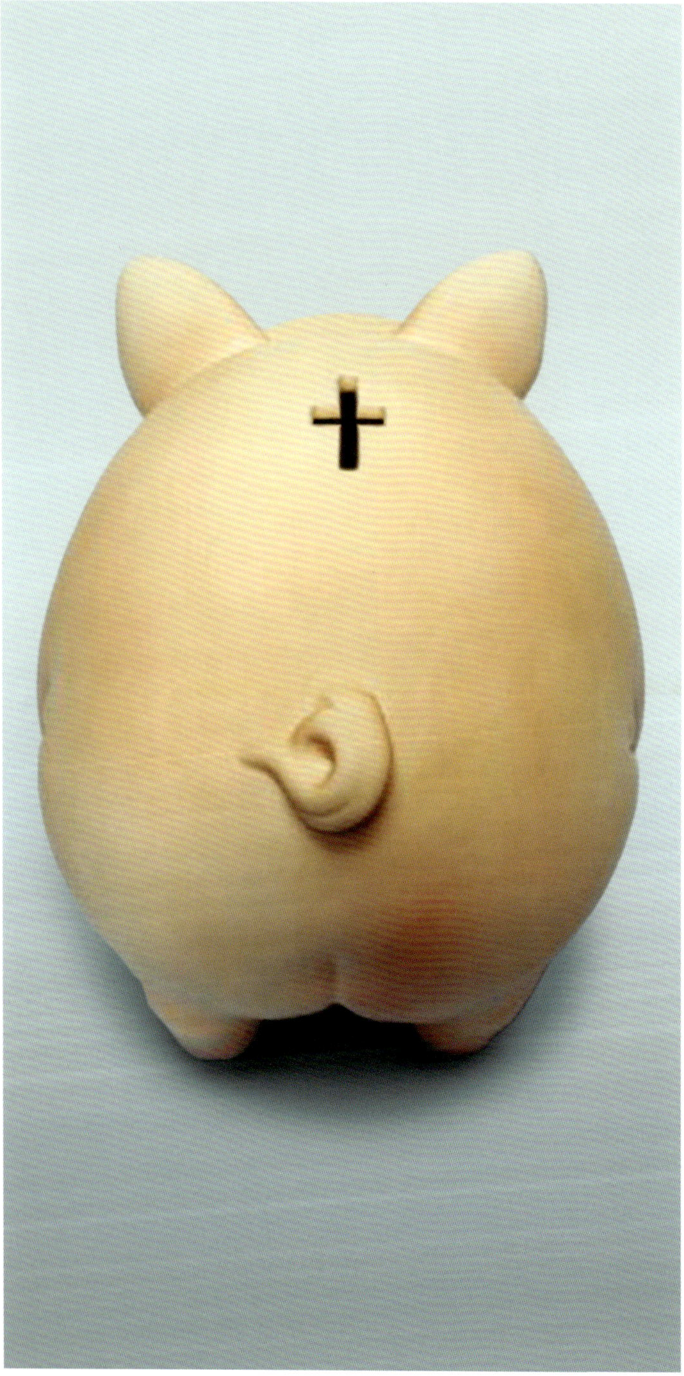

Penna, 2007

Mela Invado, 2006

Risparmi, 2008

OGM, 2009

GVA Studio + Tomaso Marcolla

ROUND 01

GVA Studio

Tomaso Marcolla

Will: Good evening all and welcome to the world's first ever live design battle between Switzerland and Italy! You've got live posters coming out of Trento, Geneva and commentary straight out of Marrakech. That's how we're rolling tonight. And speaking of rolling, GVA and Marcolla have just set the ball rolling with their first posters. Commendable efforts both, but I have to say I think Marcolla's ahead on points at this early stage. GVA, what have you got in your engine? Apparently they're stocked up on onions and beer, so whatever it is, it should be good…

Tommaso: Mentre Will mi chiede se "can you be funny?" a proposito di questi commenti, vorrei per prima cosa concentrarmi sulla qualità dei poster. Marcolla è nettamente davanti, mentre vedo gli Svizzeri già in difficolta. Due parole vanno spese per l'organizzazione particolarmente internazionale della serata: i designer vengono da Trento e Geneva, mentre al momento io e Will ci troviamo (in maniera improbabile, per lavoro) a Marrakech.

GVA Studio **Tomaso Marcolla**

Will: Well, after the first round, Signor Marcolla is indeed ahead on points according to our live studio audience (hello! ciao! bonsai!). So let's see what's happened in the meantime… GVA have matched Marcolla's colour scheme and raised it with the addition of some pencils in the middle! remarkable! and Marcolla, wow. what has he done? He looks like he's thrown it all away… we cut now to our to our live studio guest, the distinguished french designer Fabrice Praeger. This is what he's got to say: 'huge boobies.' Merci Fabrice!

Tommaso: Entrambi gli sfidanti vergono sul tricolore. Le proposte si stanno anche verticalizzando, ma sembra esserci confusione a centro campo. Speriamo che Marcolla si riprenda, era partito meglio. GVA deve spingere più a fondo se vuole superare la difesa dell'azzurro.

GVA Studio + Tomaso Marcolla

ROUND 03

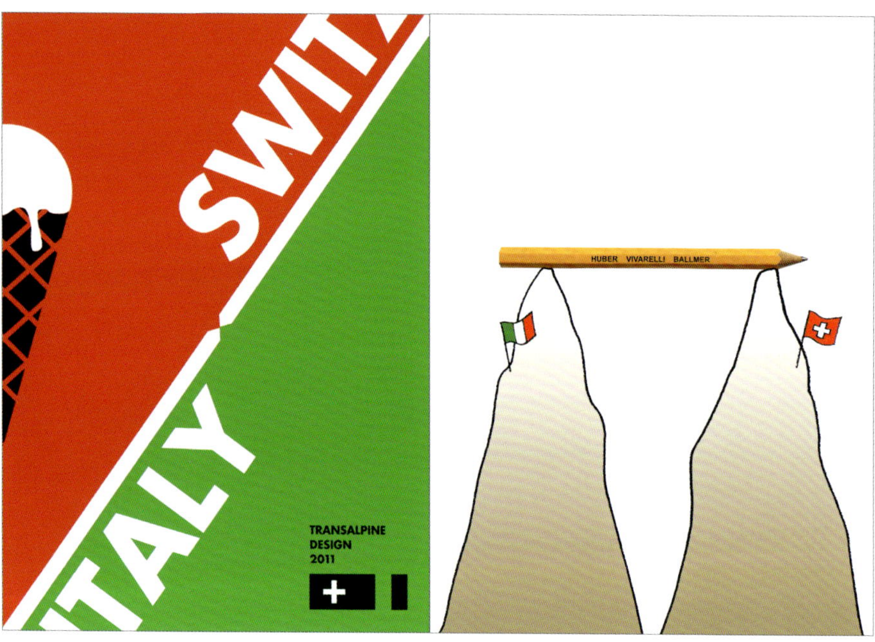

GVA Studio   **Tomaso Marcolla**

Will: and we're back… GVA definitely pulled it back on that round, four votes each according to our Facebook friends. but what's this? GVA have thrown a cornetto into the mixer! that's what i call coming out of leftfield. And this (http://www.youtube.com/watch?v=biL6zAMkOQs) is what i call great advertising. And Marcolla, well, Marcolla's clearly a man after our friend fabrice's heart. But is Tomaso's poster the breast, or has it gone tits up? You decide…

Tommaso: GVA seguono la strada tracciata sin dal primo poster, con un rigore piuttosto degno di Müller-Brockmann. È una strategia che paga perché al secondo turno i due si sono trovati in pareggio. Marcolla invece offre una matita a simboleggiare una pacifica connessione tra Italia e Svizzera. Ci vorrà ben più del cuore di panna di GVA per far scendere il guru dalla sua montagna.

ROUND 04

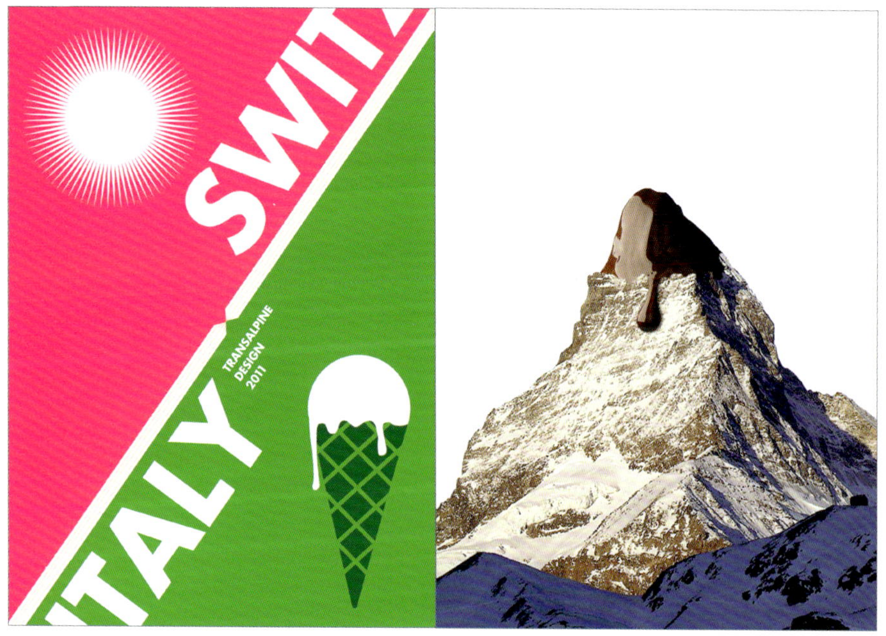

GVA Studio   **Tomaso Marcolla**

Will: so alas, my friends, we face the final curtain, the penultimate round of our design battle. And it looks like melting is theme of the day; Marcolla drops the chocolate bomb (tasty, very tasty) while GVA let the sunshine in. That's enough to bring a glow to everyone's heart…

Tommaso: Il Cervino si sta sciogliendo sotto i potenti colpi del Marcolla, sembra di rivedere Rossi vincere l'oro mentre tra le Alpi rimbomba la voce della telecronaca del Galeazzone nazionale http://www.youtube.com/watch?v=sMz-4EtbbMo. Il sole di GVA è invece buono giusto per una tintarella di luna. Tira una brutta aria a Ginevra.

GVA Studio
Tomaso Marcolla

Will: pencils down. It's 8.06 and the battle draws to a close. Glasses chink around across the world to toast the success of the most fun I've had behind a monitor since I discovered porn. Luckily both these posters are something I'd be proud to show my mother; I'm particularly fond of GVA's colourscheme here and Marcolla's final poster is, well, sharp. To the point. You get the idea.

Tommaso: L'approccio metodico di GVA sembra non essere stato capace di sviare il brio dell'estroso Marcolla. Il suo ultimo poster mostra una bandiera svizzera letteralmente polverizzata dalla matita pungente del design italiano. Mi sarei aspettato di più da GVA, ma la loro ciliegina sulla torta (o sul cornetto) arriva troppo tardi.

Will: and the winner is (drum roll please)…Signor Marcolla. Bravo Tomaso. And bravi GVA. I think you'll join me in saying that the real winner this evening has been design. No, art. And thank you too for watching, it's been a blast. Huge thanks must go to GVA, Tomaso Marcolla, the Casablanca brewery and Luca Comino. Grazie a tutti! (oh, and you can see the results of all 11 collaborations at an exhibition or in a bookshop near you soon! check italiandesigniscominghome.ch for more details!) Peace out! (and Hello Mum!)

Tommaso: Grazie a tutti per la partecipazione. Abbiamo un vincitore: Marcolla. Bravo. MA un grazie speciale anche a GVA, che hanno dimostrato comunque una grande integrità nelle loro scelte durante il match. Per la cronaca, il conteggio finale alle 20.15 è stato di 59 a 24 (tra tweets e "mi piace") Vi ricordiamo ancora una volta che potrete vedere questa e altre 10 collaborazioni tra designer svizzeri e italiani nel prossimo futuro sia in mostra che in un libro. Per tenervi aggiornati basta visitare italiandesigniscominghome.ch

GVA Studio

GVA Studio
"Transalpine Design"

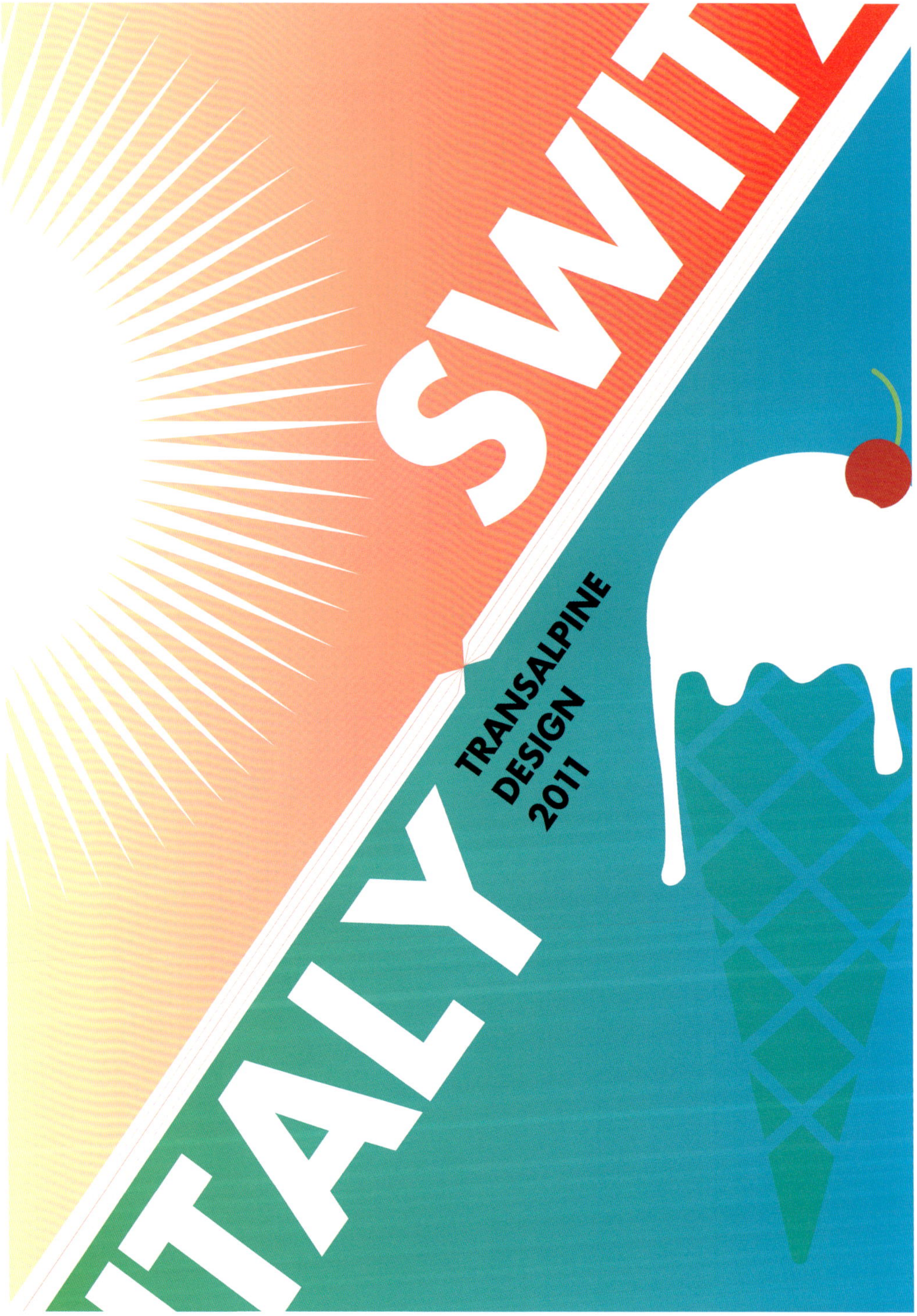

Tomaso Marcolla
"Trucioli"

Melchior Imboden

ENG

Melchior Imboden lives and works in Buochs, Central Switzerland. In 1972 he began his studies as an interior designer and worked in this profession until 1984. During this period he discovered a passion for design and typography that led him to study graphic design at the Art School in Lucerne.

Since 1992 he has worked as an independent graphic designer and photographer, and teaches in both disciplines as well. His posters, many of which deal with the arts, have been honoured with numerous national and international awards. In 1998 he became a member of the Alliance Graphique Internationale (AGI) and has served as the President of AGI Switzerland since 2006.

DE

Melchior Imboden lebt und arbeitet in Buochs in der Zentralschweiz. 1972 begann er sein Studium als Innenarchitekt und arbeitete in diesem Beruf bis 1984. In dieser Zeit entwickelte er eine Leidenschaft für Design und Typografie, die ihn schließlich dazu brachte, Grafikdesign and der Kunstschule in Luzern zu studieren.

Seit 1992 arbeitet Imboden als unabhängiger Grafikdesigner und Fotograf und lehrt zudem auch beide Studienfächer. Seine Poster, von denen sich viele mit Kunst beschäftigen, wurden mit zahlreichen landesweiten und internationalen Preisen ausgezeichnet. Im Jahr 1998 wurde er Mitglied der Alliance Graphique Internationale (AGI) und dort ist er seit 2006 der Vorsitzende der AGI Schweiz.

FR

Melchior Imboden habite et travaille à Buochs, au centre de la Suisse. En 1972 il commença des études de design d'intérieur et travailla en tant que tel jusqu'en 1984. Pendant cette période il découvrit une passion pour le design et la typographie qui l'ont amené à étudier le graphisme à l'École d'Art de Lucerne.

Depuis 1972, il travaille en tant que graphiste indépendant et photographe et enseigne aussi les deux disciplines. Ses posters, beaucoup d'entre eux dans le domaine de l'art, ont reçus beaucoup de prix nationaux et internationaux. En 1998 il devint membre de l'Alliance Graphique Internationale (AGI) et est président de l'AGI Suisse depuis 2006.

ITA

Melchior Imboden vive e lavora a Buochs, Svizzera centrale. Nel 1972 comincia il suo percorso di studio come interior designer e lavora in questo campo fino al 1984. È in questo periodo che scopre la passione per il design e la tipografia, che lo porta a studiare design grafico alla Scuola D'Arte di Lucerna.

Dal 1992 lavora come grafico e fotografo indipendente, insegnando inoltre entrambe le discipline. I suoi manifesti, molti dei quali hanno a che fare con l'arte, hanno avuto l'onore di ricevere numerosi premi nazionali e internazionali. Nel 1998 diventa membro dell'Alliance Graphique Internationale (AGI) ed è Presidente di AGI Svizzera dal 2006.

Leftloft

ENG

Leftloft is an independent graphic design company established in 1997 in Milan by Andrea Braccaloni, Francesco Cavalli, Bruno Genovese and David Pasquali. They met at the Politecnico University of Milan while studying architecture and urban planning. The studio now operates with a team of designers and opened a New York office in 2009. Leftloft has developed projects locally and internationally for some of the most important Italian companies and institutions including: Pirelli, Moleskine, Corriere della Sera, Emergency and Internazionale F.C. In addition the partners teach design at the Politecnico University of Milan and the studio is one of the founders of the Ministero della Grafica, a cultural association promoting design culture.

DE

Leftloft ist eine unabhängige Grafikdesignfirma, die 1997 von Andrea Braccaloni, Francesco Cavalli, Bruno Genovese und David Pasquali in Mailand gegründet wurde. Die Gründer lernten sich während Ihres Studiums für Architektur und Stadtplanung an der Politecnico Universität in Mailand kennen. Das Studio umfasst heute ein Team an Designern und hat seit 2009 ein Büro in New York. Leftloft hat regional und international Projekte für einige der wichtigsten italienischen Unternehmen und Organisationen entwickelt, unter anderem für Pirelli, Moleskine, Corriere della Sera, Emergency und Internazionale F.C. Zudem lehren die Partner auch Design an der polytechnischen Universität in Mailand und das Studio ist einer der Mitbegründer der Ministero della Grafica, einer kulturellen Organisation, die Designkultur fördert.

FR

Leftloft est une entreprise de graphisme indépendante établie à Milan en 1997 par Andrea Braccaloni, Francesco Cavalli, Bruno Genovese et David Pasquali. Ils se sont rencontrés à l'Université Polytechnique de Milan alors qu'ils étudiaient l'architecture et la planification urbaine. Aujourd'hui, le studio comprend une équipe de graphistes et a ouvert un bureau à New York en 2009. Leftloft a développé des projets localement et à l'international pour quelques unes des plus grandes entreprises et institutions italiennes y compris : Pirelli, Moleskine, Corriere della Sera, Emergency et Internazionale F.C. De plus ses collaborateurs enseignent le design à l'Université Polytechnique de Milan et le studio est l'un des fondateurs du Ministerio della Grafica, une association culturelle qui promeut la culture du design.

ITA

Leftloft è una società indipendente di progettazione grafica, fondata a Milano nel 1997 da Andrea Braccaloni, Francesco Cavalli, Bruno Genovese e David Pasquali. Essi si sono conosciuti durante gli studi di architettura e urbanistica al Politecnico di Milano. Lo studio attualmente è composto da un gruppo di designer e ha aperto una nuova sede a New York nel 2009. Leftloft ha sviluppato progetti locali e internazionali, collaborando con alcune fra le più importanti società italiane tra le quali Pirelli, Moleskine, Corriere della Sera, Emergency e Internazionale F.C. I soci inoltre, insegnano Design al Politecnico di Milano e lo studio è uno dei fondatori del Ministero della Grafica, un'associazione culturale per la promozione della cultura del design.

Melchior Imboden

Self-designed Poster for Permanent Exhibition of Melchior Imboden's work. Lucerne 2009

Black and White Poster for Exhibition at the GGG Gallery in Tokyo, Japan, 2005

30 Years of the Ermitage Art Gallery, Beckenried, Switzerland, 2009

Leftloft

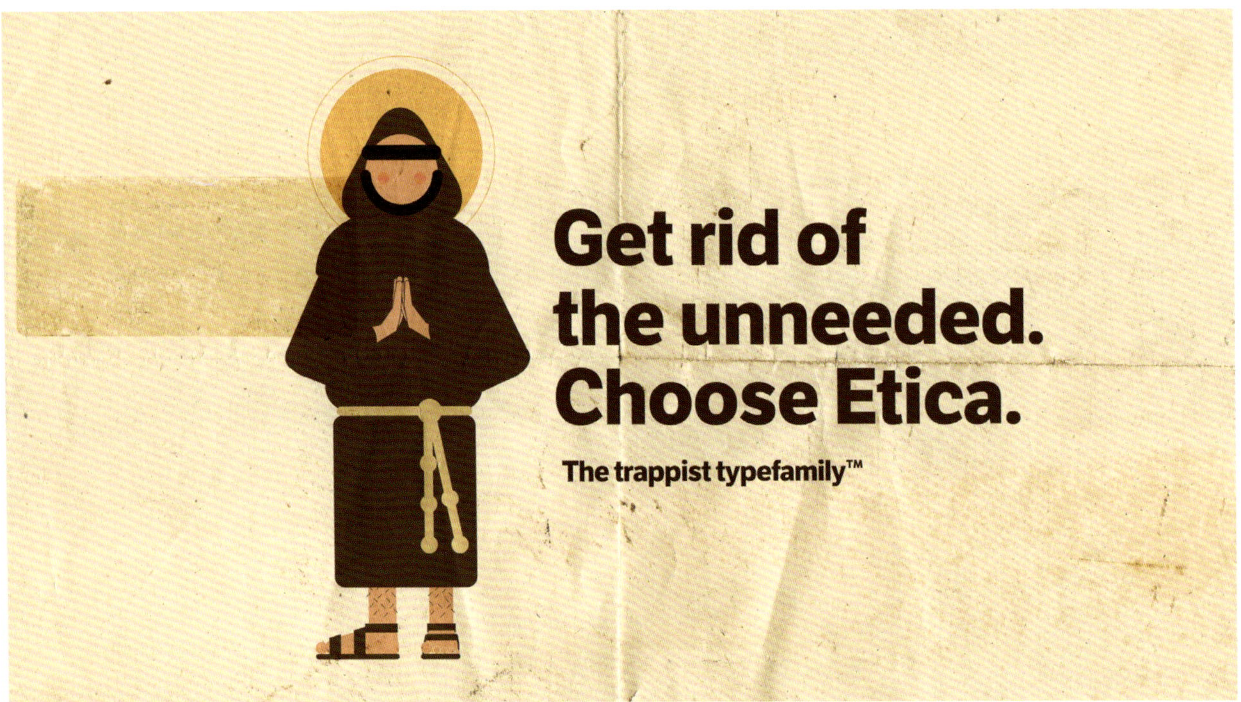

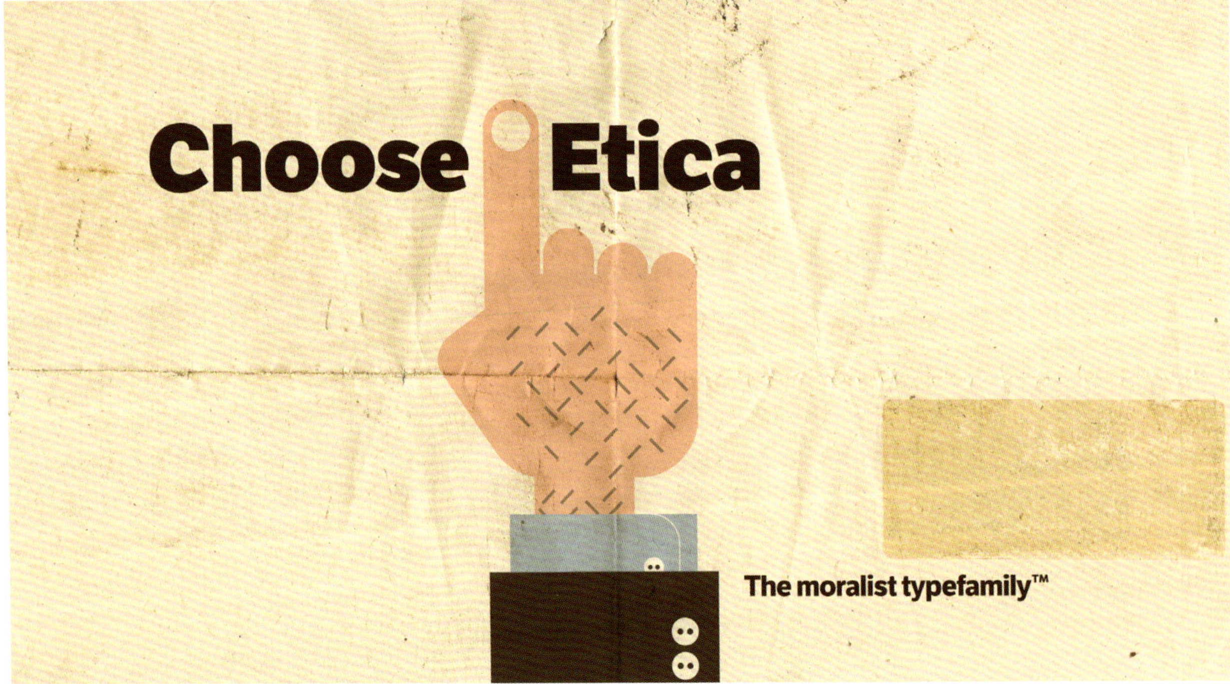

Etica, the moralist typefamily project. An ongoing and evolving project born in 2000

Solferino Text, the new typeface for Corriere della Sera

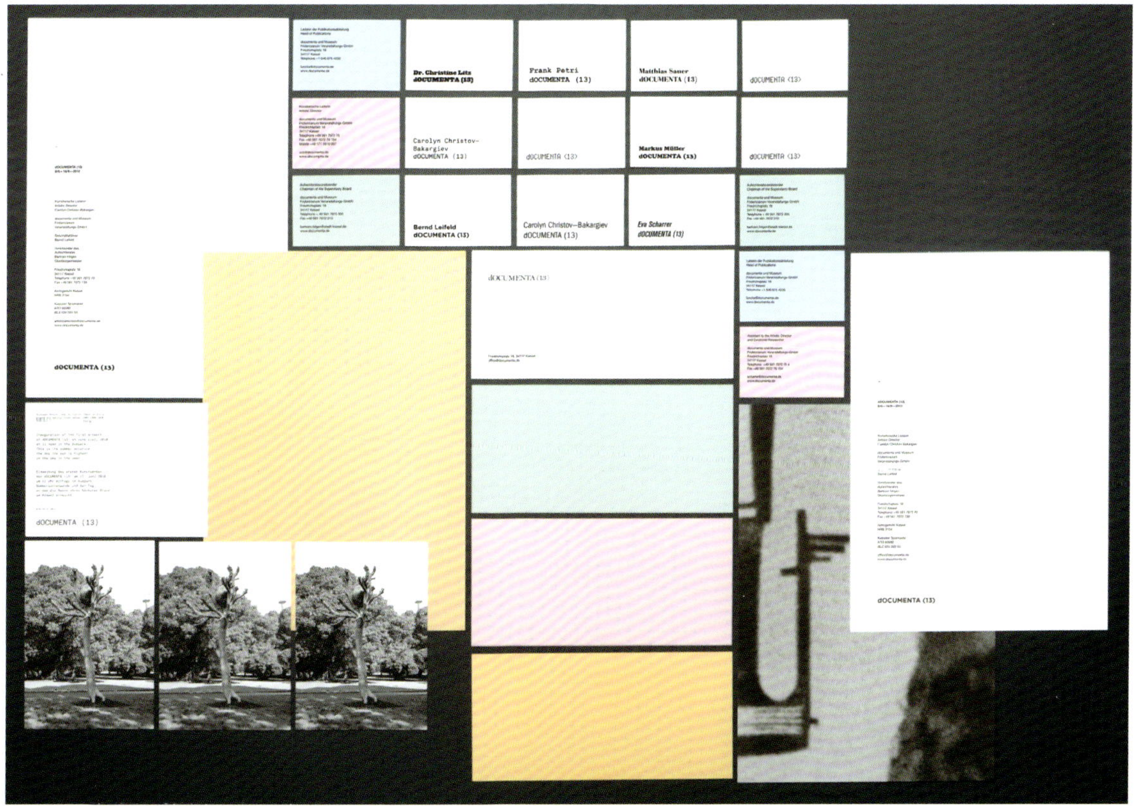

Visual Identity for dOCUMENTA (13), the world's most important exhibition for contemporary art, held every five years in Kassel, Germany

Melchior Imboden

Melchior Imboden
"Neue Formen"

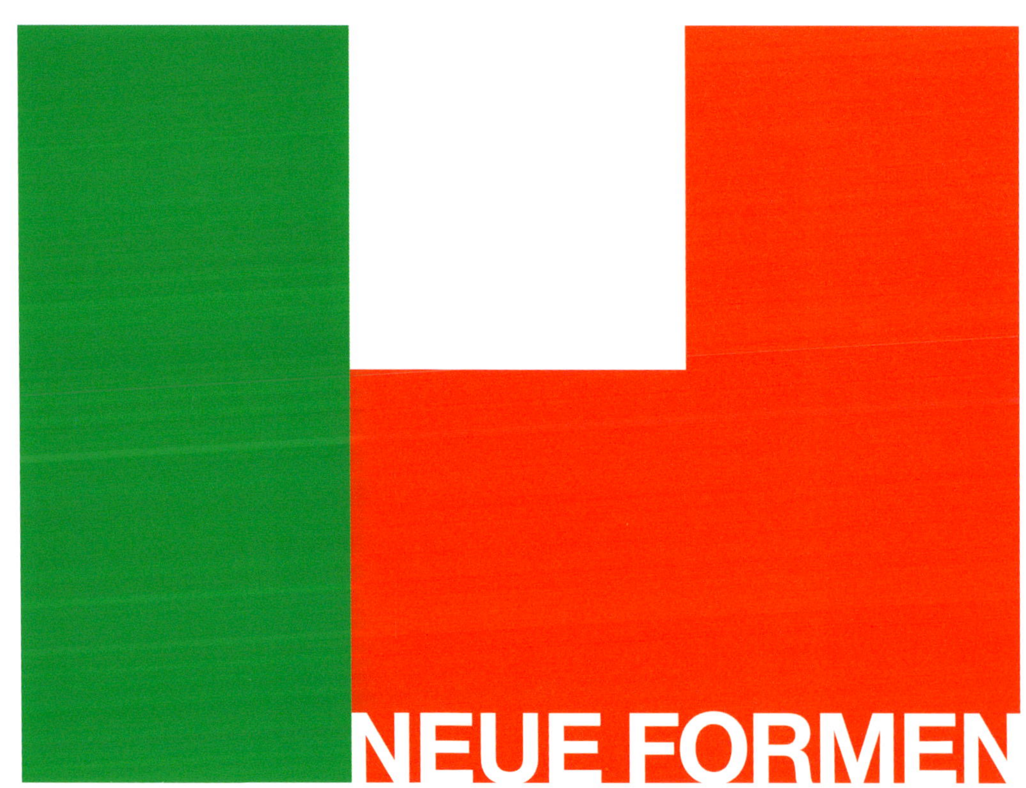

Leftloft
"Nuove Forme"

NUOVE FORME

Dafi Kühne

ENG

A MacBook, a laser cutter, wood type, a plate maker and presses from the 1960s are just some of the tools that Dafi Kühne uses in his day job as a graphic designer and letterpress printmaker. After his studies at the Visual Communications Department at Zurich University of the Arts and an internship with Hatch Showprint in Nashville, Tennessee (one of the oldest letterpress poster shops still in operation in the States) he started his own studio babyinktwice near Zurich. He uses new self-made printing blocks alongside old ones in the production of posters, flyers and magazines for music, art and film projects.

DE

Ein MacBook, ein Laserschneidegerät, Holzbuchstaben, ein PlateMaker und Pressen aus den sechziger Jahren – dies sind nur einige der Werkzeuge, die Dafi Kühn in seiner täglichen Arbeit als Grafikdesigner und Druckgrafiker anwendet. Nach seinem Studium im Bereich der visuellen Kommunikation an der Züricher Kunsthochschule und einem Praktikum bei Hatch Showprint in Nashville, Tennessee (einer der ältesten Plakatdruckerläden in den USA, der noch in Betrieb ist), gründete er sein eigenes Studio babyinktwice in der Nähe von Zürich. Kühne mischt neue, selbstgemachte und alte, gebrauchte Druckformen in seiner Herstellung von Plakaten, Flyern und Zeitschriften für Musik-, Kunst- und Filmprojekte.

FR

Un MacBook, un coupeur laser, des lettres de bois, un PlateMaker et une presse des années 1960 sont juste quelques uns des outils que Dafi Kühne utilise dans son travail de tous les jours en tant que graphiste et graveur de typographie. Après ses études au Département de Communications Visuelles à l'Université des Beaux-arts de Zurich et un stage chez Hatch Showprint à Nashville, Tenesse (l'un des plus vieux magasins graveur de posters encore opérationnel aux Etats Unis) il créa son propre studio appelé babyinktwice à côté de Zurich. Il utilise des nouveaux blocs d'impression qu'il a fabriqué lui-même ainsi que de plus vieux dans la production de posters, flyers et magasines dans le domaine de la musique, de l'art et des films.

ITA

Un MacBook, una macchina da taglio laser, caratteri in legno, un plate maker e torchi tipografici degli anni '60, sono solo alcuni degli strumenti che Dafi Kühne utilizza nel suo lavoro da grafico e stampatore rilievografico. Dopo i suoi studi nel dipartimento di Comunicazione Visiva all'Università delle Arti di Zurigo e uno stage con Hatch Showprint a Nashville, Tennessee (uno dei negozi di manifesti rilievografici più vecchi rimasti in attività negli Stati Uniti), apre il suo studio babyinktwice vicino a Zurigo. Utilizza, insieme a quelle vecchie, nuove matrici di stampa fabbricate da lui stesso, per produrre manifesti, volantini e riviste per progetti di musica, arte e film.

Marco Nicotra

ENG

Marco Nicotra was born in Milan and still works there today as a graphic designer. After graduating in Communication Design at the Politecnico di Milano, he worked at a few agencies for several years before finally turning freelance. He currently specializes in editorial and online projects. He has a passion for collage, vintage, photo editing and printing techniques. He also has several self-produced projects that mainly concern the press, like Super8, a free magazine that features collaborations with designers from around the world.

DE

Marco Nicotra wurde in Mailand geboren und arbeitet auch heute noch als Grafikdesigner dort. Nach seinem Abschluss in Kommunikationsdesign von der Politecnico di Milano er für einige Jahre bei verschiedenen Agenturen, bevor er sich schließlich selbstständig machte. Er spezialisiert sich momentan auf Editorial- und Online-Projekte. Er hat eine Leidenschaft für Collagen, Vintage, Fotobearbeitung und Drucktechniken. Er hat zudem eigene Projekte produziert, hauptsächlich im Bereich der Presse - zum Beispiel Super8, eine kostenlose Zeitschrift, in der Gemeinschaftsproduktionen mit anderen Designern weltweit vorgestellt werden.

FR

Marco Nicotra est né à Milan et y travaille encore aujourd'hui en tant que graphiste. Après avoir obtenu son diplôme en Design de Communication à la Politecnico di Milano, il a travaillé au sein de plusieurs agences avant de devenir freelance. Il se spécialise aujourd'hui en projets éditoriaux et en ligne. Il a une passion pour les techniques de collage, de vintage, d'édition photo et d'imprimerie. Il a aussi crée lui-même des projets qui se situent principalement dans le domaine de la presse comme Super8, un magasine gratuit qui traite des collaborations entre designers à travers le monde.

ITA

Marco Nicotra nasce a Milano e ancora oggi ci lavora come grafico. Dopo la laurea in Communication Design al Politecnico di Milano, lavora per alcuni anni in varie agenzie, prima di dedicarsi alla carriera freelance. Ora è specializzato in progetti editoriali e web. Ha la passione per i collage, il vintage, il fotoritocco e le tecniche di stampa. Porta avanti, inoltre, alcuni progetti autoprodotti che riguardano soprattutto la stampa, come Super8, una rivista gratuita che presenta collaborazioni con designer di tutto il mondo.

Dafi Kühne

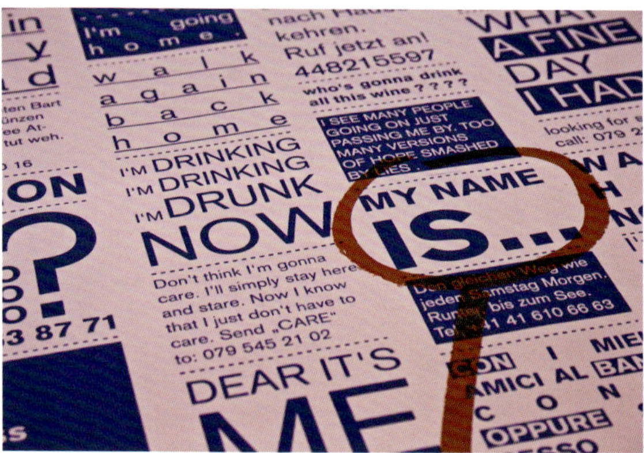

The Pussywarmers. 2c letterpress prints from photopolymer plates and a little leadtype. For more information about this project: http://www.babyinktwice.ch/index28.php

As Bad As It Gets. 8c letterpress magazines from photopolymer-plates. For more information about this project: http://www.babyinktwice.ch/index26.php

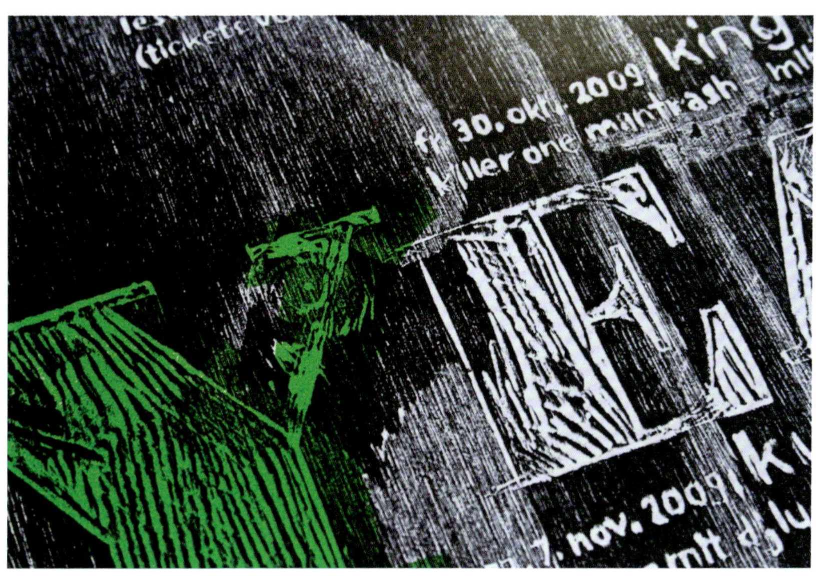

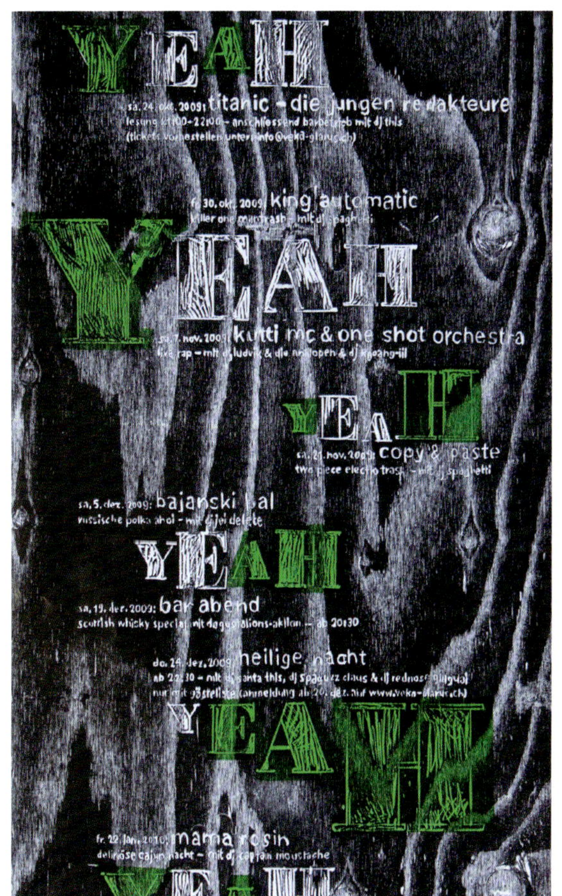

Yeah (Small). 2c letterpress prints from a plywood plate and linocut. For more information about this project: http://www.babyinktwice.ch/index19.php

Marco Nicotra

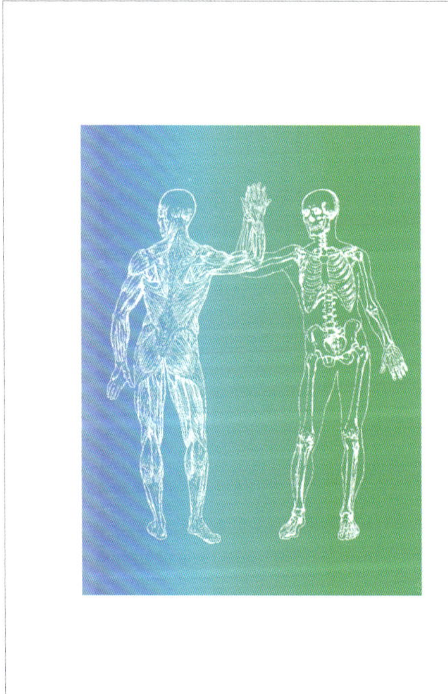

Minimal Posters. A series of posters for my apartment.

Dafi Kühne prints his poster *Zürich Milano*

4 colour letterpress prints from lasercut plexiglass and handset leadtype.

Design: **Dafi Kühne**

Print: **Dafi Kühne on a FAG Control 900**

Year: **2011**

Format: **50 x 70cm**

Paper: **Coated Favini 200g/m2**

Dafi Kühne

Dafi Kühne
"Zurich Milano"

Marco Nicotra
"Zurich Milano"

ENTRA IN A2
STRADA A PEDAGGIO
INGRESSO IN ITALIA
153 KM

CONTINUA SU A9
STRADA A PEDAGGIO PARZIALE
31,0 KM

PRENDI L'USCITA PER A8/E62 VERSO MILANO
CONTINUA A SEGUIRE LA A8
STRADA A PEDAGGIO PARZIALE
11,0 KM

CONTINUA SU AUTOSTRADA DEI LAGHI (INDICAZIONI PER MILANO/VIALE CERTOSA CENTRO/FIERAMILANOCITY)
3,1 KM

CONTINUA SU CAVALCAVIA CASCINA GOBBA
650 M

CONTINUA SU CAVALCAVIA DEL GHISALLO
650 M

CONTINUA SU VIALE ALCIDE DE GASPERI
1,0 KM

MANTIENI LA SINISTRA AL BIVIO
70 M

CONTINUA SU VIALE LODOVICO SCARAMPO
450 M

SVOLTA A SINISTRA IN VIALE TEODORICO
750 M

PROSEGUI DRITTO SU PIAZZA FIRENZE
M

SVOLTA A DESTRA PER RIMANERE SU PIAZZA FIRENZE
50 M

SVOLTA A DESTRA PER RIMANERE SU PIAZZA FIRENZE
37 M

CONTINUA SU CORSO SEMPIONE
1,4 KM

SVOLTA A DESTRA IN VIA ANTONIO CANOVA
500 M

CONTINUA SU VIALE GIOVANNI MILTON L'INGRESSO IN ZONA A PEDAGGIO
260 M

CONTINUA SU VIALE MOLIERE
400 M

CONTINUA SU VIA PIETRO PALEOCAPA
200 M

SVOLTA A DESTRA IN PIAZZALE LUIGI CADORNA
300 M

SVOLTA A SINISTRA IN LARGO PAOLO D'ANCONA
18 M

CONTINUA SU CORSO MAGENTA
350 M

CONTINUA SU VIA SANTA MARIA ALLA PORTA
130 M

CONTINUA SU VIA BORROMEI
220 M

SVOLTA A SINISTRA IN PIAZZA BORROMEO
110 M

CONTINUA SU VIA BOCCHETTO
260 M

SVOLTA A DESTRA IN PIAZZA CORDUSIO
37 M

CONTINUA SU VIA OREFICI
180 M

SVOLTA A DESTRA IN VIA TORINO

ARRIVO A MILANO

INGRESSO IN **ITALIA** A8/E62
PRENDI L'USCITA PER
MANTIENI LA SINISTRA AL BIVIO
MANTIENI LA SINISTRA
SVOLTA A DESTRA IN **PIAZZALE CADORNA**
SVOLTA A DESTRA IN **PIAZZA CORDUSIO**
CONTINUA SU VIA OREFICI
ARRIVO A **MILANO**

Stefan Jost

ENG

Stefan Jost was born in 1983 and grew up in a small town near Bern. He was inspired to take on Graphic Design as a result of his fascination with Art and Design. After his apprenticeship in a printing company, he studied Visual Communications in Basel. While developing his own graphic style during this time, Stefan had several internships and worked as a freelancer for various clients, mostly in the cultural sector. Stefan would describe his work with the following terms: obscure references, typography, and clean lines. His work has been widely exhibited and published in many books.

DE

Stefan Jost wurde 1983 geboren und wuchs in einer Kleinstadt in der Nähe von Bern auf. Seine Faszination für Kunst und Design inspirierten ihn dazu, das Grafikdesign zu erlernen. Nach seiner Ausbildung bei einer Druckerei studierte er visuelle Kommunikation in Basel. In dieser Zeit entwickelte er seinen eigenen Stil, absolvierte mehrere Praktika und arbeitete als Freiberufler für verschiedene Kunden, hauptsächlich im kulturellen Bereich. So würde Stefan seine Arbeit beschreiben: obskure Referenzen, Typografie und klare Linien. Seine Werke sind in zahlreichen Ausstellungen zu sehen und in vielen Büchern veröffentlicht.

FR

Stefan Jost est né en 1983 et a grandi dans une petite ville à côté de Berne. Il a été poussé à se lancer dans le graphisme à cause de sa fascination pour les Arts et le Design. Après son apprentissage dans une imprimerie, il a étudié la Communication Visuelle à Bâle. Alors qu'il développait son propre style en graphisme, Stefan a fait plusieurs stages et a travaillé en tant que freelance pour de nombreux clients, principalement dans le secteur culturel. Stefan décrirait son travail avec les mots suivants : références obscures, typographie et lignes droites. Son travail a été largement exposé et publié dans de nombreux livres.

ITA

Stefan Jost nasce nel 1983 e cresce in una piccola località vicino a Berna. La sua passione per l'arte e il design, lo porta ad apprendere il design grafico. Dopo un apprendistato in un'azienda di stampa, studia Comunicazione Visiva a Basilea. In questo periodo Stefan sviluppa il proprio stile grafico, svolgendo contemporaneamente alcuni stage e lavorando come libero professionista per vari clienti, per la maggior parte nel settore culturale. Stefan descriverebbe i suoi lavori con questi termini: spunti inusuali, tipografia, e linee pulite. I suoi lavori sono stati ampiamente esposti e pubblicati in molti libri.

Alessandro Gori

ENG

Alessandro Gori is one of the founders of Laboratorium, which came to life in 2004 with Florence as its base. Laboratorium's core values are research and experimentation.

Gori's work ranges from book design (A New Italian Fashion, 2011, Walter Albini And His Time, 2010, A Modern Day, 2010), to communication (Pitti Immagine, Altaroma, Furla), to exhibition design (Fashion at the Time of Fascism, London College of Fashion, 2010; The Colored Rooms, Emilio Pucci, 2007) and installations (Atlante. collective House and modern living 1930-1980, The Architecture Biennale, Venice 2008, Notebook, Neon, Milan, 2008). He has been a lecturer of Graphic Design and corporate identity at the University of Bologna since 2005.

DE

Alessandro Gori ist einer der Mitbegründer von Laboratorium, das 2004 ins Leben gerufen wurde und in Florenz seinen Standort hat. Die Grundwerte Laboratoriums sind Forschung und Experimentieren.

Goris Werke reichen von Buchdesign (A New Italian Fashion, 2011, Walter Albini And His Time, 2010, A Modern Day, 2010) über Kommunikation (Pitti Immagine, Altaroma, Furla), bis hin zu Messedesign (Fashion at the Time of Fascism, London College of Fashion, 2010; The Colored Rooms, Emilio Pucci, 2007) und Installationen (Atlante. collective House and modern living 1930-1980, The Architecture Biennale, Venedig 2008, Notebook, Neon, Mailand, 2008). Er lehrt seit 2005 die Studienfächer Grafikdesign und Corporate Identity an der Universität Bologna.

FR

Alessandro Gori est l'un des fondateurs de Laboratorium, qui a été crée en 2004 à Florence. Les valeurs principales de Laboratorium sont la recherche et l'expérimentation.

Le travail de Gori va du design de livres (A New Italian Fashion, 2011, Walter Albini And His Time, 2010, A Modern Day, 2010) à la communication (Pitti Immagine, Altaroma, Furla), au design d'exposition (Fashion at the Time of Fascism, London College of Fashion, 2010; The Colored Rooms, Emilio Pucci, 2007) jusqu'aux installations (Atlante. collective House and modern living 1930-1980, The Architecture Biennale, Venise 2008, Notebook, Neon, Milan, 2008). Il est professeur de Graphisme et d'image de marque à l'Université de Bologne depuis 2005.

ITA

Alessandro Gori è tra i fondatori del progetto Laboratorium, che diventa studio nel 2004 e che ha base a Firenze. I valori fondanti di Laboratorium sono la ricerca e la sperimentazione.

Il lavoro di Gori spazia dal design del libro (Una nuova moda italiana, 2011; Walter Albini e il suo tempo, 2010; Una giornata moderna, 2010), al design di esposizioni (Fashion at the Time of Fascism, London College of Fashion, 2010; The coloured rooms, Emilio Pucci, 2007) fino alle installazioni (Atlante. Casa collettiva e abitare moderno 1930-1980, La Biennale di architettura, Venezia 2008; Notebook, Neon, Milano, 2008). Dal 2005 è docente di Grafica e immagine coordinata presso l'Università di Bologna.

Stefan Jost

EINSXEINS - made with Dominic Rechsteiner

Alessandro Gori

Altaroma LVPA

:MMVIII Notebook

Una Nuova Moda Italiana

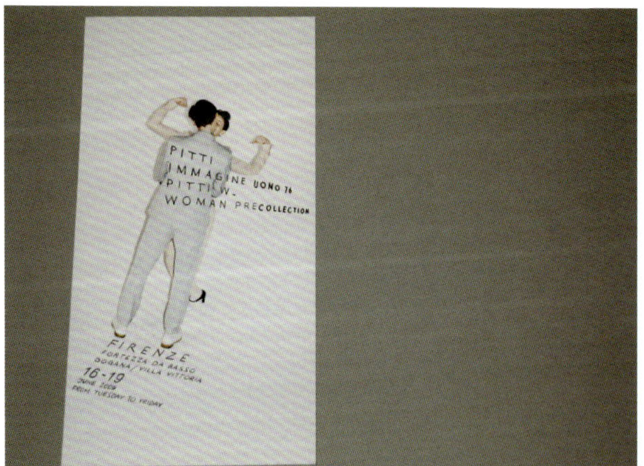

Pitti Immagine Uomo 76

Rosa Emilio 00 399	Bruciato 001 468	Verde 2 245	Pavone (0) 444
Rosa Emilio 398	Bruciato 03 461	Verde 03 249	Pavone 0 443
Rosa 0205 404	Rame (0) 471	Verde 3 248	Pavone 0 Bis 446
Rosa 205 403	Rame 63 459	Verde 002 247	Pavone 442
Rosa (0)137 402	Bordeaux (0)2 456	Verde 02 246	Lavanda 00 450
Rosa 0137 401	Bordeaux 02 455	Verde 2 245	Lavanda 448
Rosa 137 400	Bordeaux 112 458	Verde 005 253	Lavanda 0 449
Ciclano (0) 408	Talpa 181 494	Verde 05 252	Lavanda 0 Bis 513
Ciclano 0 407	Talpa 0 486	Verde 5 251	Lavanda 0020 453
Ciclano 0 406	Talpa 485	Cobalto 00 232	Lavanda 0220 452
Rosa Peonia 134 396	Talpa 00194 493	Cobalto 0 231	Lavanda 220 451
Rosa Peonia 0134 395	Beige 0049 484	Cobalto 230	Grigio 65 119
Rosa Peonia 00134 394	Beige 049 483	Nilo 227	Grigio 065 120
Viola 003 417	Corda 0 498	Nilo 0 228	524
Pavone (0) Bis 447	Corda 497	Nilo 00 229	Acciaio 01 111
Viola 06 419	Senape 00224 502	Capri 00146 226	Grigio Perla 116
Viola 6 418	Senape 0224 501	Capri 0146 225	Luna
Viola 007 423	Senape 224 5(0)	Capri 146 224	Luna 109
Viola 07 422	Miele 488	Acqua 352 221	Luna 00 107
Viola 7 921	Zucca 00 328	Acqua 0170 216	Moon Shine 113
Prugna 00 411	Zucca 327	Acqua 170 215	Moon Shine 0 114
Prugna 0 410	Arancio 167 320	Acqua 0197 220	Moon Shine 00 115
Prugna 409	Arancio 328 326	Acqua 330 203	Antracite 00 103
Viola 0095 429	Arancio 04 324	Acqua 001 214	Antracite 0 102
Viola 95 427	Arancio 004 325	Turchese 0030 196	Antracite 101
Rosa Quiana 1 382	Giallo Oro 0 308	Turchese 0300 195	Polvere 00 155
Rosa Quiana 01 383	Mattone 00 318	Turchese 30 194	Polvere 00 157
Rosa Quiana 001 384	Albicocca 314	Turchese (0)117 187	Zaffiro 001 136
Rosa Quiana 2 385	Albicocca 0 315	Turchese 0117 186	Zaffiro 01 135

Stefan Jost

Stefan Jost
"Pizza, Pasta, Pergola"

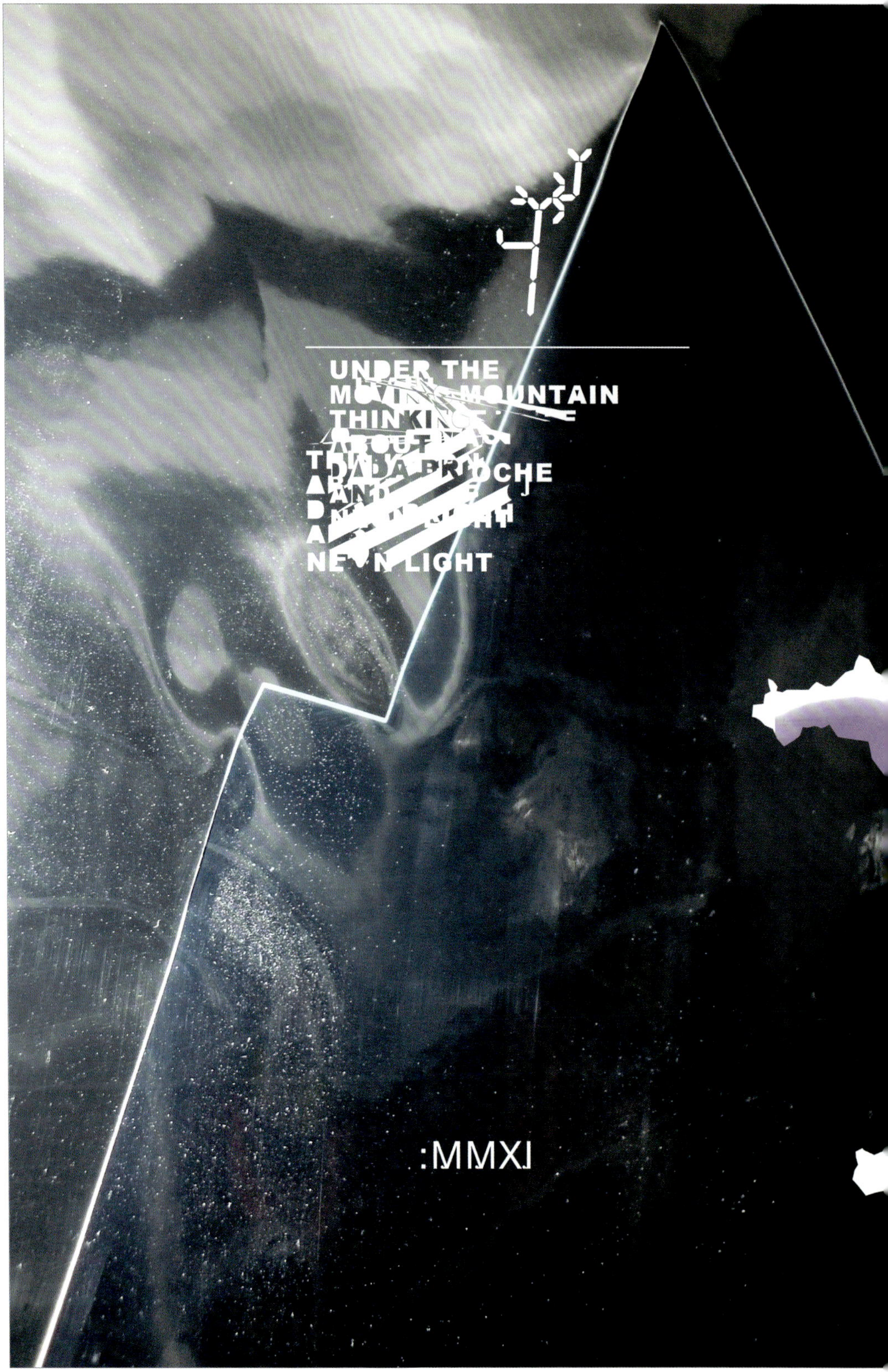

Alessandro Gori
*"Under the moving mountain
thinking about dada brioche
and neon light"*

Nerves

ENG

Nerves is a multidisciplinary agency that offers design and engineering under one roof. The combined knowledge of designers, illustrators, artists and engineers shapes its core competence for complete, distinct communications design. Always at the forefront of emerging techniques and technology, Nerves produces cutting edge products in both old and new media, from pocketknives to interactive multimedia terminals. Since its creation in 2009, Nerves has worked for international clients such as Microsoft, Porsche, Victorinox, Unicef, Absolut Vodka, Nescafé and the Swiss Embassy. Nerves is located in the heart of Zurich next to the Sihl river.

DE

Nerves ist eine multidisziplinäre Agentur, die Design und Ingenieurwesen unter einem Dach zusammenbringt. Das gemeinsame Fachwissen der Designer, Illustratoren, Künstler und Ingenieure formt einen Kompetenzkern für komplettes und individuelles Kommunikationsdesign. Nerves befindet sich immer an der Spitze der neuesten Techniken und Technologien und produziert innovative Produkte in alten und neuen Medien, von Taschenmessern bis zu interaktiven Multimedia-Terminals. Seit seiner Gründung in 2009 hat Nerves für internationale Kunden wie Microsoft, Porsche, Victorinox, Unicef, Absolut Vodka, Nescafé und der schweizerischen Botschaft gearbeitet. Nerves befindet sich am Ufer des Flusses Sihl im Herzen von Zürich.

FR

Nerves est une agence pluridisciplinaire qui offre design et ingénierie sous un même toit. Le savoir combiné des designers, illustrateurs, artistes et ingénieurs lui donne les moyens essentiels pour créer des design de communication complets et qui se différencient. Toujours à la tête de techniques et de technologies nouvelles, Nerves produit des produits de pointe dans l'ancien comme dans le nouveau média, des couteaux de poches aux écrans médiatiques interactifs. Depuis sa création en 2009, Nerves a travaillé pour des clients internationaux comme Microsoft, Porsche, Victorinox, Unicef, Absolut Vodka, Nescafé et l'Ambassade Suisse. Nerves se situe au cœur de Zurich, à côté de la rivière Sihl.

ITA

Nerves è un'agenzia multidisciplinare che offre e ospita servizi di design e ingegneria sotto un unico tetto. Le conoscenze congiunte di designer, illustratori, artisti e ingegneri, costituiscono la sua competenza distintiva per un design della comunicazione completo e unico. Sempre all'avanguardia nelle tecniche e tecnologie emergenti, Nerves produce prodotti innovativi usando media vecchi e nuovi: da temperini a stazioni multimediali e interattive. Dalla sua nascita nel 2009, Nerves lavora per clienti internazionali come Microsoft, Porsche, Victorinox, Unicef, Absolut Vodka, Nescafé e l'ambasciata svizzera. Nerves si trova nel cuore di Zurigo sulla riva del fiume Sihl.

Studio Kmzero

ENG

Studio Kmzero was founded in 2002 by Francesco Canovaro, Cosimo Lorenzo Pancini and Debora Manetti. After many years experience as creative directors in advertising and web design they joined forces to create a place to experiment with graphic design, new media and digital art: a space to mix visual arts research, television advertising, 3D animation and graphic storytelling.

Their goal is to find an original way into the digital media conflux by marrying experience and professionalism with enthusiasm, curiosity and creativity. They search for a dialectic, non-conflict relationship between our cultural roots, local reality and the global influences absorbed from the online world.

DE

Studio Kmzero wurde 2002 von Francesco Canovaro, Cosimo Lorenzo Pancini und Debora Manetti gegründet. Nach vielen Jahren Erfahrung als künstlerische Leiter in Werbung und Webdesign schlossen sie sich zusammen, um einen Ort zu schaffen, an dem sie mit Grafikdesign, neuen Medien und digitaler Kunst experimentieren konnten – ein Ort, an dem Recherche der visuellen Kunst, Fernsehwerbung, 3D-Animation und grafische Geschichtencrzählung miteinander verbunden werden.

Ihr Ziel ist es, einen originellen Weg in den Zusammenfluss digitaler Medien zu finden, indem Erfahrung und Professionalität mit Enthusiasmus, Neugier und Kreativität gepaart werden. Sie suchen nach einer dialektischen, konfliktfreien Beziehung zwischen unseren kulturellen Wurzeln, der eigentlichen Realität vor Ort und den globalen Einflüssen, die durch die Online-Welt absorbiert werden.

FR

Studio Kmzero a été créé en 2002 par Francesco Canovaro, Cosimo Lorenzo Pancini et Debora Manetti. Après de nombreuses années d'expérience en tant que directeurs artistiques dans le domaine de la publicité et du design de sites web, ils s'associèrent pour créer un endroit afin d'expérimenter avec le graphisme, nouveau média et art digital : un espace pour mélanger la recherche en arts visuels, publicité à la télévision, animation 3D et graphisme de l'art de conter.

Leur objectif est de se frayer un chemin original dans le confluent du média digital en alliant expérience et professionnalisme avec enthousiasme, curiosité et créativité. Ils recherchent une relation dialectique et non conflictuelle entre nos racines culturelles, réalité locale et influences globales absorbés du monde en ligne.

ITA

Studio Kmzero è stato fondato nel 2002 da Francesco Canovaro, Cosimo Lorenzo Pancini e Debora Manetti. Dopo tanti anni di esperienza come direttori creativi per la pubblicità e il web design, hanno unito le loro professionalità per creare un luogo dove sperimentare, al confine tra il design grafico, i nuovi media e l'arte digitale: uno spazio dove unire la ricerca sulle arti visive, la pubblicità televisiva, l'animazione 3D e la narrazione grafica.

Il loro obiettivo è quello di trovare un linguaggio originale per arrivare al cuore dei media digitali, unendo a esperienza e professionalità, entusiasmo, curiosità e creatività. Studio Kmzero cerca un rapporto dialettico e non conflittuale tra le nostre radici culturali, le realtà locali e le influenze globali assorbite dal mondo online.

Nerves

Social media campaign for the Absolut Vodka anti-prejudices claim «In An Absolut World There Are No Labels». Based on social psychology research findings, especially the Rosen- thal-Effect, Nerves decided to sensitise our fellow beings by creating the «No Label Task Force».
Everybody who sees the person and not the label can join as a fighter against well-established spurious prejudices. Absolut Vodka, Sweden.

Studio Kmzero

Alphaposter

Images for the Alphaposter project from Scalacolore.

Sex, power and money

A series for "Italian Renaissance 2" to express the studio's personality via personality, typography, desires and primary colours.

Nerves + Studio Kmzero

Stage 1: Knowing me, knowing you

<table>
<tr><td valign="top" width="50%">

E-mail_01

On Wed, Nov 10, 2010 at 1:22 PM, Raphael Krastev wrote:

Buongiorno Studio km zero!

How are you? Good I hope. Finally, we did a brainstorming and we would like to explain our most-loved idea, so that we hopefully can inspire you. We considered a lot about how we can work together on one poster, when you sit in Florence and we in Zürich. However, we can make two posters and your studio will determine what is the graphic content on our poster and vice versa. Which means, you will create a Swiss poster with graphic stuff from Zürich/Switzerland, selected by Nerves and we will create an Italian poster with graphic stuff from Firenze/Italia selected by you.

How will it work? It is very simple: Both studios send each other an envelope with 10 different product labels (beermat, bag of chips, bottle label, etc.) from your surroundings of your every day life. These 10 product labels will be the graphic inspirations for the poster. Integrate them in a way. For example, you can use the fonts of the labels or you can try to imagine how the product of the label should look like, make sketches, scan, multiply and so on... The idea would also contain some sort of documentation process, where for example we would document our discovery of your product labels with a glass of fine Barolo to create an Italian atmosphere. This images/impressions could possibly be included in the book/show alongside our final works.

Final format of the poster could be A1 (594 x 841mm).

What do you think? If you like the idea, we would suggest sending these 10 product labels per post as soon as possible, at best later this week. We could also send a first schedule so that we can orientate our selves.

All the best from Zürich

Raphael

</td><td valign="top" width="50%">

E-mail_02

On 12 November 2010 15:24:47, Cosimo Pancini wrote:

Hello Nerves!

We received your proposal and are already hunting for Italian products. In the meanwhile - we wanted to propose you an alternate collaboration route - it may be just for fun, or be part of the final project. We thought it would be nice to have a photographical comparision of similar things in italy and switzerland. We could both start a half-filled grid, so that the other studio finds the corresponding image. That would lead to have a series of double images that could have inside jokes or lead to thoughtful references. We could even think about a swiss/ita memory game, with different images... So, here is our half filled grid examples: a looser one and a tighter one, all based on photos from our studio. (since we did them without preparation, it seems our studio is really a bit messy... but it m ay be funny if you have a very clean "swiss" studio! :) . You could provide anot her similar grid with any sort of images, or we could integrate the label in the game. Let us know what you think - we will be sending you a package with the products (some of them have nice packages, so we will send not only the labels but the products too) on Monday.

Bye!

Cosimo

</td></tr>
</table>

E-mail_03

On 12/03/2010 01:48 PM, Cosimo Pancini wrote:

Hi everybody at Nerves!

Just checking if our package has arrived and wondering if you already sent yours. Can't wait to start playing with our ideas. In the meanwhile, an Italian product that didn't make it to your package seemed fit to describe us (Cosimo is not black but if he was, he definitely would be a better jazz player).

Waiting for your news!

Bye!

Cosimo

E-mail_04

On Fri, Dec 3, 2010 at 2:53 PM, Dan Krusi wrote:

Hi Cosimo!

Yes thank you very much - your package arrived well! We are already at work on our poster based on your products. We are shocked to hear you have not recieved our package yet. We sent it on the 16.11.2010, so it should have arrived by the latest 22.11.2010. We are trying to contact the postal service to see if they can track it down in any way. Do you have any ideas? Could it be you need to pick it up at the post?

Best,

Dan
(Attached - Our package in the making...)

E-mail_05

On 3 December 2010 15:08:43, "kmzero + design positive" wrote:

Hi Dan,

the address is ok, but I'm sorry to confirm that we didn't receive it.

:(

Let us know!

Bye bye,

Debora

E-mail_06

On Fri, Dec 3, 2010 at 4:12 PM, Dan Krusi wrote:

That's really sad to hear... Sorry, we had some good Swiss Chocolates! I guess we will collect some new stuff and send it over as soon as possible.

Best,

Dan

E-mail_07

On 3 December 2010 17:13:55 CET, "kmzero + design positive" wrote:

Ok Dan,

thank you!

Debora (very very sad for chocolate dispersion!)

Nerves + Studio Kmzero

Stage 2: Nerves kick off…

Work in Progress

Contents of Kmzero's package

Focusing on the brands

The first sketch

Nerves' story

Having exchanged packages with Studio Kmzero containing various local products and brands, Nerves took inspiration from the Italian goods to create a posse of football stars sponsored by the package contents.

Stage 3: Kmzero counter…

The first thought – the studio exchange grid

Making the package

Playing with stereotypes

The first ideas: ItEntity

KMzero's story

The match between StudioKmzero and Nerves was played in the classical tradition on a level playing field. In the first phase of study and research, the two teams engaged on the field of brand design, with an exchange of products via mail. In the meantime a friendly match took place via a further exchange of photos of the two studios, resulting (after a couple of rallies) in the poster "Kmzero versus Nerves - Carambolage agency. " As in any self-respecting game, Nerves then took the offensive to counter-attack with a politically themed poster to score the first goal. Studio Kmzero then responded first with an attack on "Stereotype" before proceeding to burst the net with a kick at "(Helv) Ethics." In the end, it was a lot of good, clean fun. And the chocolate was very good, thanks Nerves!

Stage 4: The Result

For the final result, please turn the page…

Nerves

Nerves
"Footballmania"

Kmzero
"HelvEtica"

Sabina Oberholzer & Renato Tagli

ENG

In 1983, after an internship at Rudolph de Harak's prestigious studio in New York for Sabina, and work experience for them both in Zurich, Sabina Oberholzer and Renato Tagli decided to found their own studio in Cevio, Switzerland. It was a conscious (and contentious) decision to start a professional venture in a small village in Valmaggia, a world away from the big city focus that prevailed in the 1980s.

Their pioneering spirit and love of creative contradiction has seen their work travel way beyond the boundaries of Valmaggia to win numerous national and international awards.

DE

1983, nach Sabinas Praktikum bei Rudolph de Haraks renommiertem Studio in New York und Sabinas und Renatos Berufspraktika in Zürich, entschieden sich die beiden Designer, ihr eigenes Studio in Cevio in der Schweiz zu gründen. Es war eine bewusste (und umstrittene) Entscheidung, ein Geschäft in einem kleinen Dorf in Valmaggia aufzubauen, weit entfernt von den kreativen Ballungszentren der Großstädte, die in den achtziger Jahren dominierten.

Mit ihrem Pioniergeist und ihrer Liebe für kreative Gegensätze schaffen sie Werke, die weit über Valmaggia hinaus Anerkennung finden und schon mit zahlreichen nationalen und internationalen Auszeichnungen honoriert wurden.

FR

En 1983, après un stage au prestigieux studio de Rudolph de Harak à New York pour Sabina et avoir travaillé pour eux deux à Zurich, Sabina Oberholzer et Renato Tagli décidèrent de créer leur propre studio à Cevio, Suisse. Ce fut une décision consciente (et contentieuse) de démarrer une aventure professionnelle dans un petit village de Valmaggia, un monde coupé du focus mis sur les villes qui régnait dans les années 1980.

Leur esprit avant-gardiste et leur amour pour la création contradictoire a vu leur travail voyager au-delà des frontières de Valmaggia pour remporter de nombreux prix nationaux et internationaux.

ITA

Nel 1983, dopo lo stage di Sabina presso il prestigioso studio di Rudolph de Harak a New York, ed esperienze di lavoro per entrambi a Zurigo, Sabina Oberholzer e Renato Tagli decidono di aprire il proprio studio a Cevio, Svizzera. Quella di avviare un'attività professionale in un piccolo villaggio in Valmaggia è una decisione cosciente (e controversa), molto diversa da quella che prevaleva negli anni '80 e che vedeva una particolare tensione verso la grande città.

Il loro spirito pionieristico e l'amore per la contraddizione creativa, hanno portato i loro lavori a viaggiare molto oltre il confine di Valmaggia per vincere numerosi premi nazionali e internazionali.

Paolo Palma

ENG

Paolo Palma (1973) is a graduate of the ISIA in Urbino, Italy, the only undergraduate university in the world devoted solely to graphic design. After two years of working with the Dolcini Associati studio in Pesaro, he joined Fabrica in 2000, before co-founding Collective Heads in 2006. His main passion is typographic experimentation and he edited a book on the work of Wim Crouwel's typeface New Alphabet: Wim Crouwel and Experimenta Typography, that was awarded the Certificate of Excellence at the International TypoGraphi Awards 2004.

DE

Paolo Palma (1973) ist ein Absolvent der ISIA in Urbino, Italien, der einzigen studentischen Universität, die sich ausschließlich dem Grafikdesign widmet. Nach seiner zweijährigen Anstellung bei dem Studio Dolcini Associati in Pesaro schloss er sich im Jahr 2000 Fabrica an, bevor er 2006 Collective Hands mitbegründete. Seine größte Leidenschaft ist typografisches Experimentieren und er hat ein Buch über die Arbeit von Wim Crouwels Schriftart New Alphabet editiert: Wim Crouwel and Experimenta Typography - welches bei den International TypoGraphi Awards 2004 das Certificate of Excellence gewann.

FR

Paolo Palma (1973) est diplômé de la ISIA à Urbino, Italie, la seule université au monde dévoué uniquement au graphisme. Après avoir travaillé deux ans avec le studio Dolcini Associati à Pesaro, il a rejoint Fabrica en 2000 avant de cofonder Collective Heads en 2006. Sa principale passion est l'expérimentation typographique et il a édité un livre sur l'œuvre de Wim Crouwel sur la police New Alphabet : Wim Crouwel and Experimenta Typography qui a reçue le Certificat d'Excellence à la remise de Prix Internationale TypoGraphi en 2004.

ITA

Paolo Palma (1973), si è diplomato presso l'ISIA di Urbino, l'unico istituto al mondo di livello universitario, dedicato esclusivamente alla progettazione grafica. Dopo una collaborazione di due anni con lo studio Dolcini Associati di Pesaro, nel 2000 è entrato a far parte di Fabrica, prima di co-fondare nel 2006 Heads Collective. Il suo interesse è rivolto in particolar modo alla sperimentazione tipografica. Ha curato un libro sul lavoro tipografico, New Alphabet di Wim Crouwel: Wim Crouwel e la tipografia sperimentale, premiato dall'International Typographic Awards 2004 con il Certificate of Excellence.

Sabina Oberholzer
& Renato Tagli

Angel's Psalms. Poster for Mostafa Majidi, Poet. Tehran, Iran, 2008

Series of three stamps (wedding, birth, anniversary) designed for the
Swiss Federal Post Office, 2009

Love, Art & Agony. Frida Kahlo & Diego Rivera Tribute, Mexico, 2008

Paolo Palma

"Four Legs Good, Two Legs Bad", Aluminium matrix engraved for "La Granja" studio opening in Barcelona

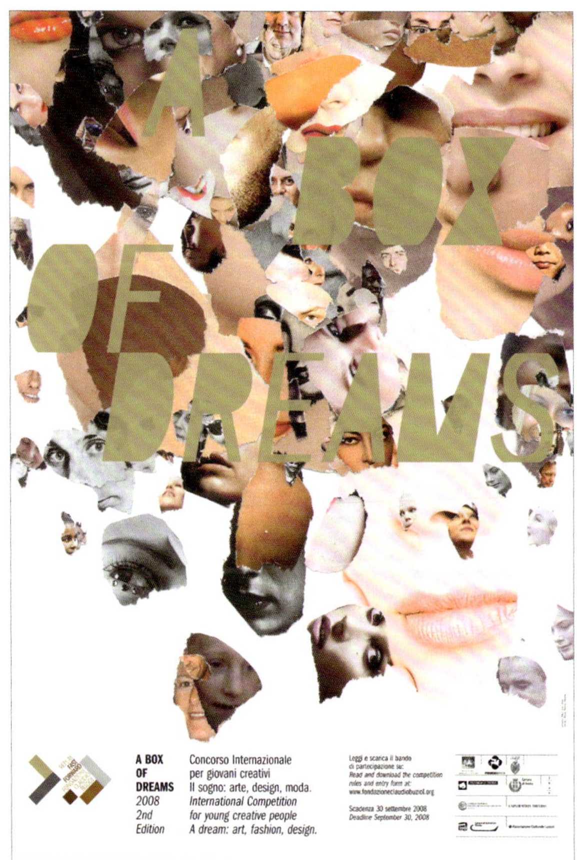

De Industria art competition 2007-2010 retrospective exhibition poster

A Box of Dreams" competition poster, Fondazione Claudio Buziol, 2008

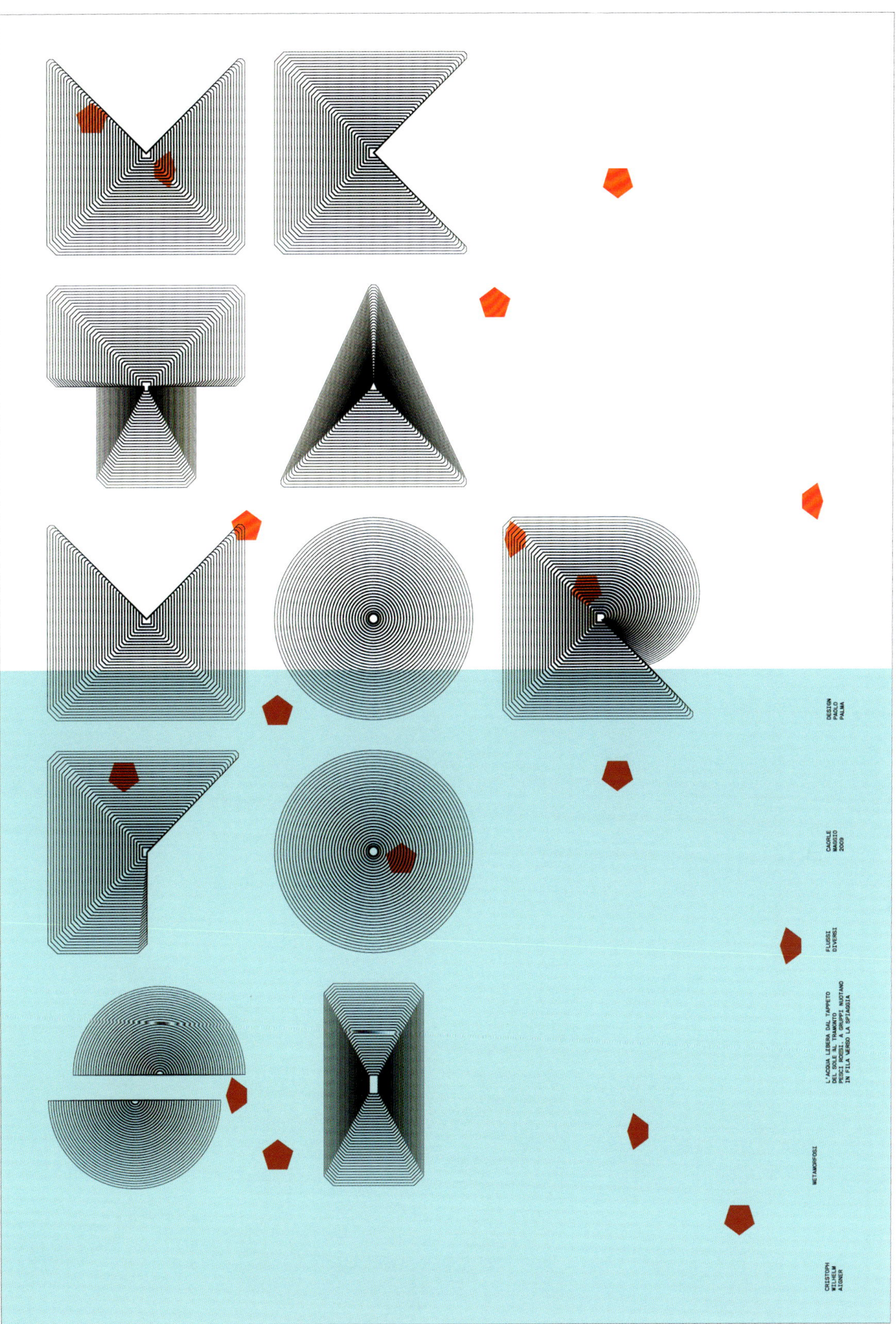

An interpretation of a poem by Austrian writer C. W. Aigner, designed for Segni Diversi graphic design exhibition in Caorle, Italy

Sabina Oberholzer & Renato Tagli

**Sabina Oberholzer
& Renato Tagli**
"O.p.t.i.ch"

Paolo Palma

Paolo Palma
"O.p.t.i.ch"

Celebrate The Future.

To support the next generation of Swiss and Italian creative talent we organized a competition for young designers to be exhibited and published alongside the established designers. The winners (and a gallery of highly commended designers) are found in this section. We salute you all.

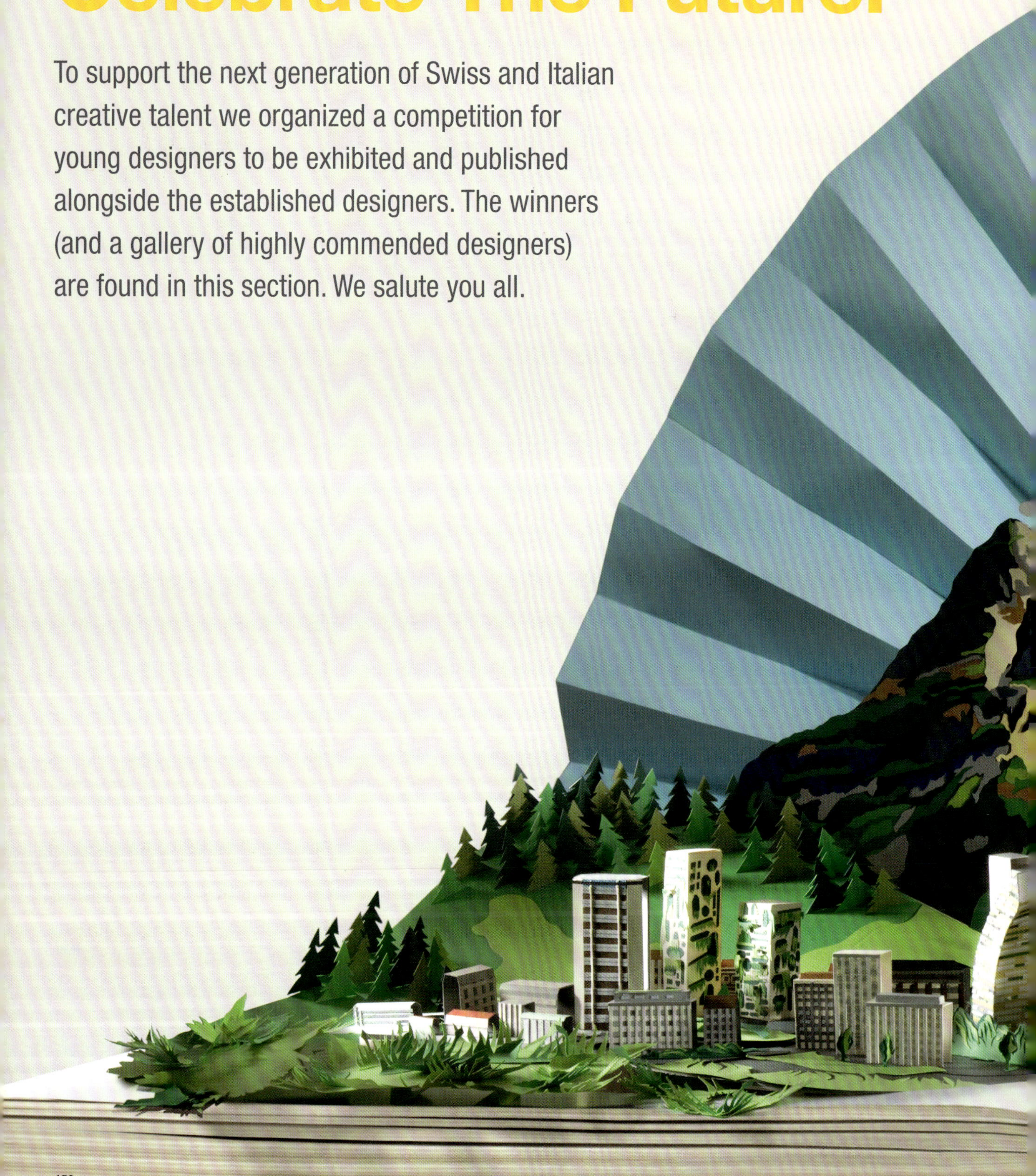

Best Swiss Student

Jonas Berthod and Louisa Gagliardi

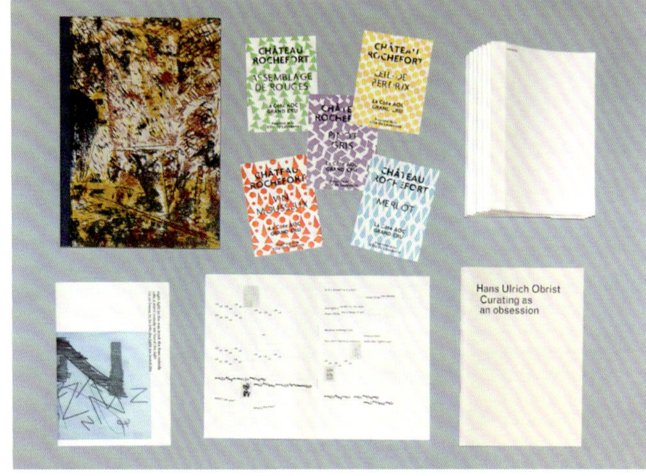

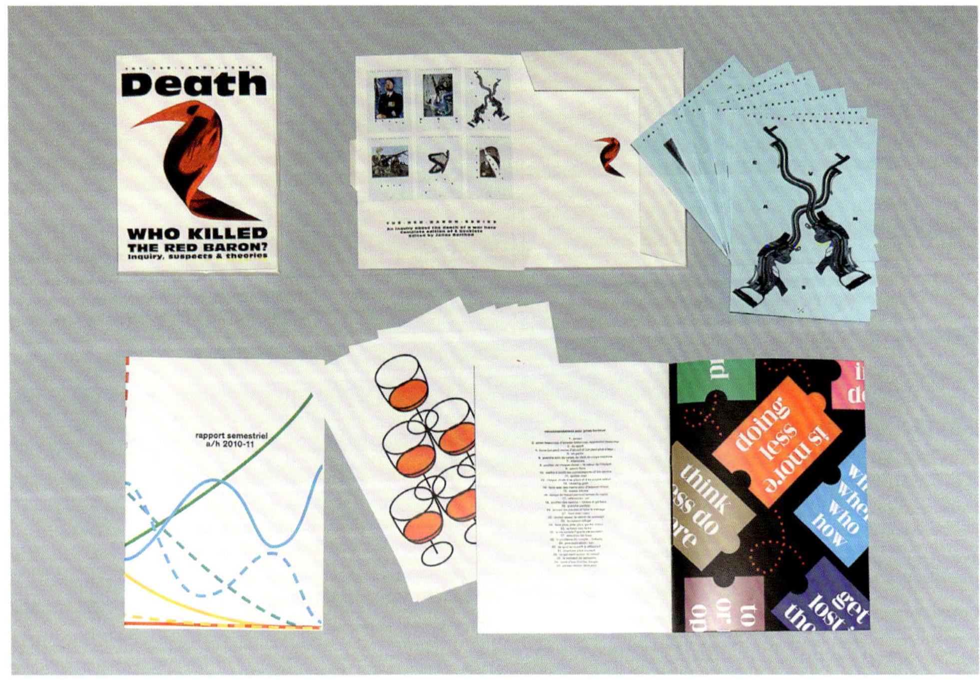

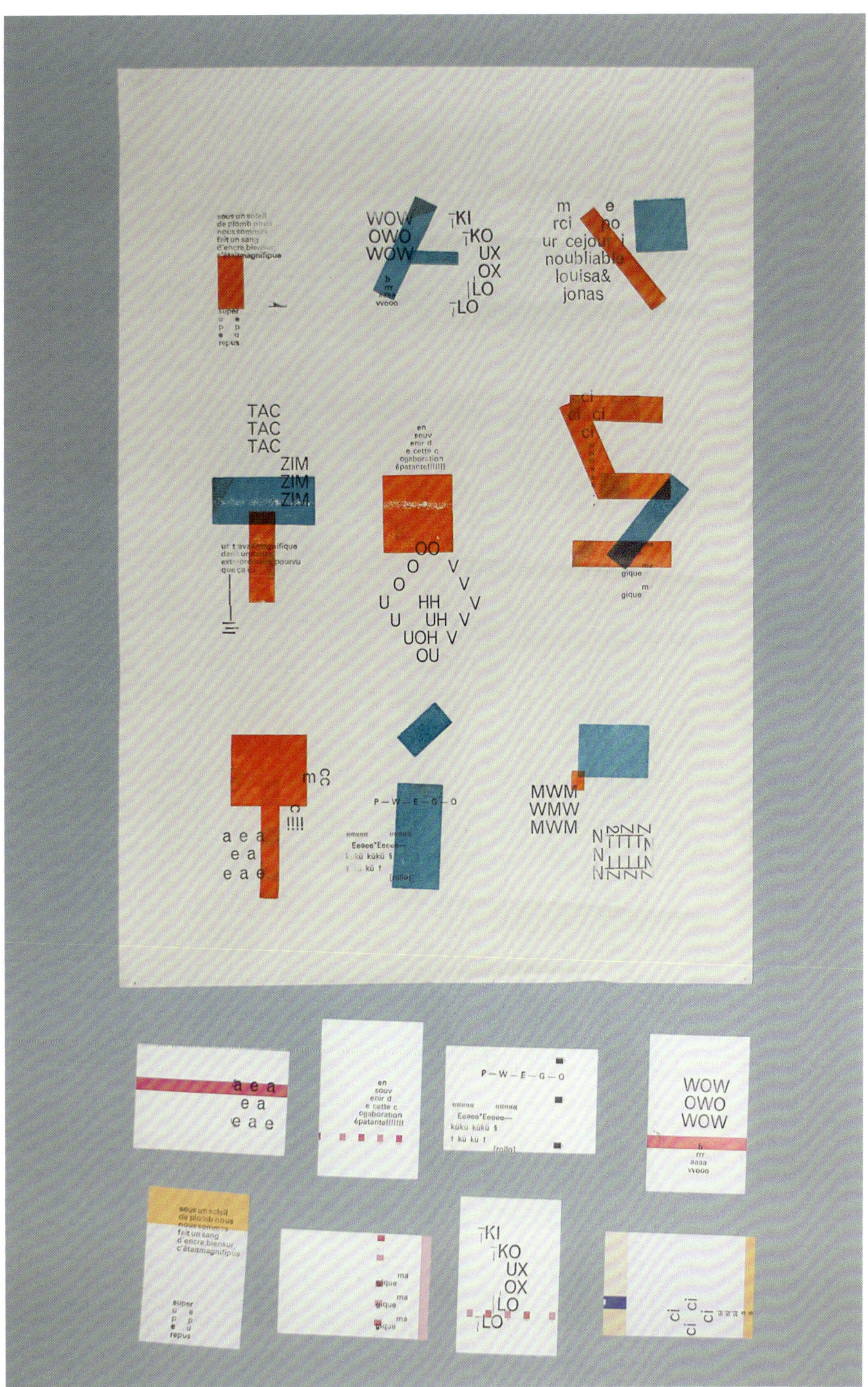

Poster Made At ECAL, University of Art
& Design, Lausanne, Switzerland

Giada Bobbera

www.dotbydotdesign.com

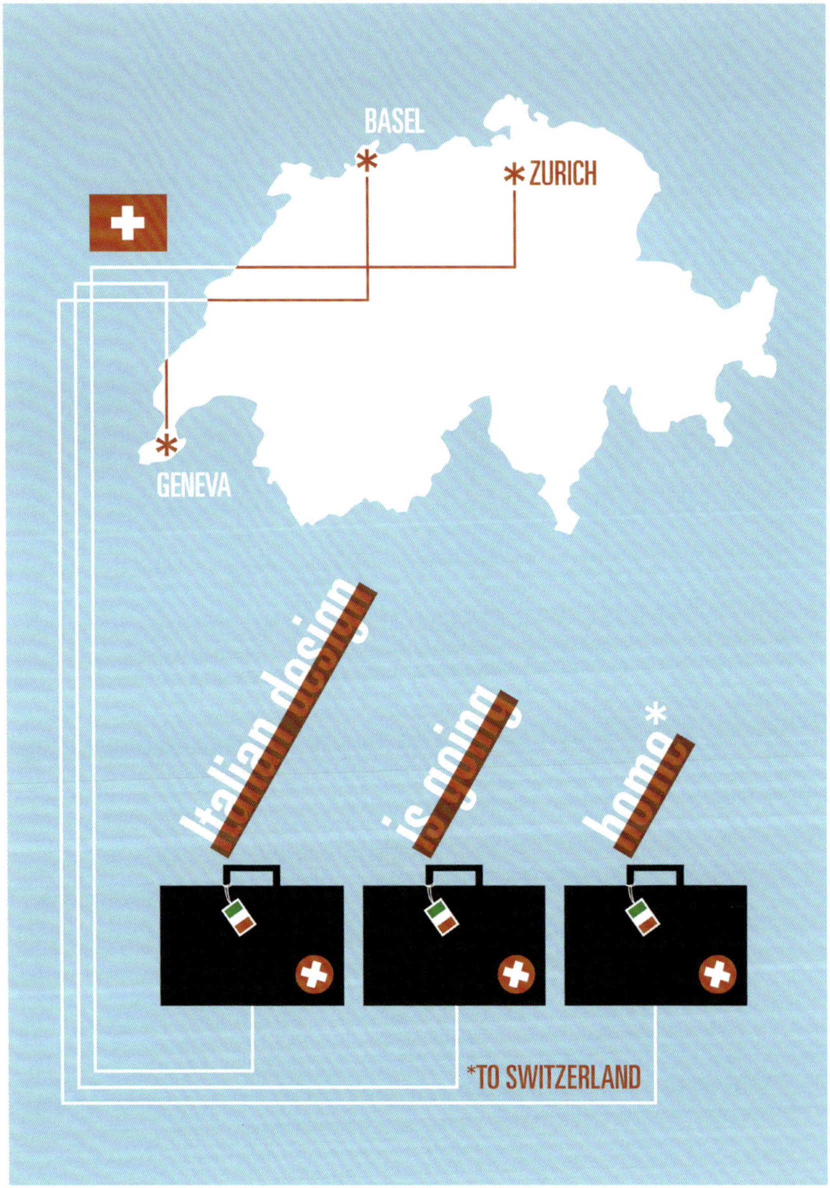

ITALIAN DESIGN IS GOING HOME*

Best Young Swiss Designer

Simone Zueger

www.simonezueger.ch

Posters made with Jonas Voegeli

ZUKUNFT
HOME OF GOOD MUSIC

PROGRAMM

November 2010

Dienerstrasse 33
8004 Zürich

DIE ABENTEUER VON MORRIS VON SER-NË

TEIL 01

Der Mann, der die
Zukunft nach Z. brachte,
kam von Westen.

Dank an: Popkredit und Stadtentwicklung
der Stadt Zürich

Unsere ausländischen Künstler reisen mit
dem Zug oder fliegen klimaneutral.

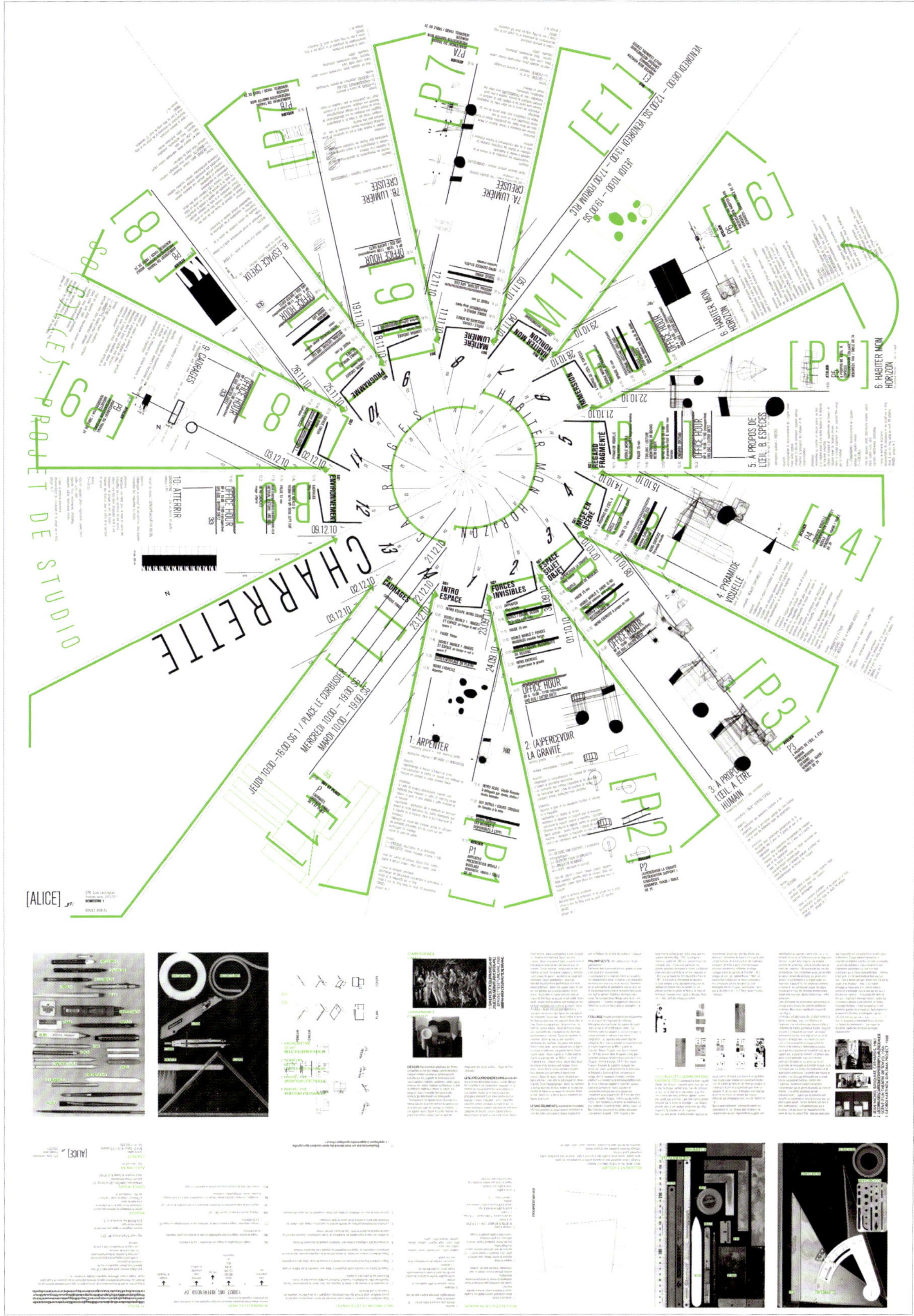

Andrea Novali

www.cargocollective.com/andren

Posters made with Jonas Voegeli.

Istituto Statale di Istruzione
Secondaria Superiore
Michele
Dell'Aquila
San Ferdinando di Puglia
(BT)

coltiva
il tuo
futuro

Una Scuola al Servizio dell'Agricoltura
e del Tavoliere meridionale che ha

Indirizzi di studio
per l'anno scolastico 2011/12

nello sviluppo rurale
la sua vocazione
economica principale.

Istruzione Tecnica Settore Economico
Amministrazione,
Finanza e Marketing
(Ex Igea, Programmatori, Linguistico aziendale)

Istruzione Tecnica – Settore Tecnologico
Sistema Moda
(Tessile, abbigliamento e moda)

Istruzione Professionale – Settore Servizi
Servizi per
l'Agricoltura
e lo Sviluppo rurale

Istruzione Professionale – Settore Servizi
Servizi commerciali
(tecnico dei servizi turistici)

Istituto Statale di Istruzione
Secondaria Superiore
Michele
Dell'Aquila

superiori
alla media

Highly Commended Gallery

Diego Fellay, Professional | Lausanne, Switzerland | diegofellay.ch

Inventarie, Studio | Bulle, Switzerland | inventaire.ch

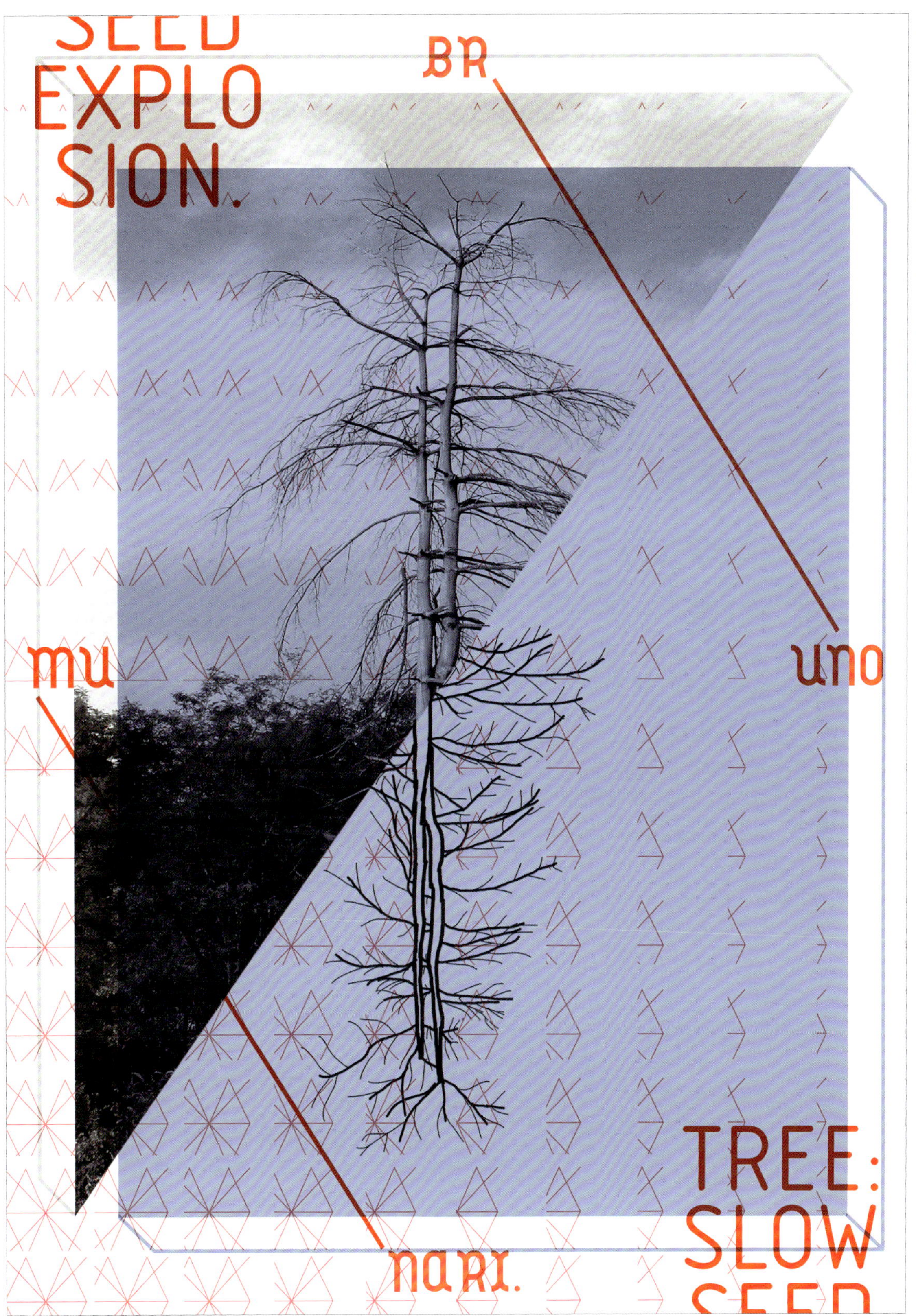
SEED
EXPLO
SION.
BR
mu
uno
nari.
TREE:
SLOW
SEED

Highly Commended Gallery

Valeria Panizza, Student | Lamone, Swtizerland | jungundbewundernswert.ch

Mathias Forbach & Charlotte Correia, Professionals | Vevey, Switzerland | hum-hum.ch

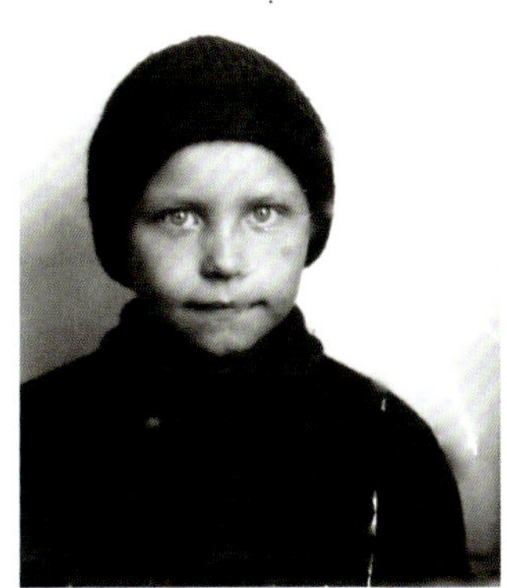

What you move away sometimes takes you back <u>home</u>.

Appendix

No paper was harmed during the making of this artwork.

A behind the scenes look at the epic production of the cover artwork for Italian Design is Coming Home. To Switzerland.

No paper was harmed during the making of this artwork.

Production Details:

Length: 2m

Width: 3m

Height: 1m

On set: 2 men. 5 knives and 30 blades. 5 glue sticks.
30 types & colours of paper.

Time of production: 350 hours

Location: Studio Alberto Parise, Milan Italy

Art direction: Tommaso Minnetti

Photography: Alberto Parise

Paper art: Alberto Parise, Giovanni Pasini

Acknowledgements

Polyedra Presents:

Italian Design Is Coming Home. To Switzerland.

A Will & Tommaso project, made possible by Polyedra.

Concept:

Will & Tommaso

How it looks:

Tommaso Minnetti

What it says:

William Georgi

Illustrations:

Elena Xausa www.ex-designer.it

Cover artwork:

Alberto Parise www.albertoparise.it

Book Design:

Jacopo Manfredini

Felix Humm Interview:

Giorgia Rossaro

Giancarlo Iliprandi Interview:

Tommaso Minnetti

Essays:

Bettina Richter, Maurizio Vitta

English to French & German Translations:

Anja Jones www.anjajonestranslation.co.uk

English to Italian Translations:

Johanna Worton

Web Design:

Pablo de Leo

This project would have been impossible without the goodwill, time and effort that many, many people have invested in it.
We would like to thank everyone involved for their generosity of spirit and enthusiasm. It's been our pleasure to work with you all and we hope you're as proud of the contents of this book as you are.
Viva Italia! Viva Switzerland!

Thank you/Merci Beaucoup/ Dankeschön/Grazie mille:

To Polyedra:

to Roberto Cavicchia in particular.

To our publisher:

To Anna Tetas and Actar.

To our media partners:

Maura Caramella at Designaside and Thierry Hausermann

To all the designers and design studios:

Alessandro Gori; Andrea Rauch; Bureau Collective; Lopetz and everyone at Büro Destruct; Christoph Frei; CCRZ; Dafi Kühne; Dan Krusi, Dario Hofstetter, Raphael Krastev and everybody at Nerves; Erich Brechbuhl; Linda Roberts and everybody at GVA Studio; Jekyll & Hyde; Leftloft; Marco Nicotra; Mauro Gatti; Melk Imboden; Paolo Palma; Sabina Oberholzer and Renato Tagli; Stefan Jost; Serena and everyone at Studio FM; Cosimo, Debora and everyone at Studio Kmzero; Tomaso Marcolla; Marco and everyone at Zetalab.

Will

To all the people who contributed to this book:

Alberto Parise and Giovanni Pasini for the stunning cover artwork; Bettina Richter; Elena Xausa for her amazing, beautiful illustrations; Felix Humm; Giancarlo Iliprandi; Giorgia Rossaro and Maurizio Vitta.

To Anja Jones, Johanna Worton, Ted van der Meulen and Google for the translations.

To all the students and young professionals who entered the contest to celebrate the future of Swiss and Italian Design, and who are sadly too many to list here. We wish you all the best for the future!

And to the jurors of the Celebrate the Future competition: Mauro Gatti, Paolo Palma, Studio CCRZ, Thierry Hausermann and Dario Hofstetter & Raphael Krastev from Nerves. Thank you for volunteering and thank you for your time.

Tommaso

Will and Tommaso were effectively homeless during the production of this book. We would therefore like to thank the following people for giving them a home and somewhere to work and sleep for the last twelve months: everyone at Gummo (ik hou van jullie); Mix Comunicazione; zia Virginia; Bas en Femke.

This book is dedicated to Dahl Doris Steenhuizen (and to Will's brother Thomas because he asked very nicely).

Will and Tommaso. Amsterdam, London, Milan, 2011.

www.willortommaso.com

Published by Actar and Polyedra
ISBN: 978-84-92861-74-3

Polyedra AG
Industriestrasse 11
4665 Oftringen, Switzerland

T +41 62 788 50 80
F +41 62 788 50 81

info.ch@polyedra.com
www.polyedra.ch

Distribution

ActarBirkhäuserD

Barcelona - Basel - New York
www.actarbirkhauser-d.com

Roca i Batlle 2
E-08023 Barcelona
T +34 93 417 49 93
F +34 93 418 67 07
salesbarcelona@actarbirkhauser.com

Viaduktstrasse 42
CH-4051 Basel
T +41 61 5689 800
F +41 61 5689 899
salesbasel@actarbirkhauser.com

151 Grand Street, 5th floor
New York, NY 10013, USA
T +1 212 966 2207
F +1 212 966 2214
salesnewyork@actarbirkhauser.com